AF323368

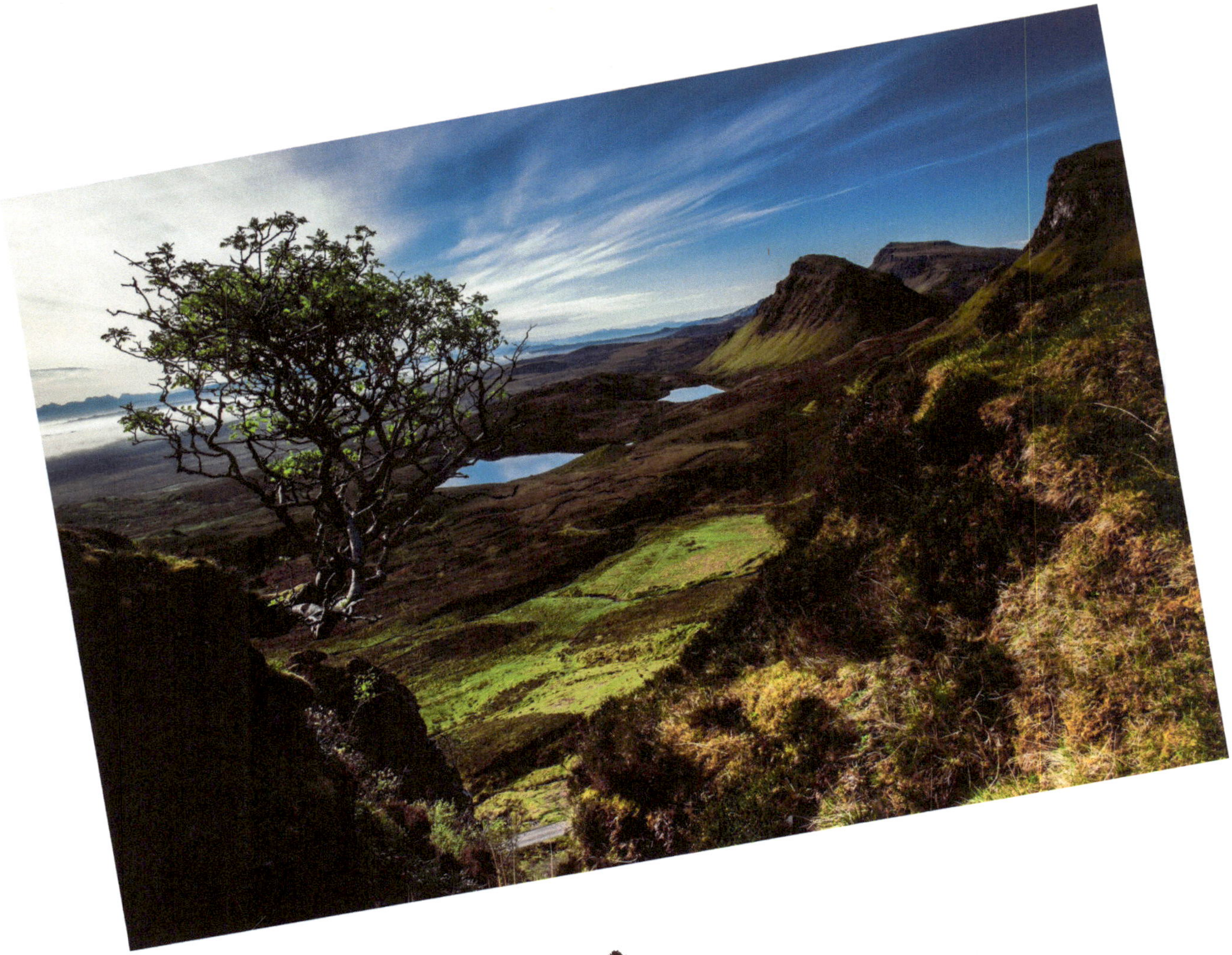

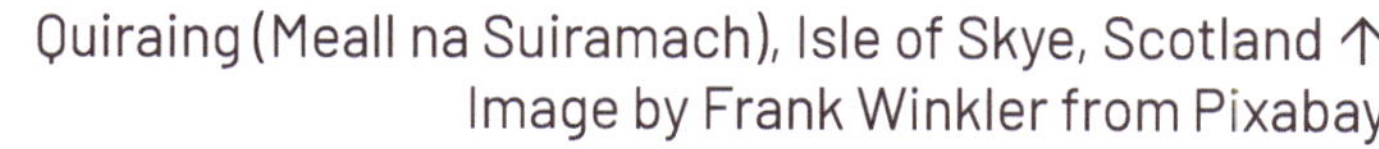

Quiraing (Meall na Suiramach), Isle of Skye, Scotland ↑
Image by Frank Winkler from Pixabay

Cover photo: Little Island, Croatia / Image by Sebastian Gößl from Pixabay

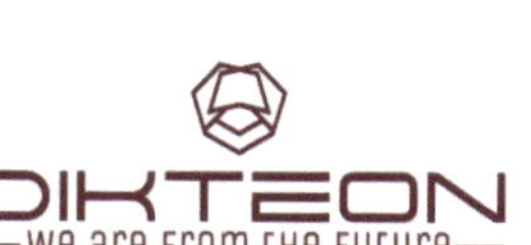

DIKTEON
—we are from the future—

Title: With or Without Trees
Author: Wirric Kouros
album@kentauron.com

"I think that I shall never see
A poem lovely as a tree.

   A tree whose hungry mouth is prest
   Against the earth's sweet flowing breast;

A tree that looks at God all day,
And lifts her leafy arms to pray;

   A tree that may in Summer wear
   A nest of robins in her hair;

Upon whose bosom snow has lain;
Who intimately lives with rain.

   Poems are made by fools like me,
   But only God can make a tree."

— Joyce Kilmer

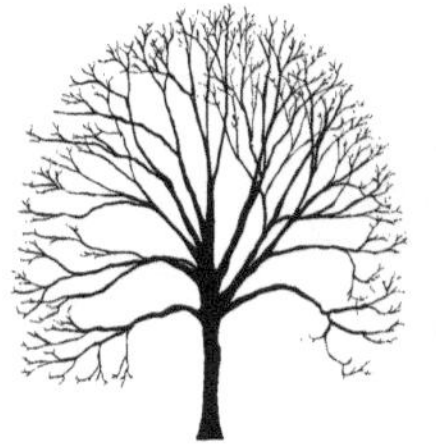

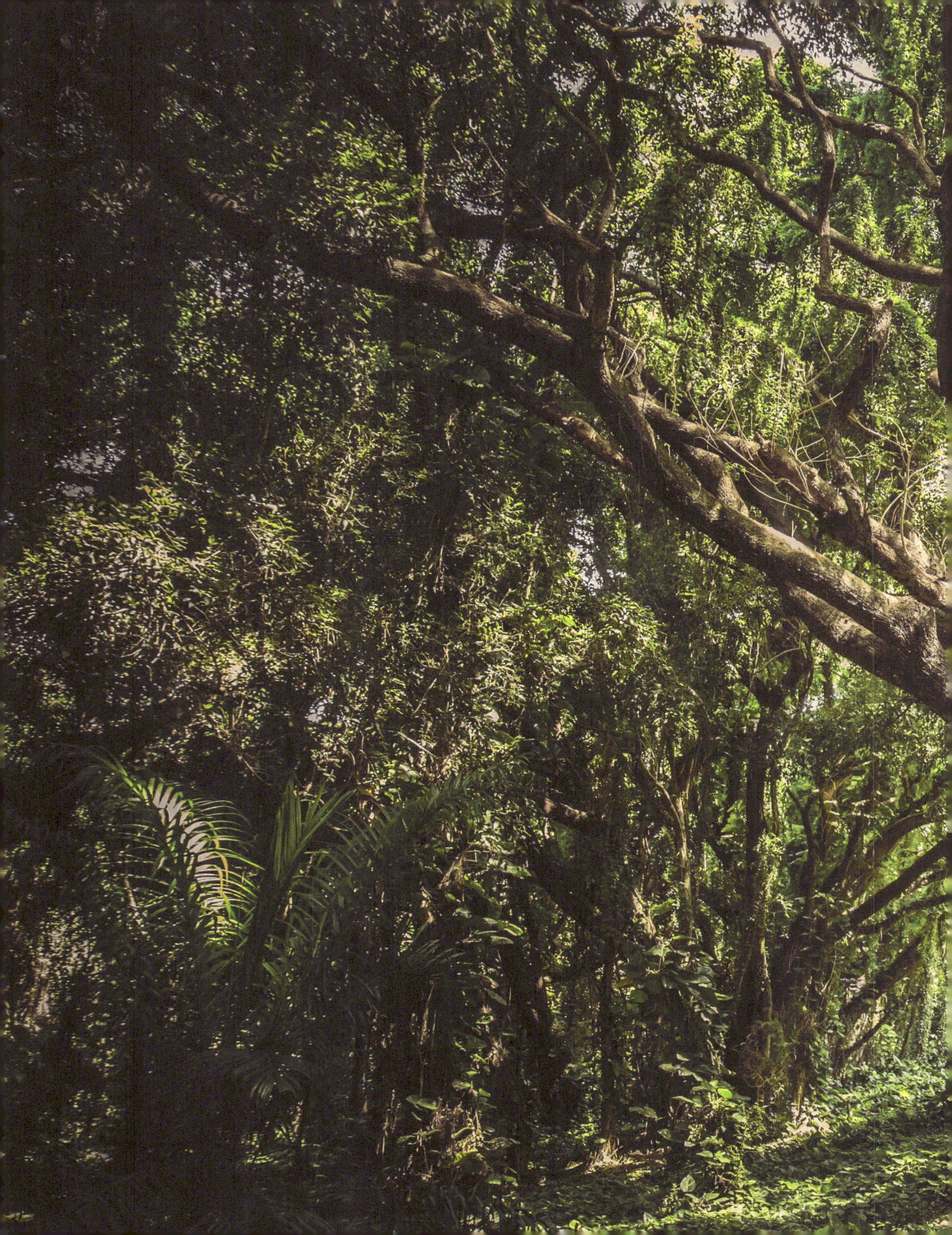

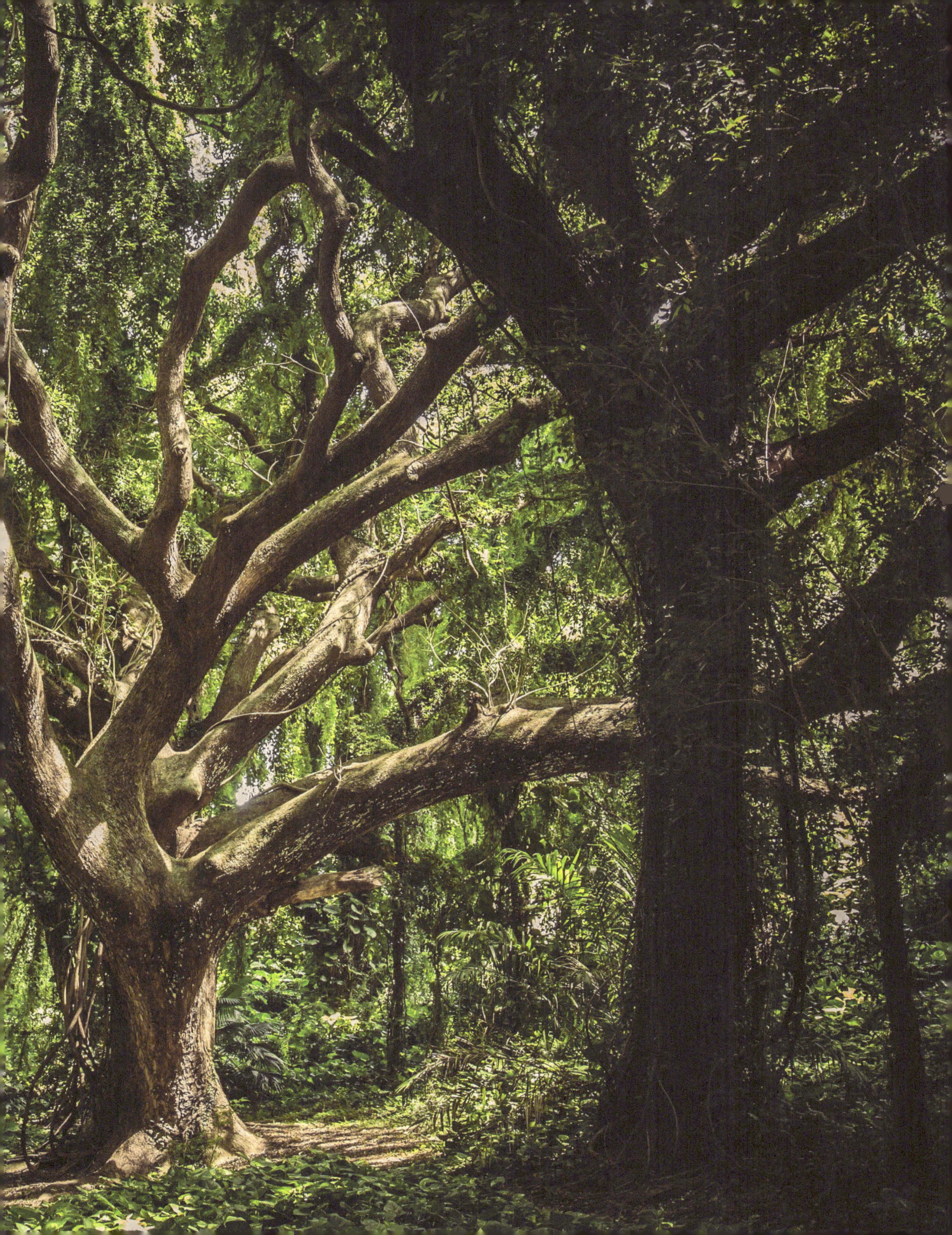

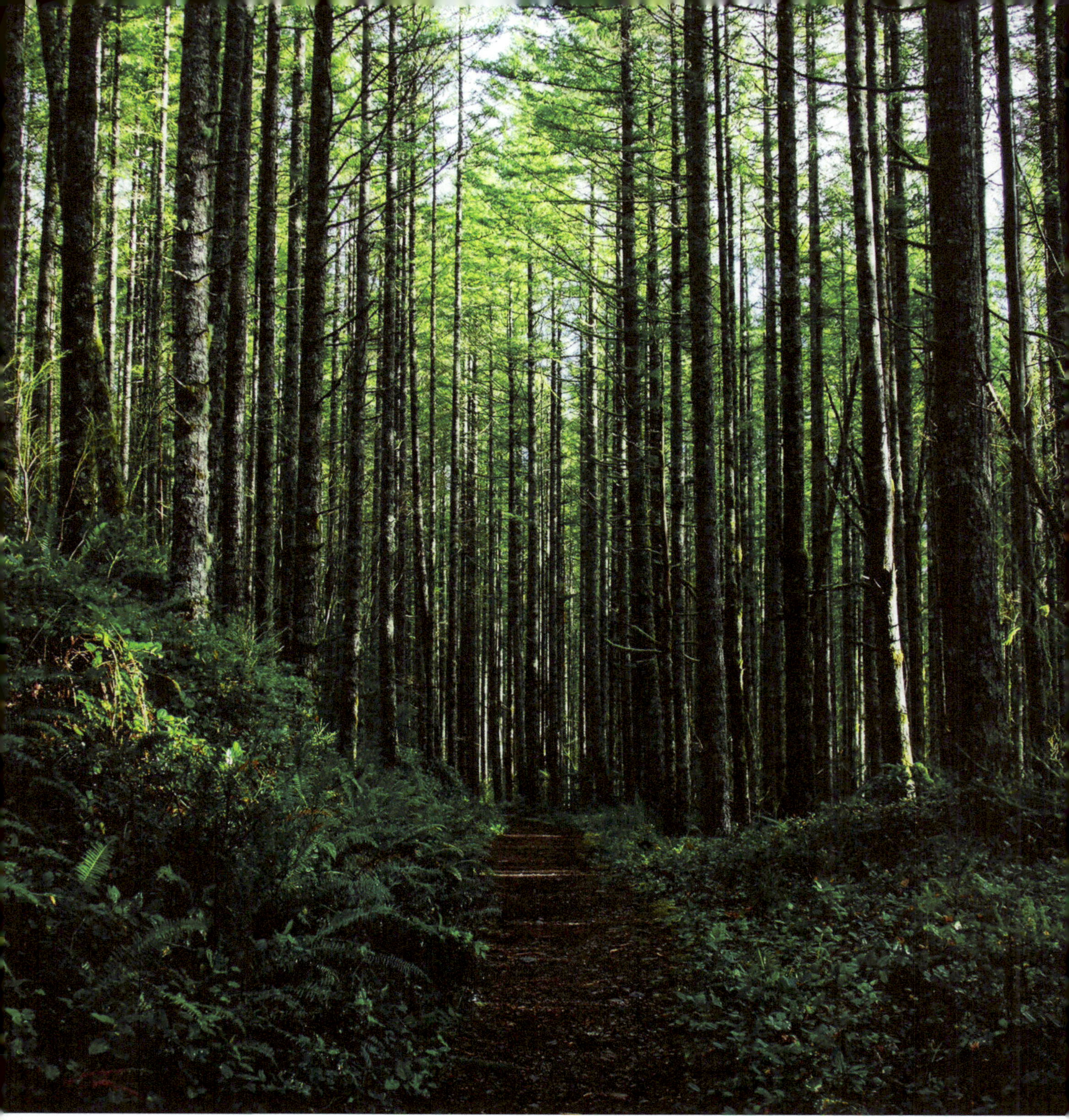

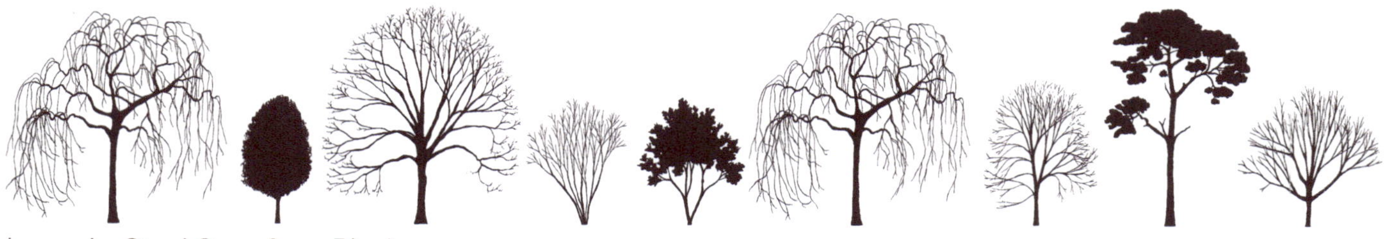

Image by StockSnap from Pixabay

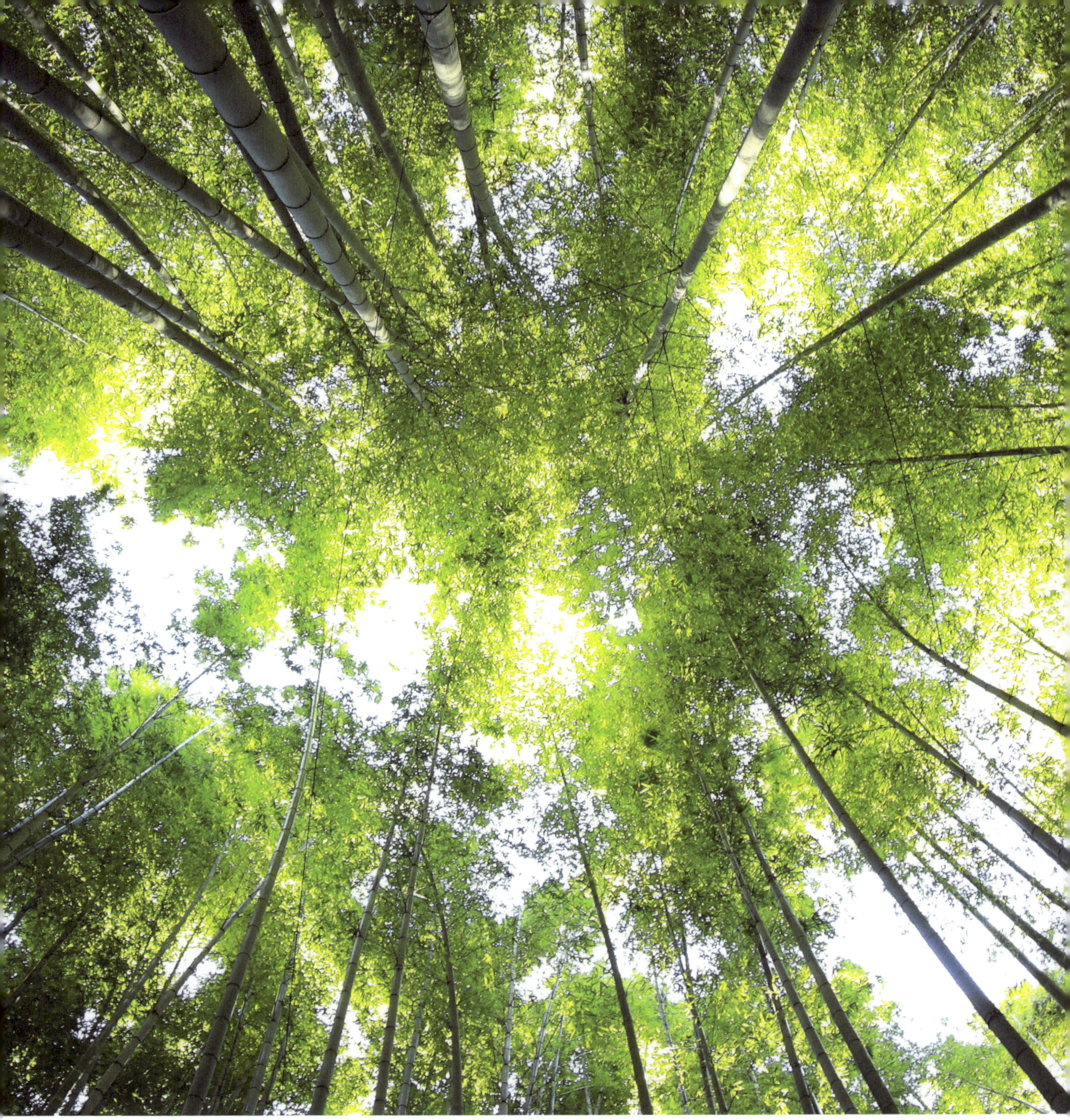

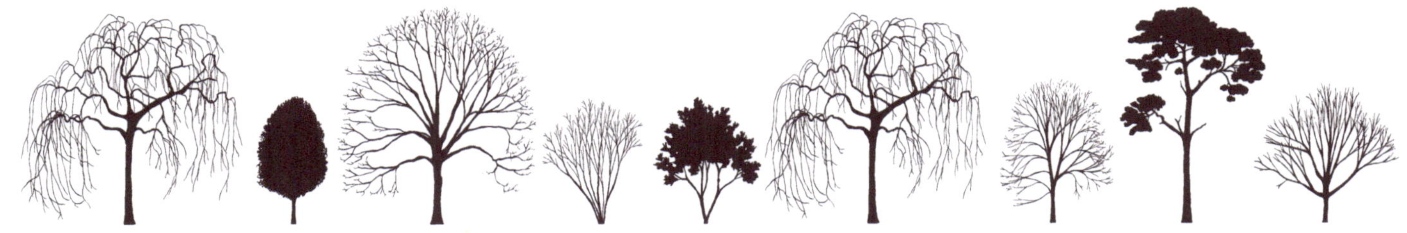

Image by StockSnap from Pixabay

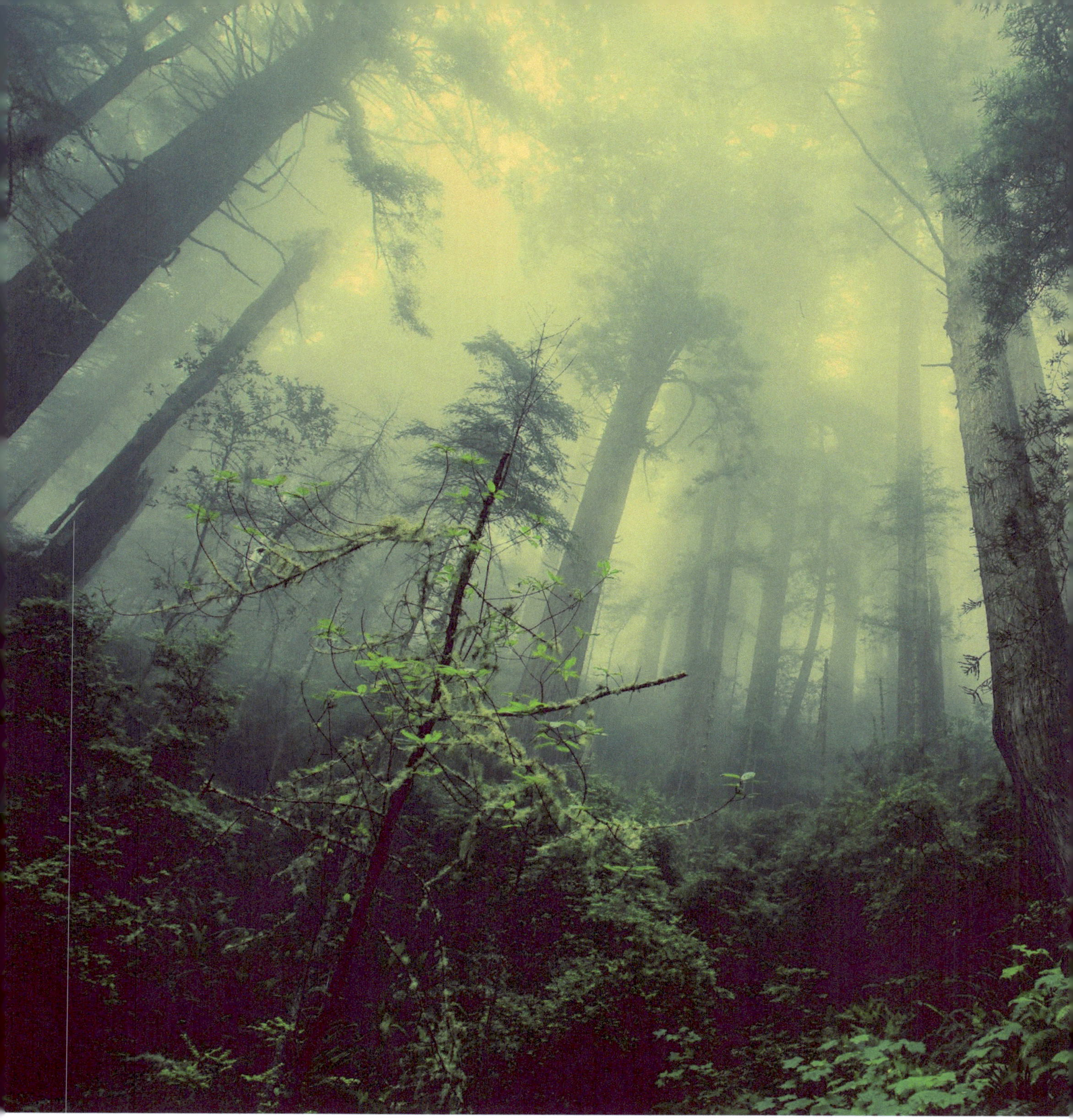

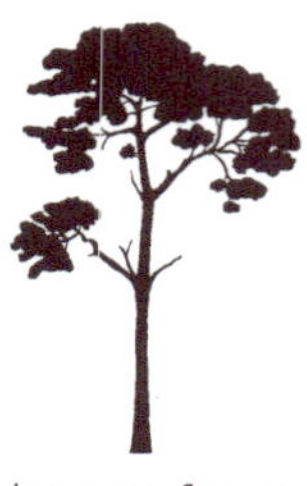

Image from Pixabay

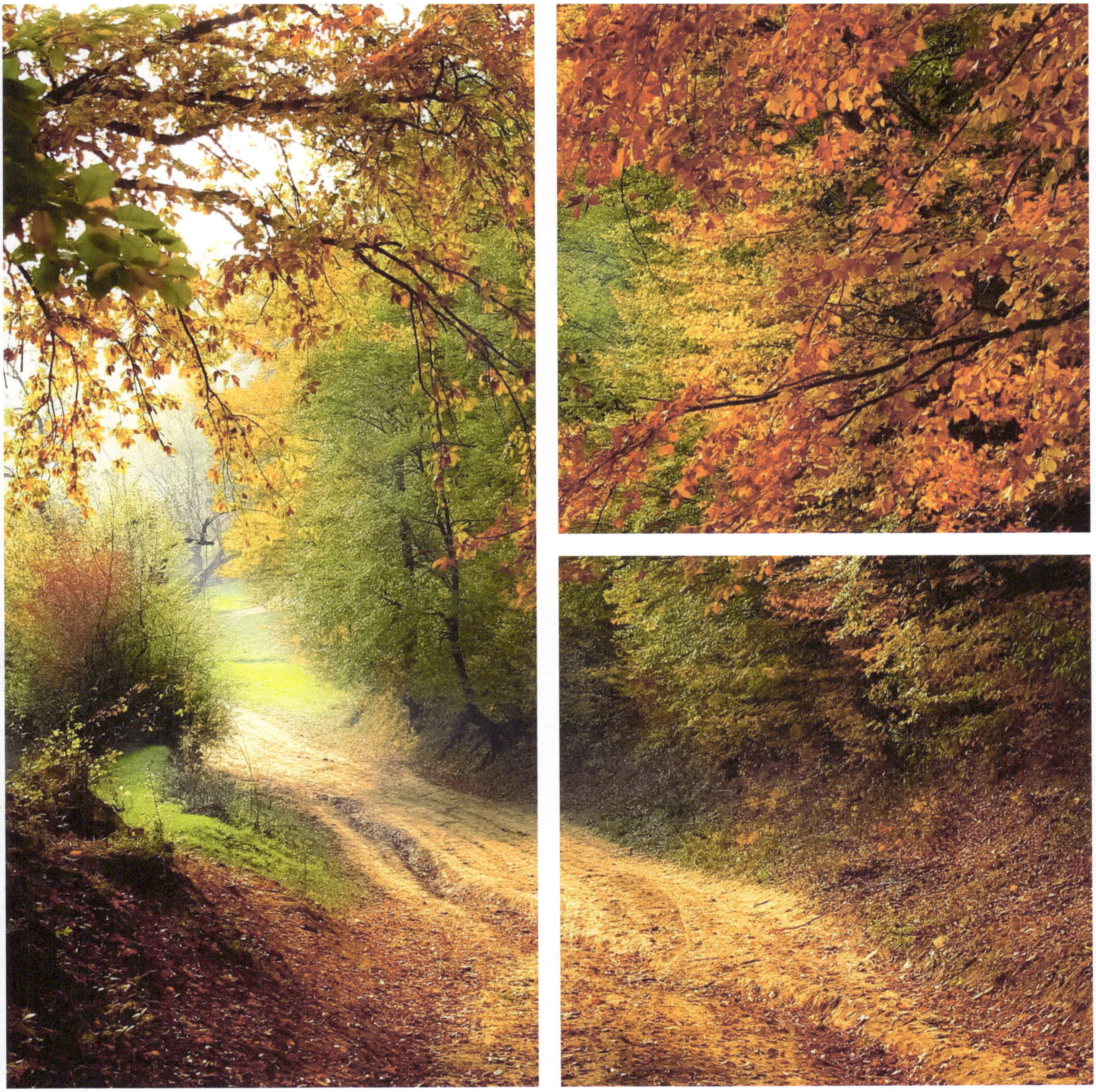

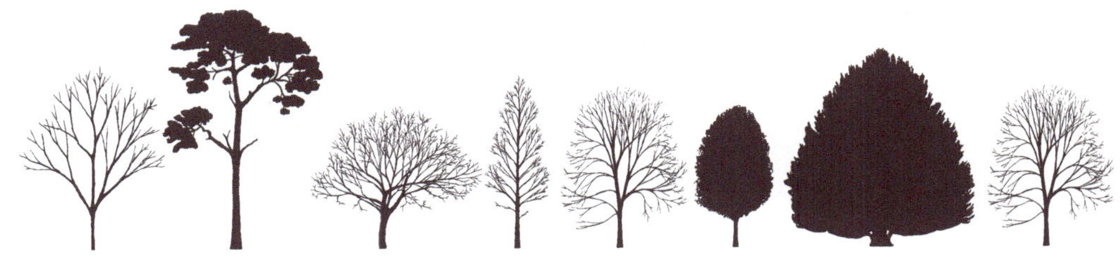

Image by Valentin Valiphotos from Pixabay

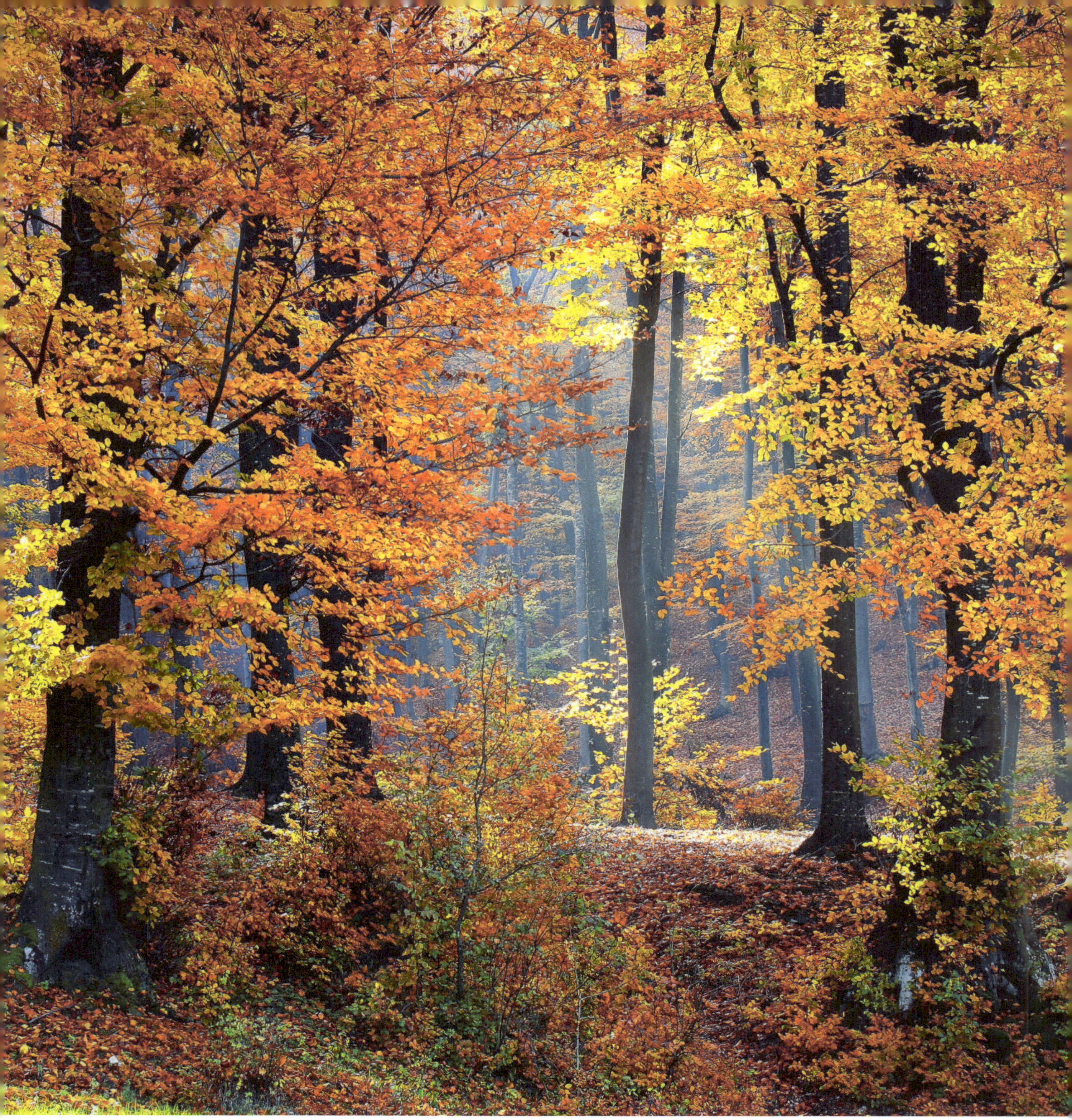

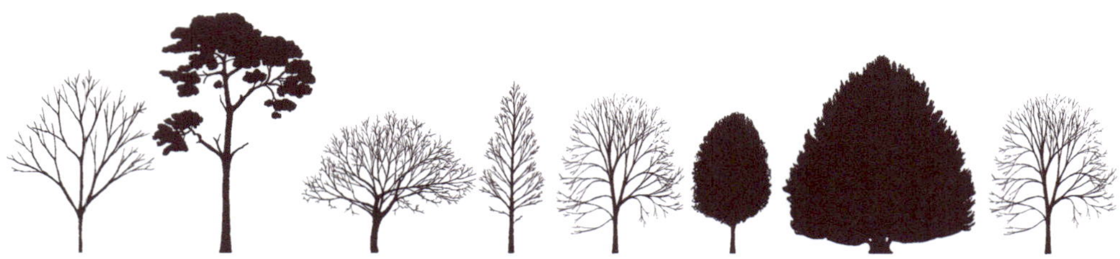

Image by Valentin Valiphotos from Pixabay

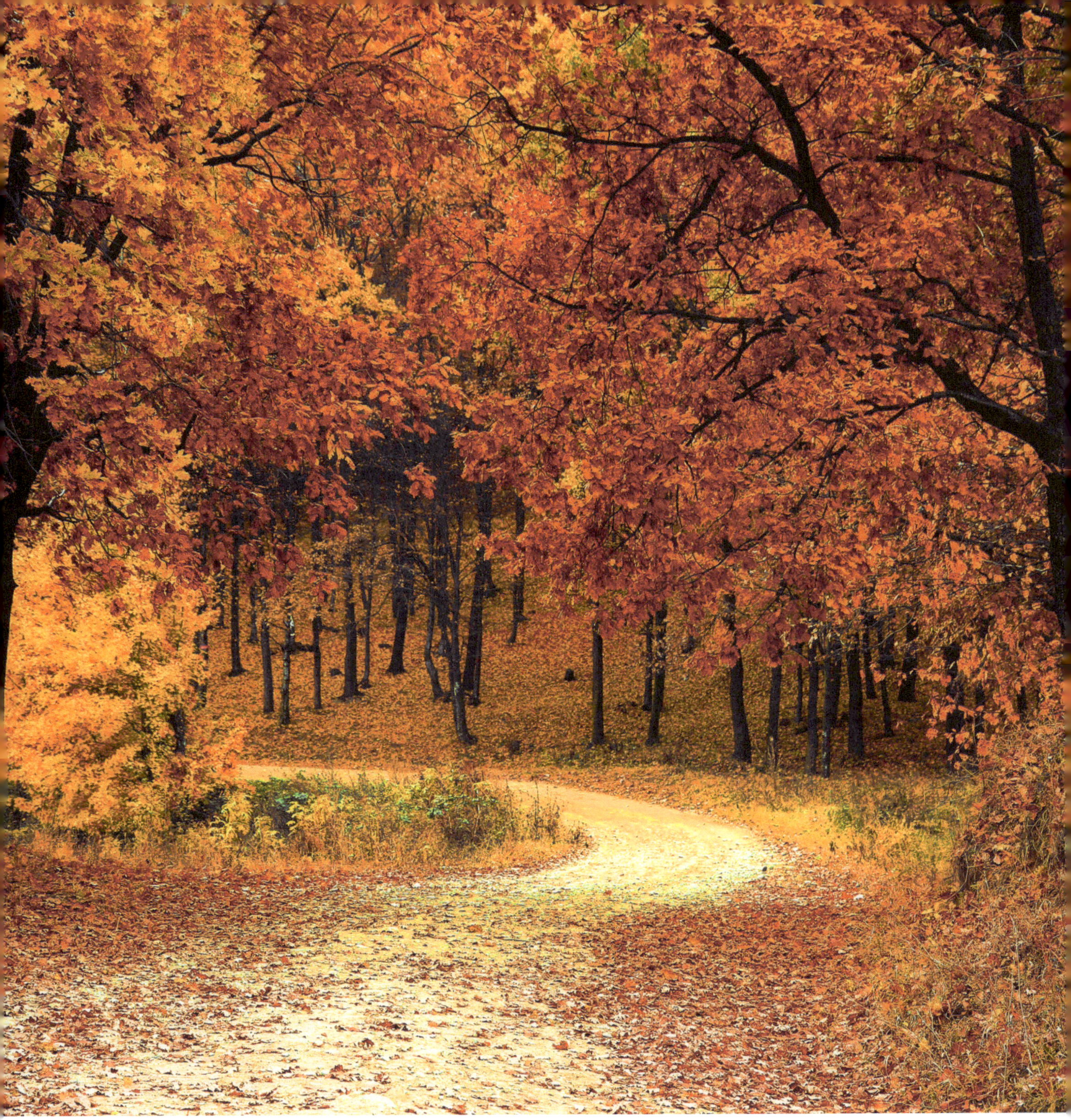

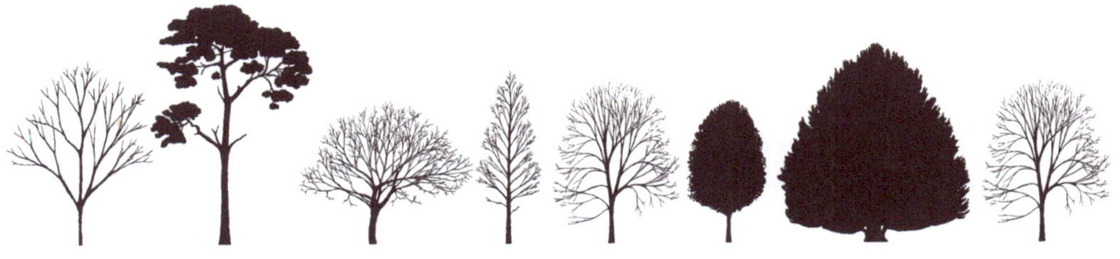

Image by Valentin Valiphotos from Pixabay

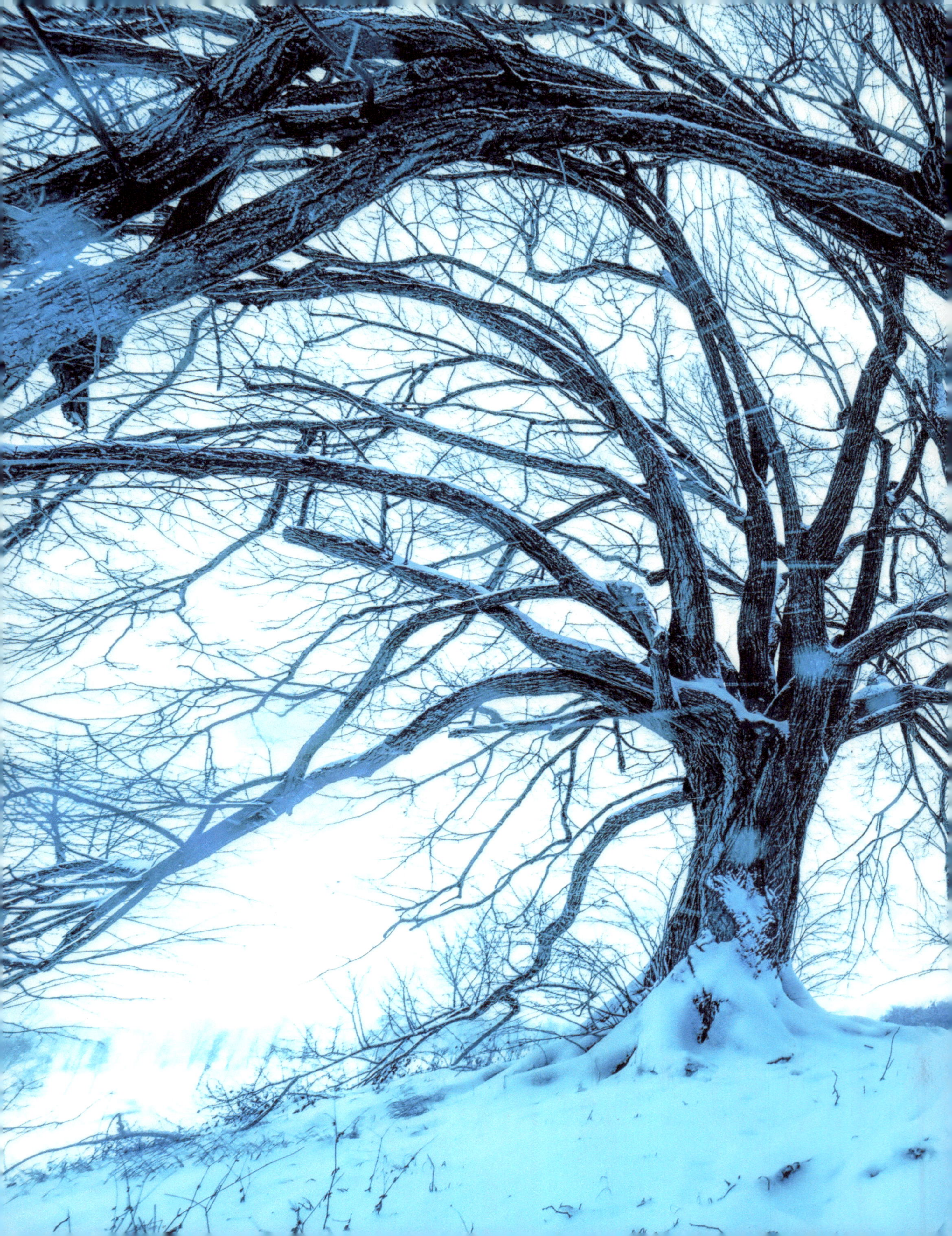

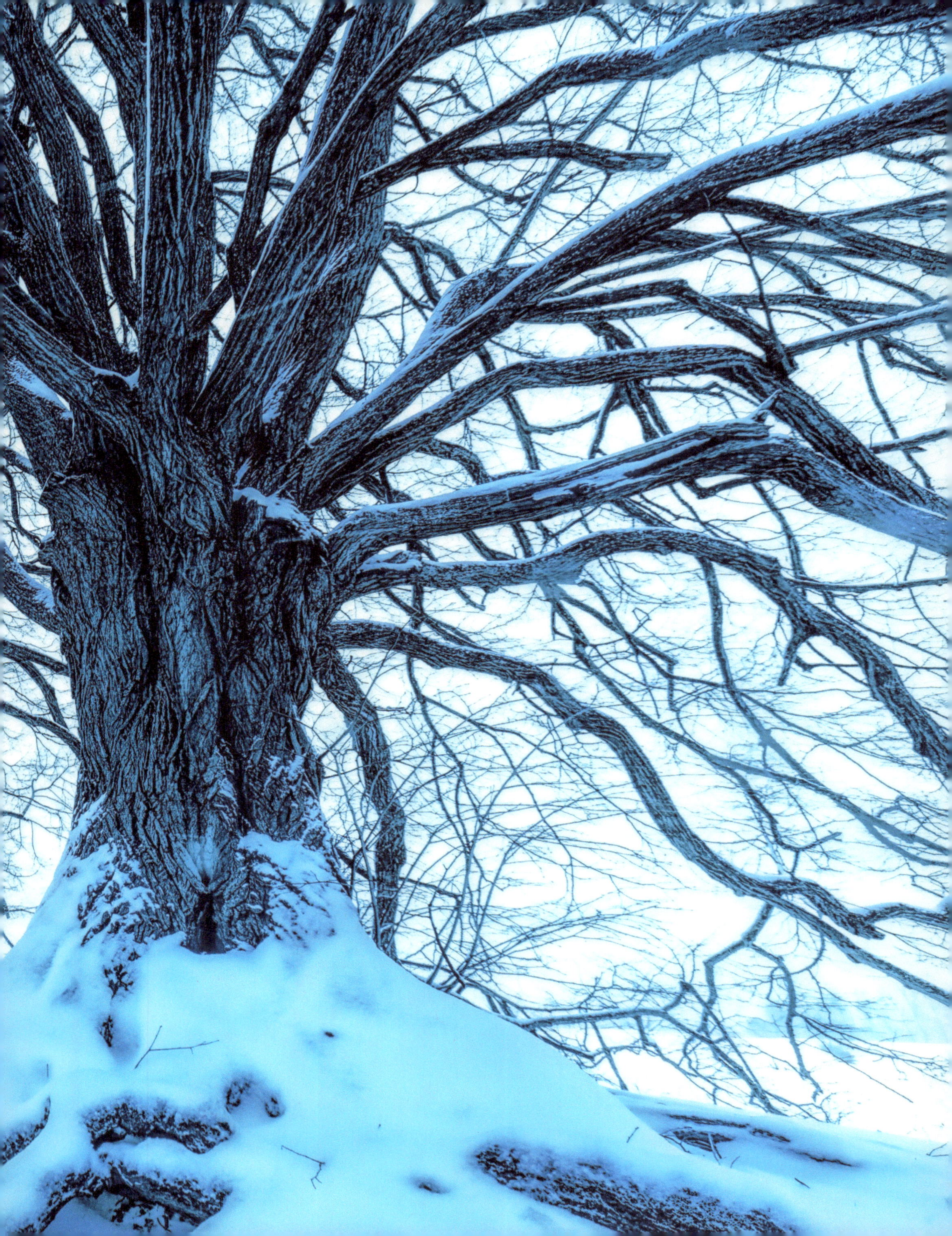

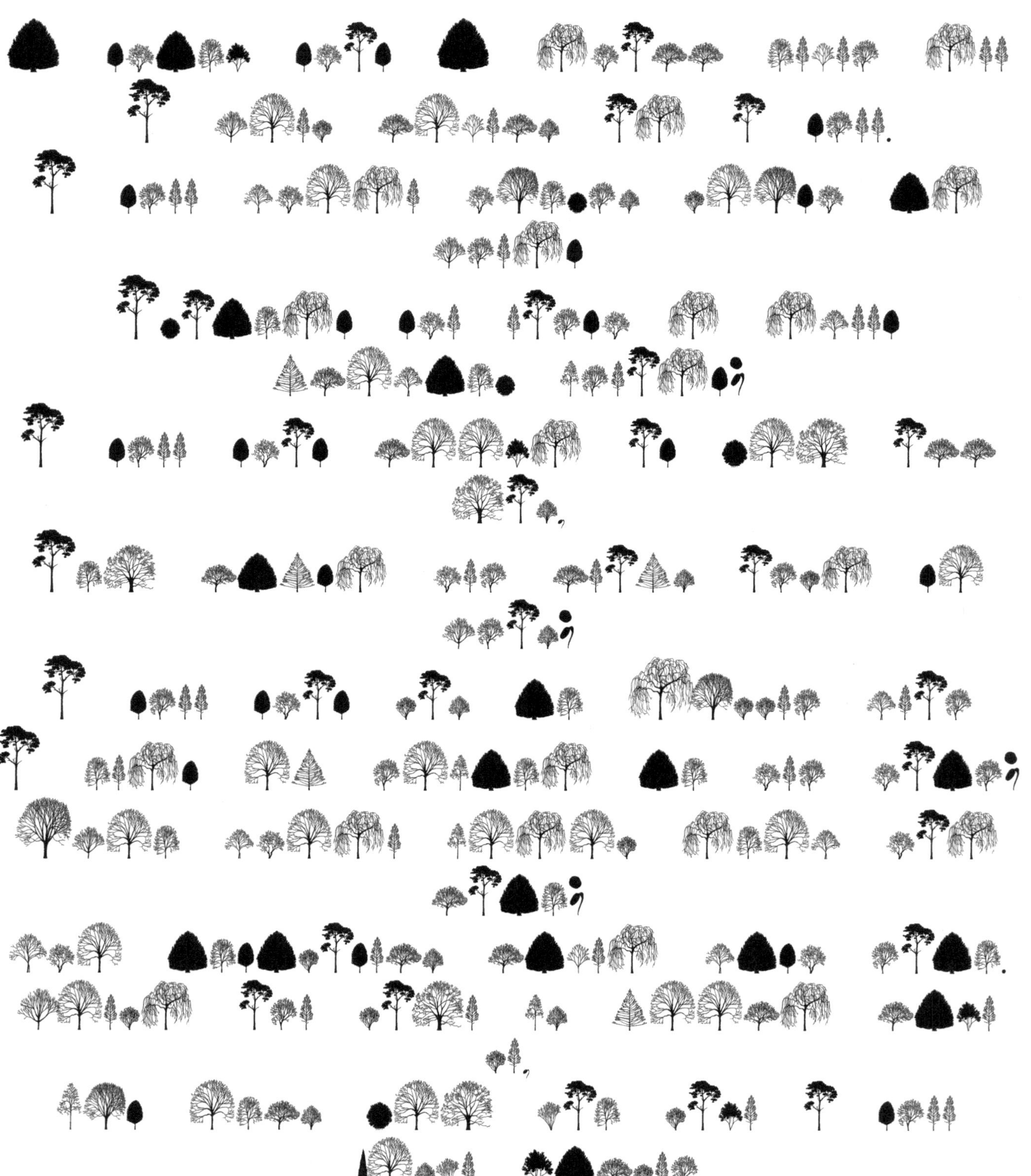

From the Forest to Savannah

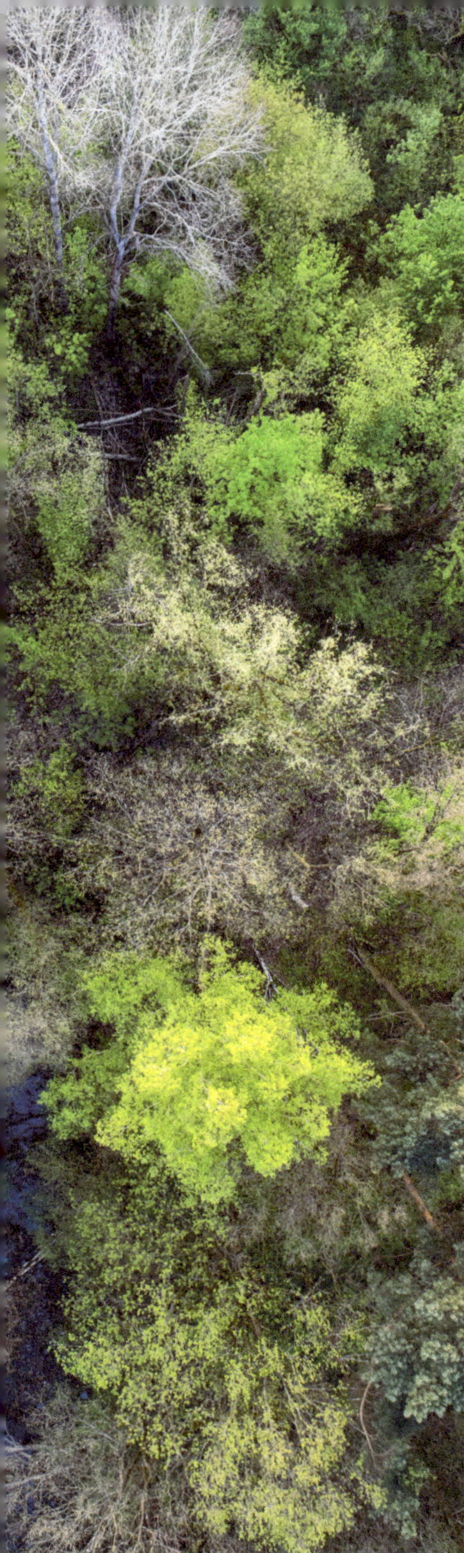 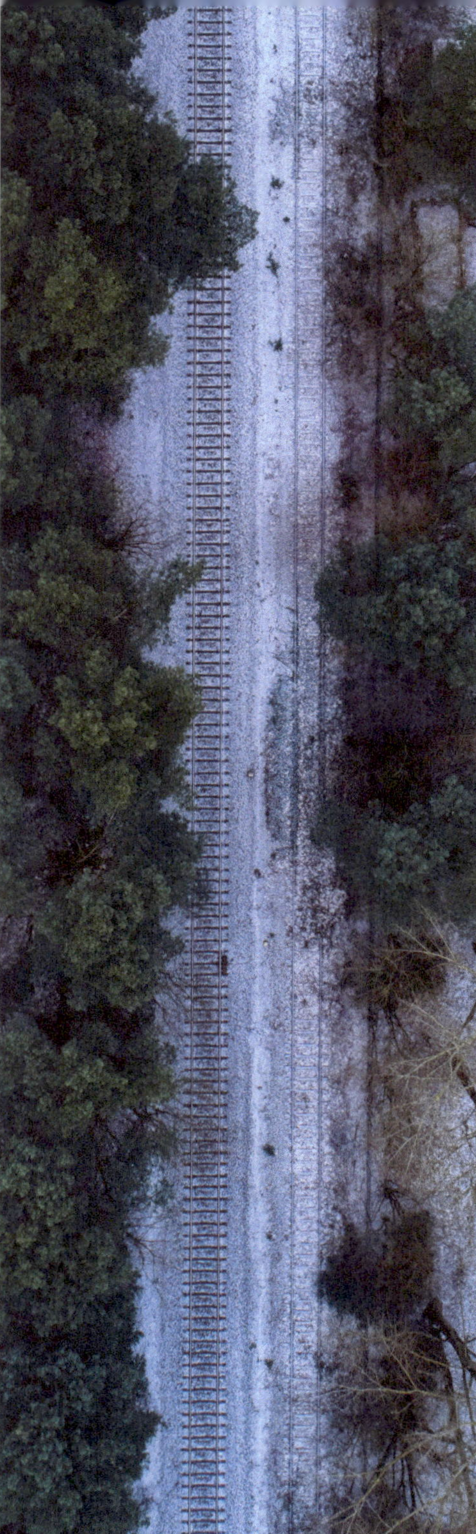 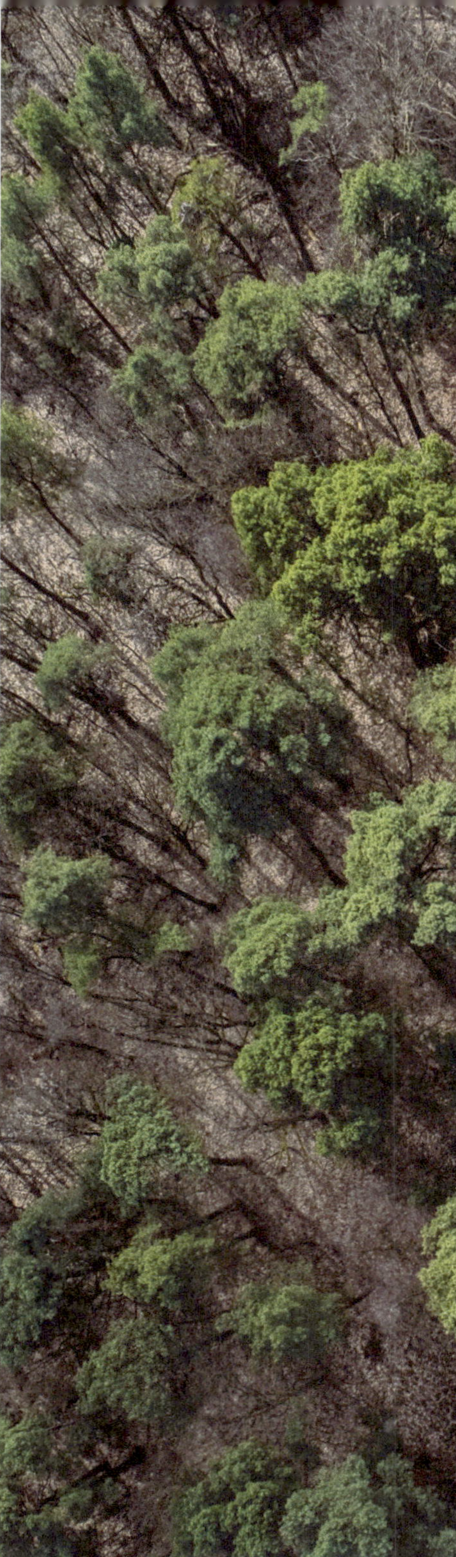

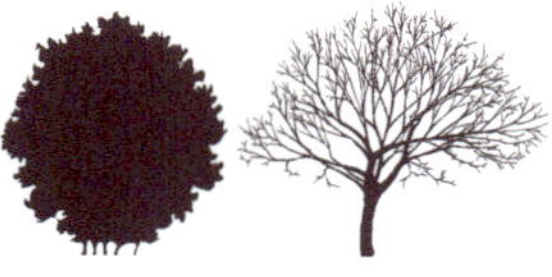
Images by Sebastian Gößl from Pixabay

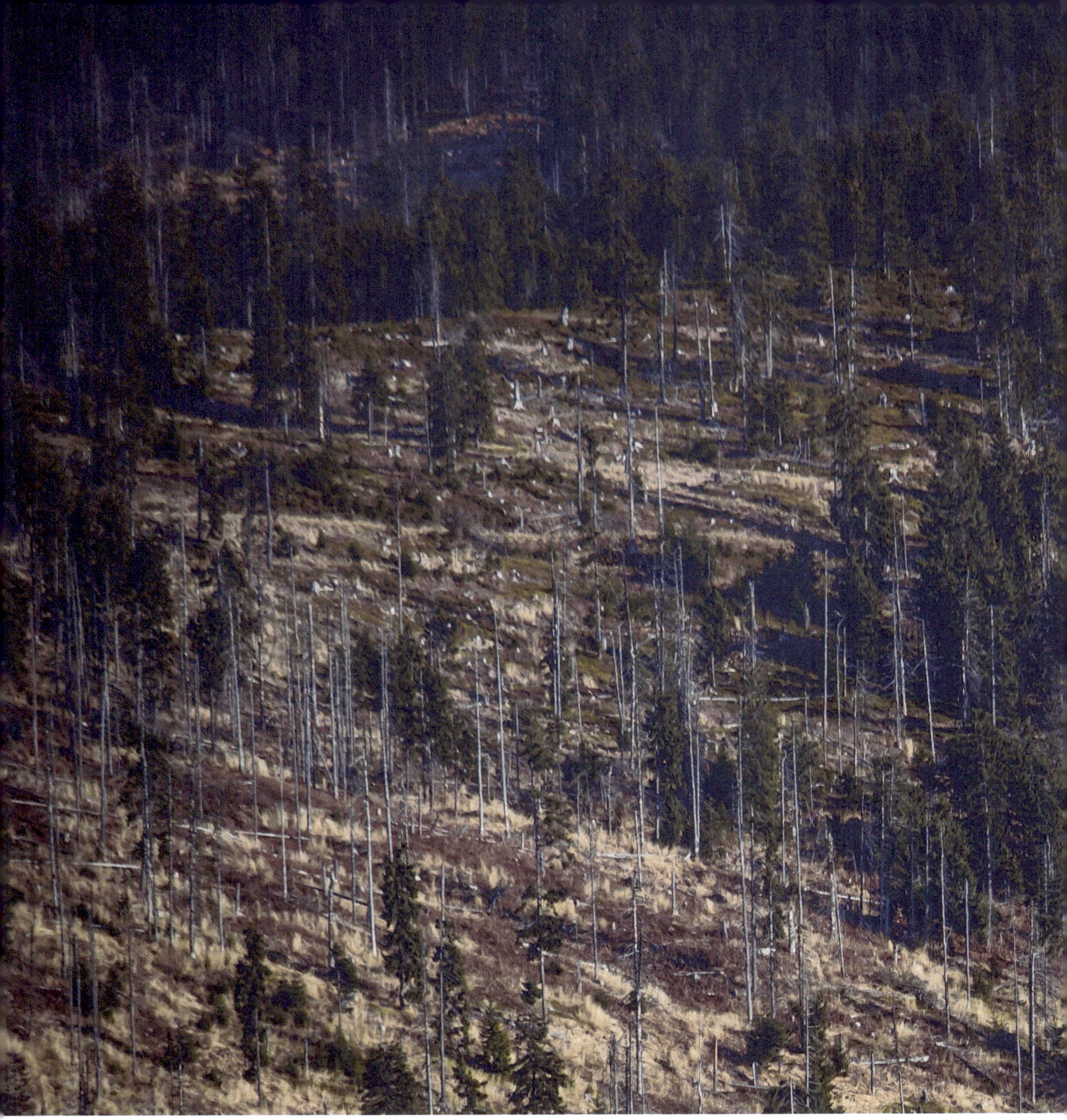

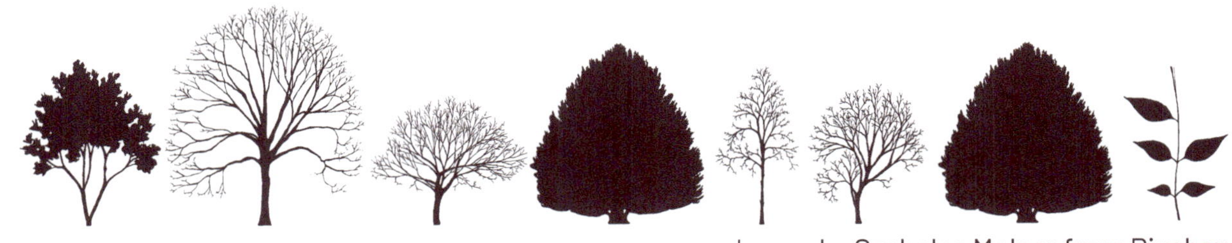

Image by Szabolcs Molnar from Pixabay

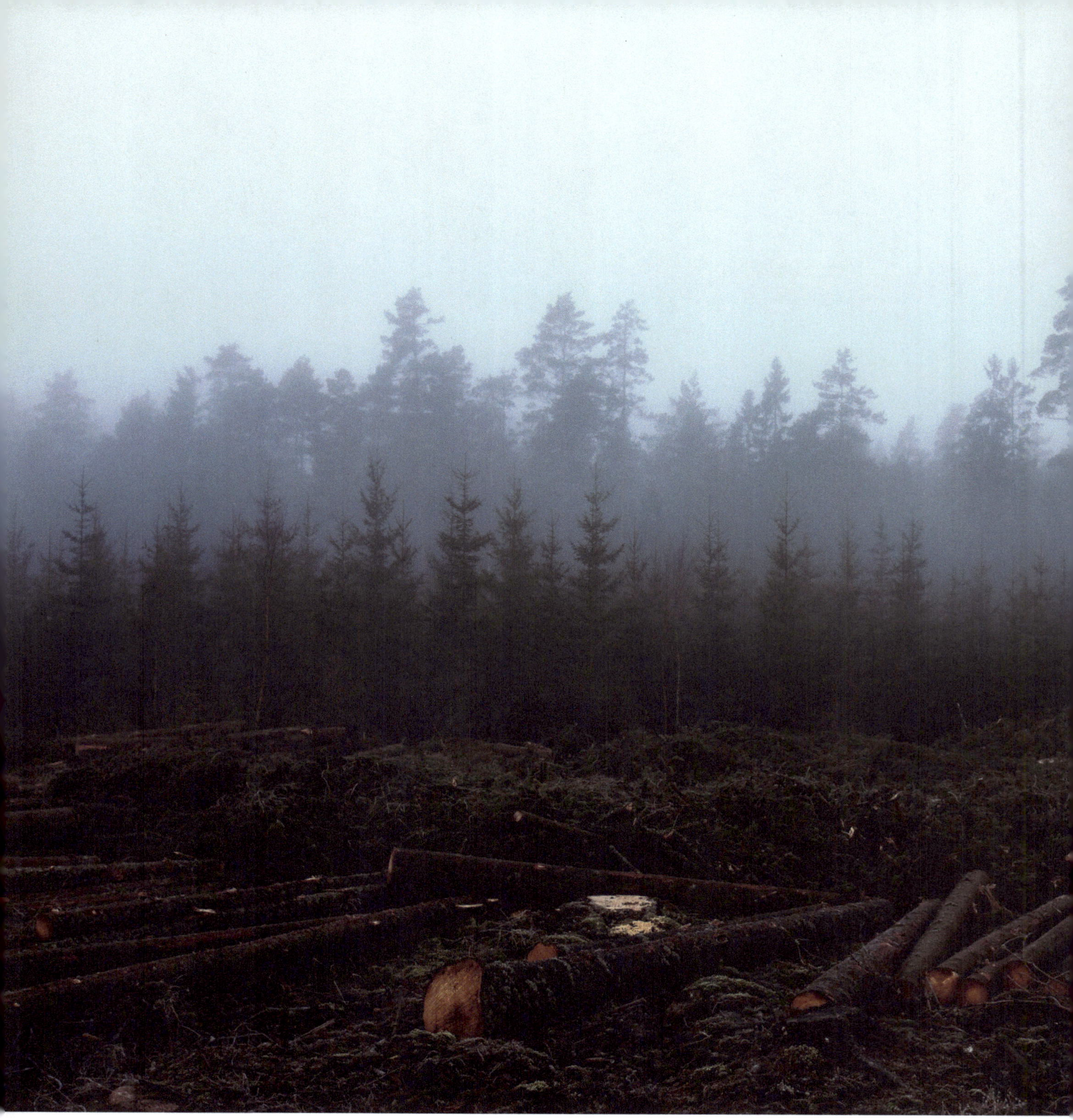

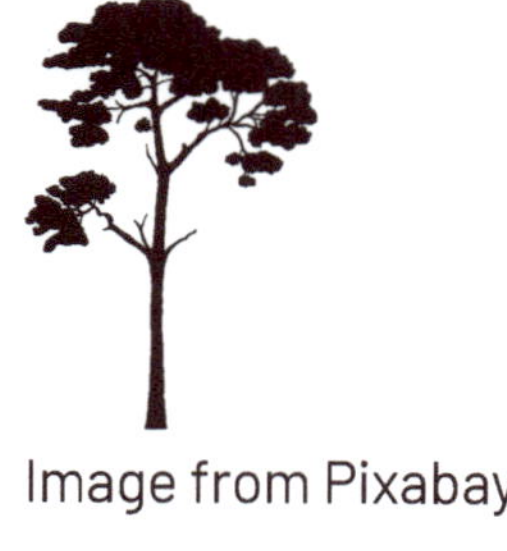

Image from Pixabay

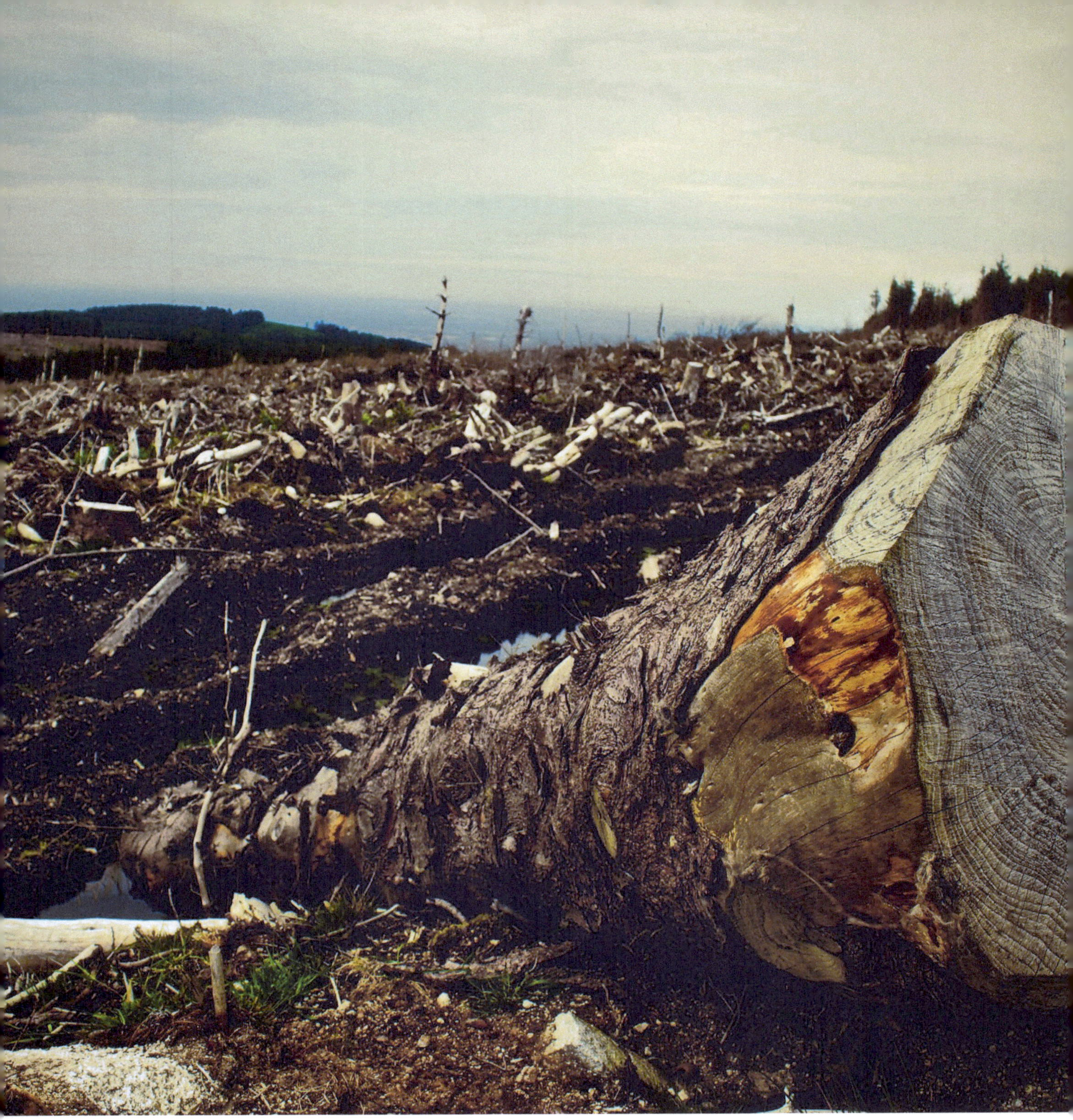

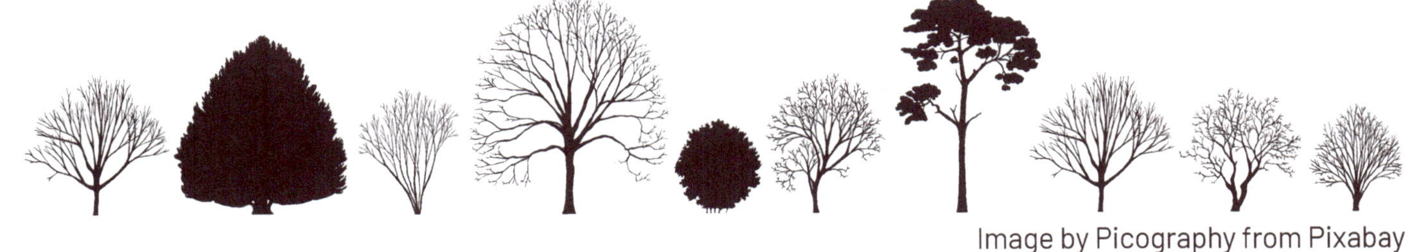
Image by Picography from Pixabay

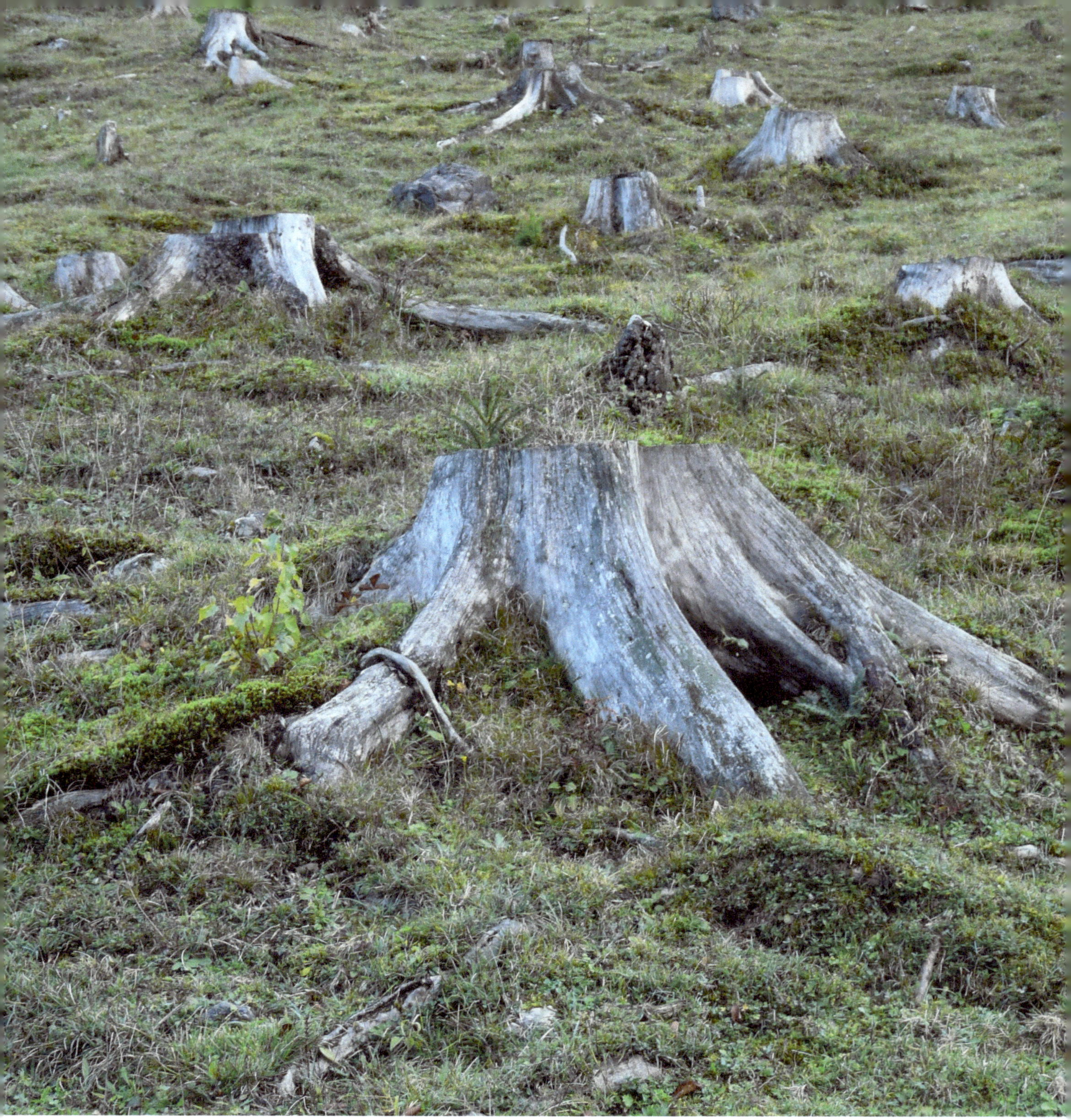

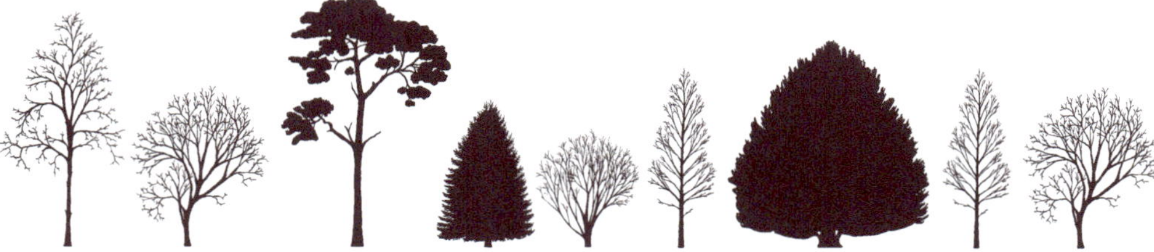

Image by Hans Braxmeier from Pixabay

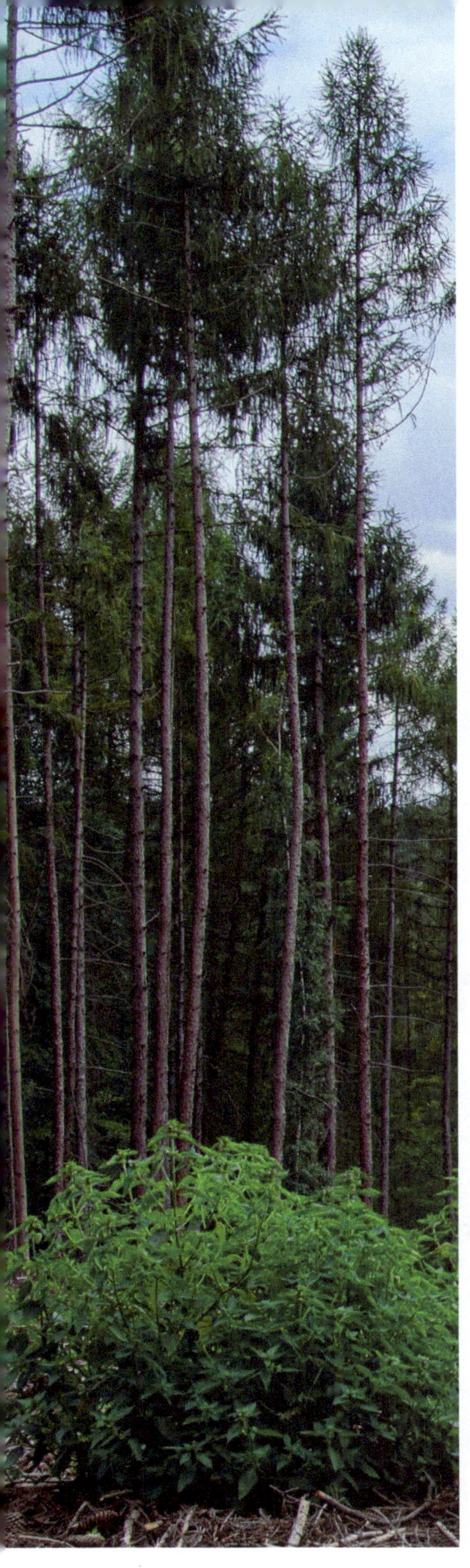
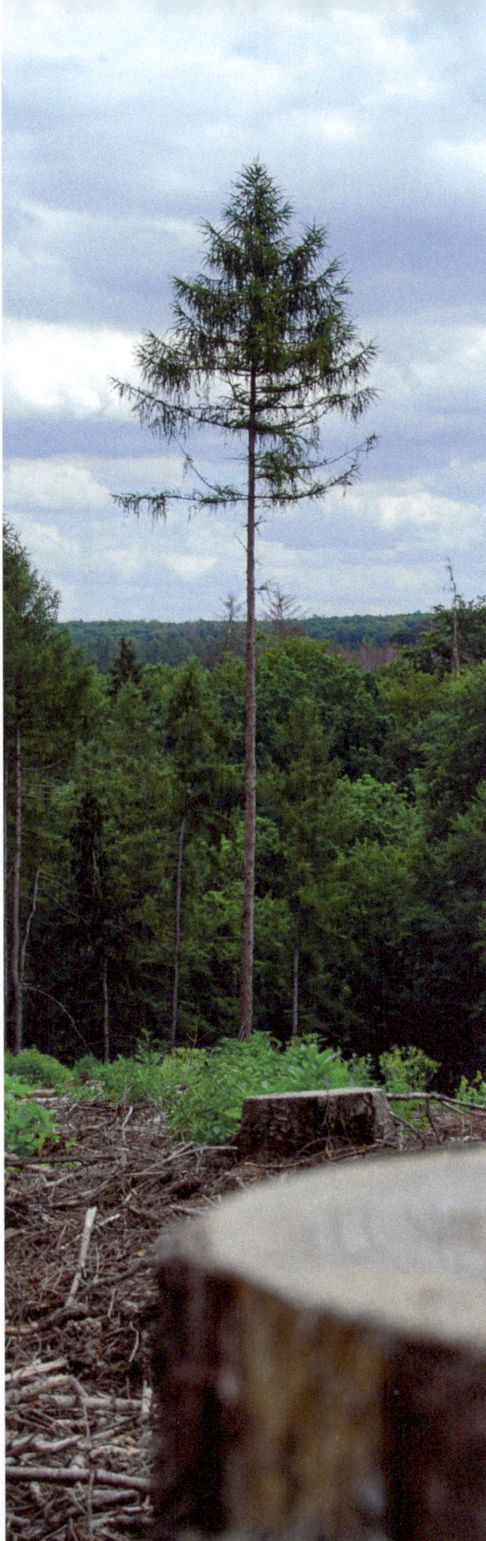
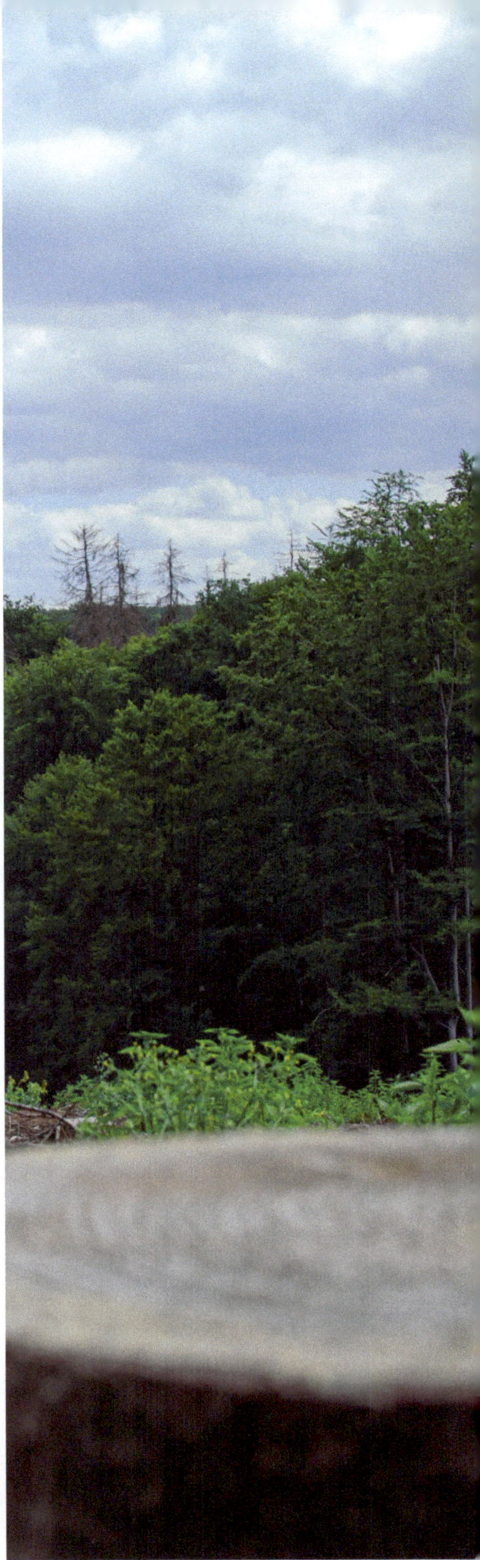
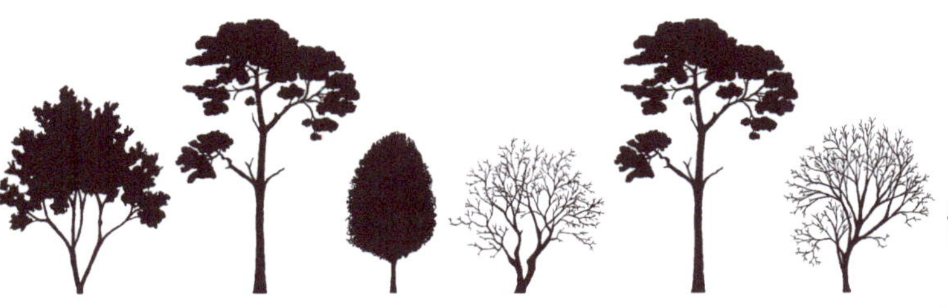
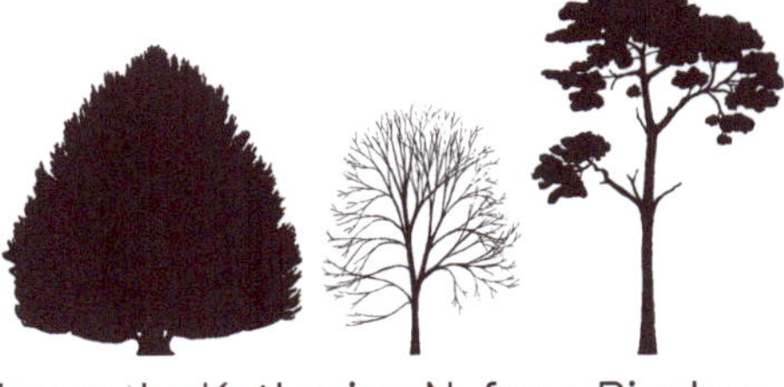

Image by Katharina N. from Pixabay

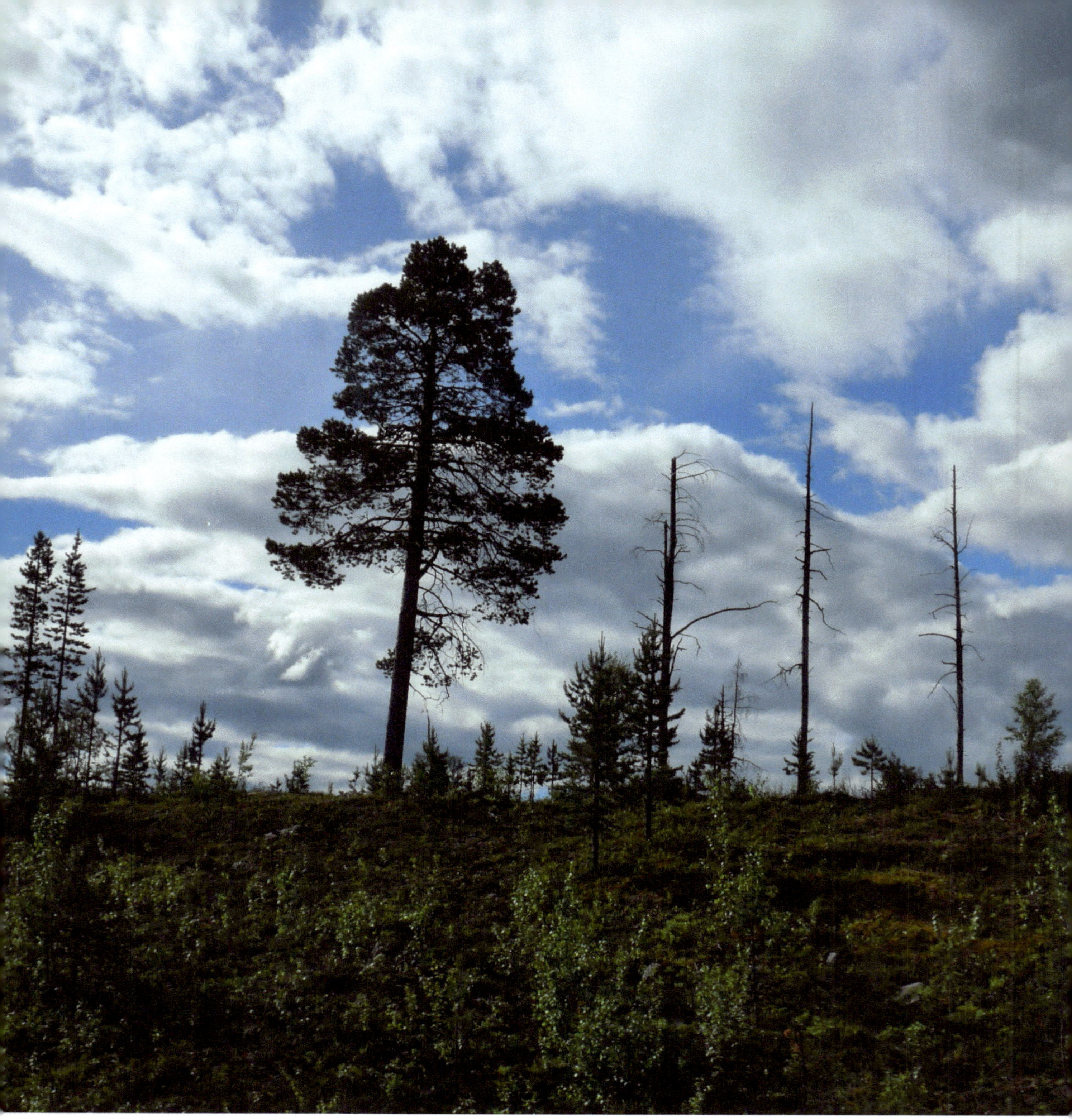

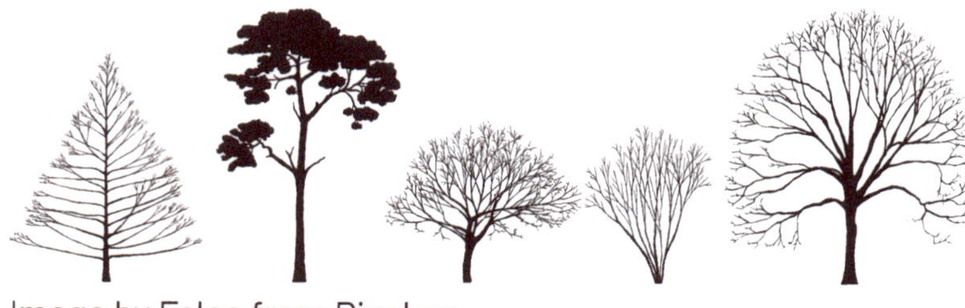

Image by Falco from Pixabay

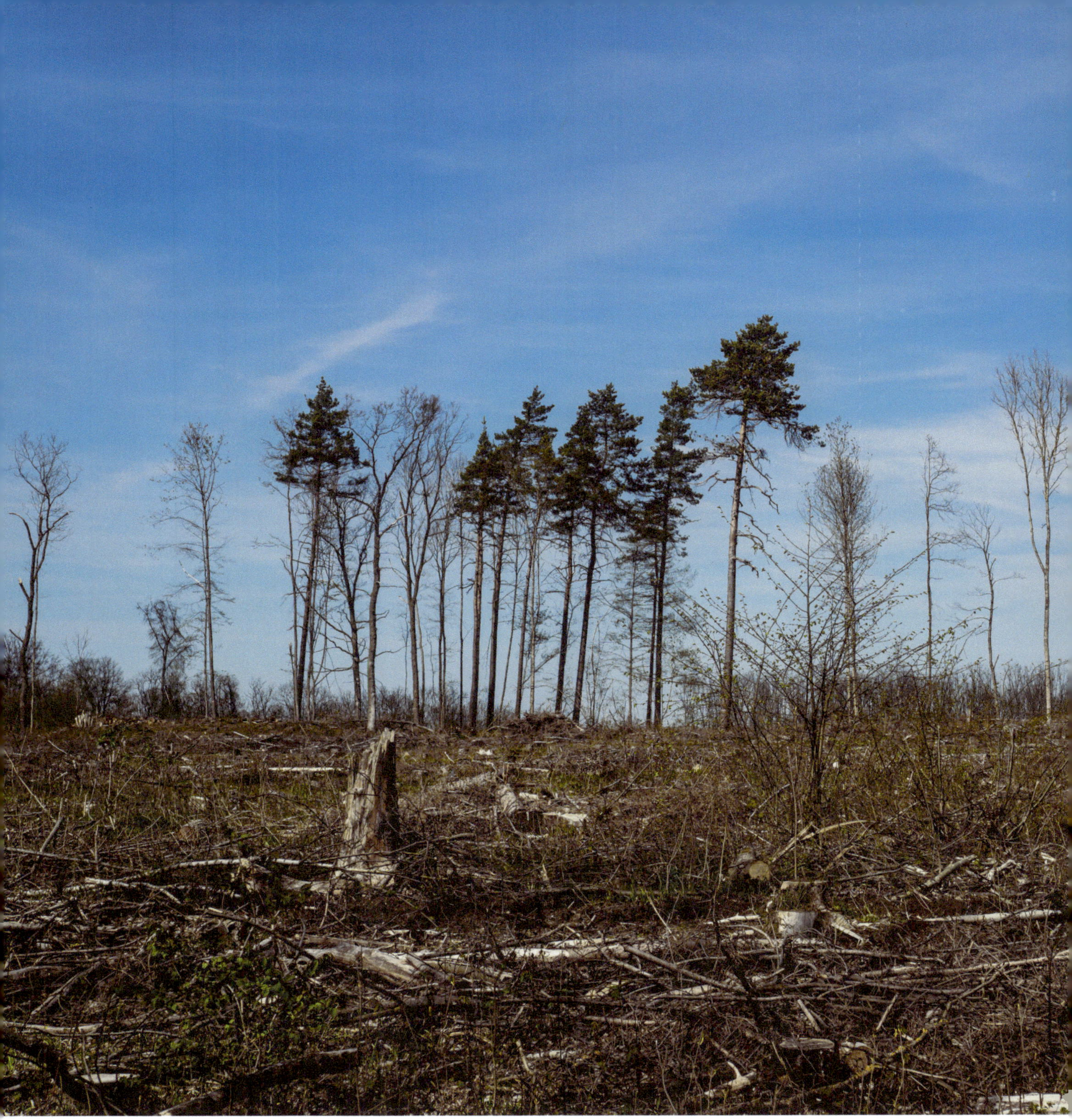

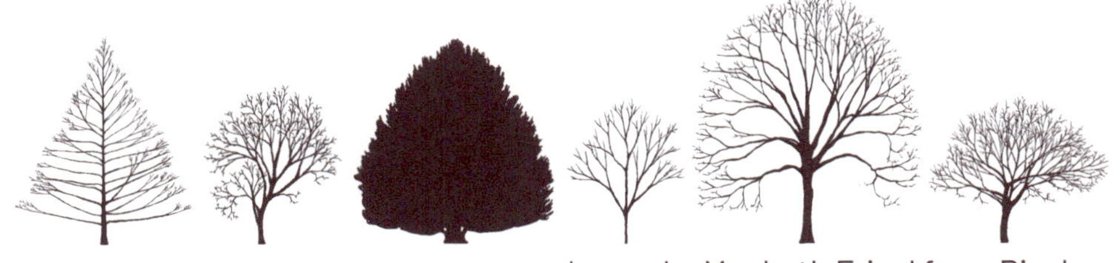

Image by Macbeth Frivol from Pixabay

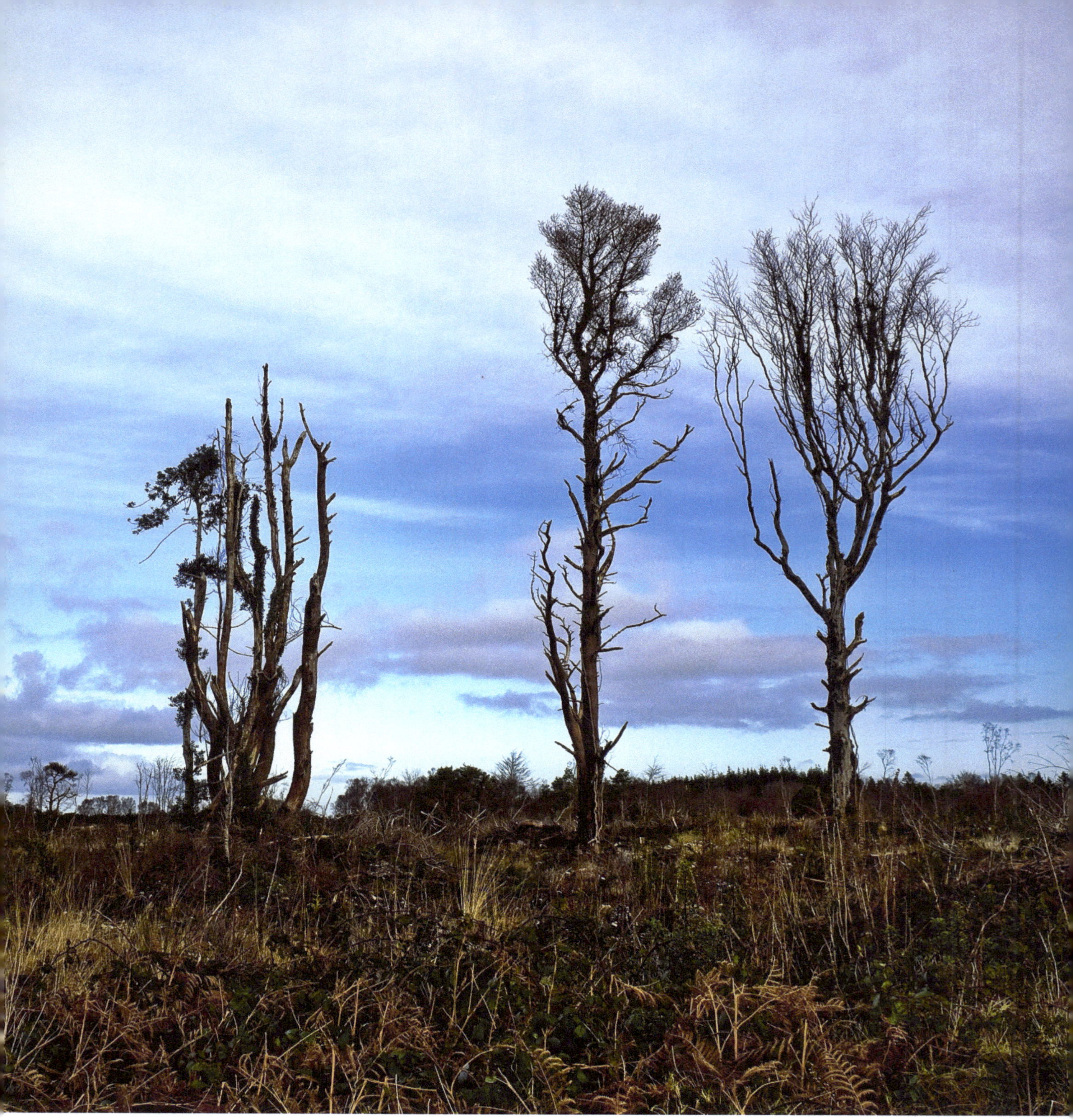

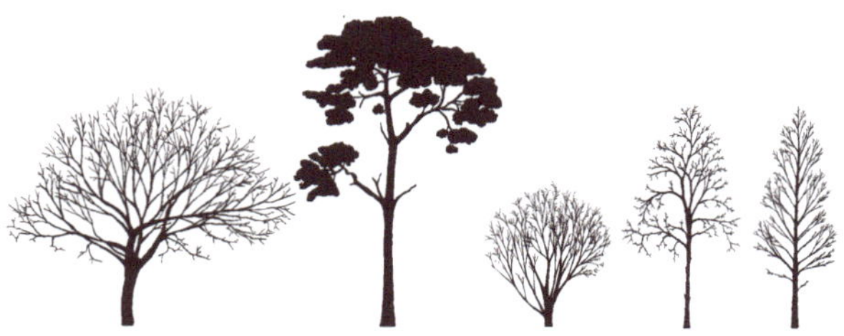

Image by Al Lambe from Pixabay

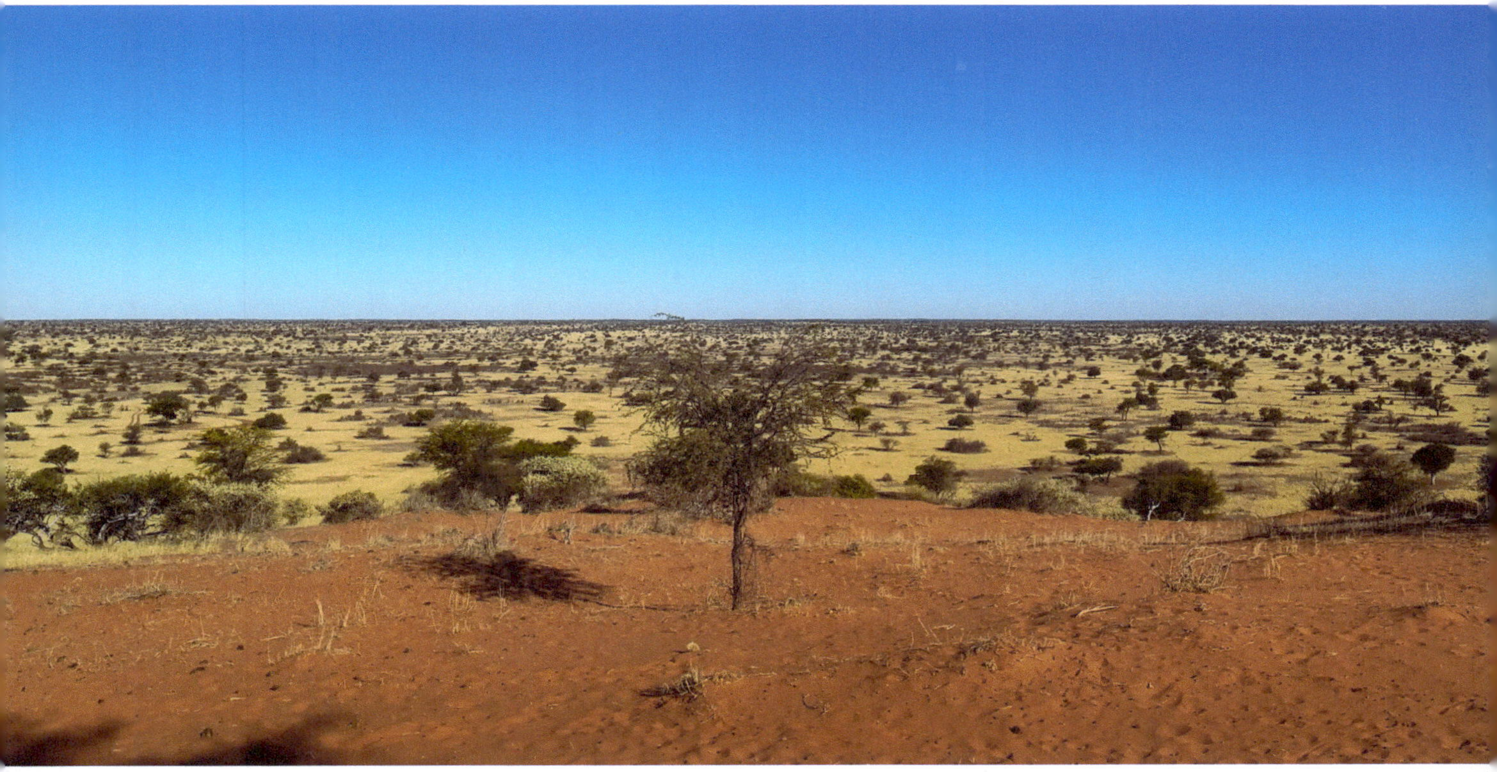

"Trees are poems the earth writes upon the sky,
We fell them down and turn them into paper,
That we may record our emptiness."
— Kahlil Gibran

Kalahari Desert, Namibia / Image by Kolibri5 from Pixabay

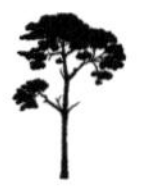

From the Savannah to Desert

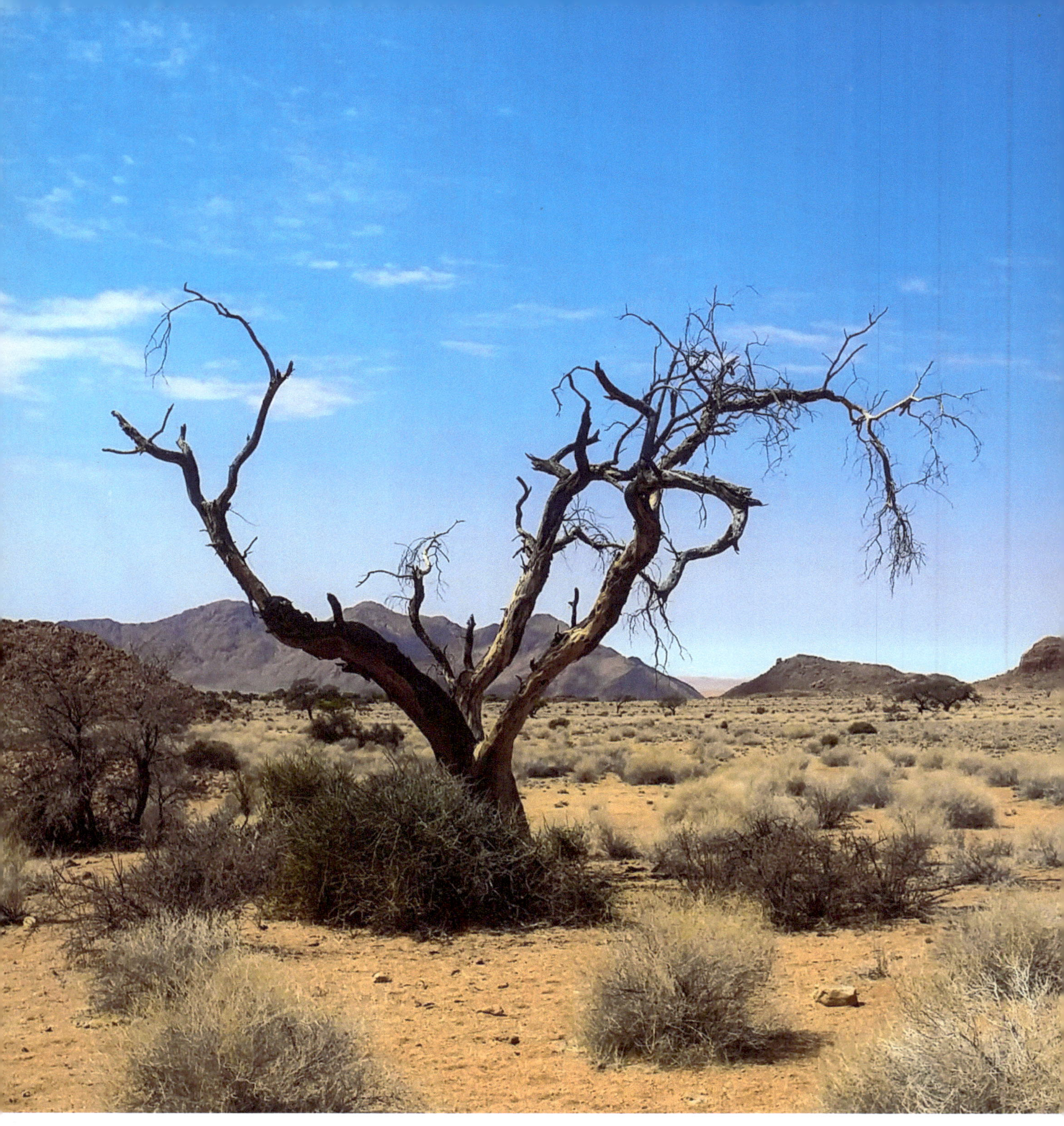

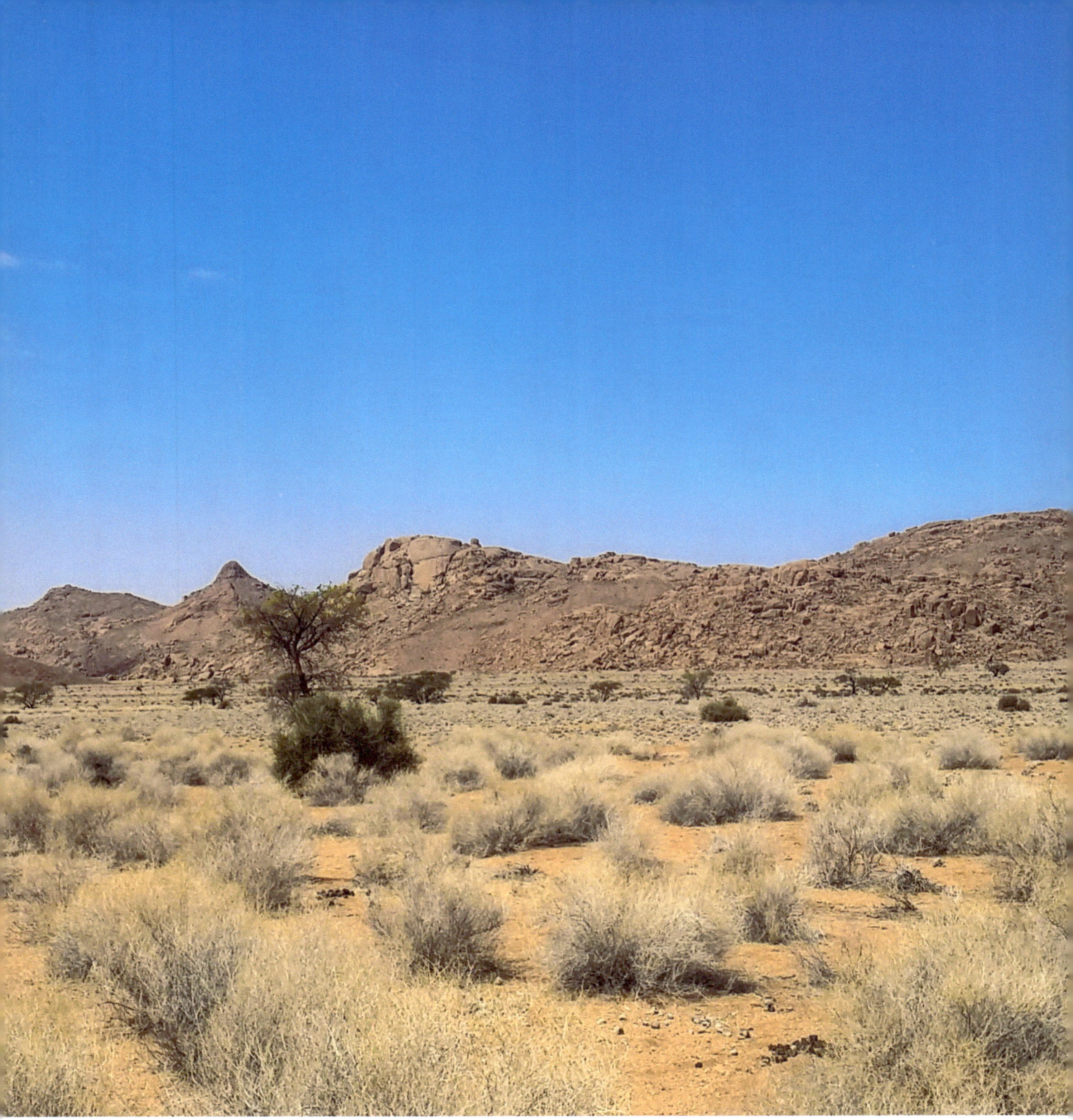

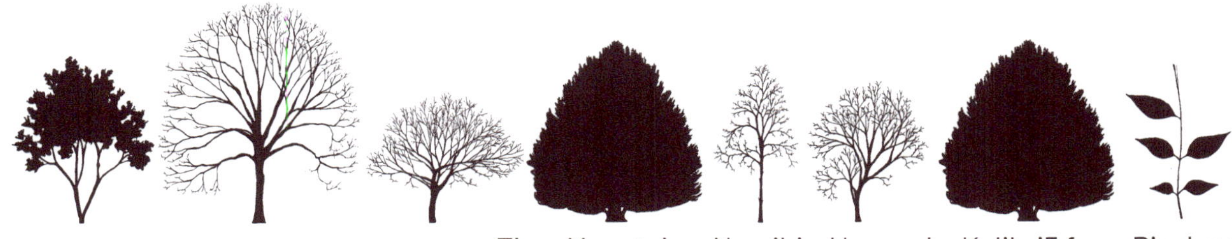

Tiras Mountains, Namibia / Image by Kolibri5 from Pixabay

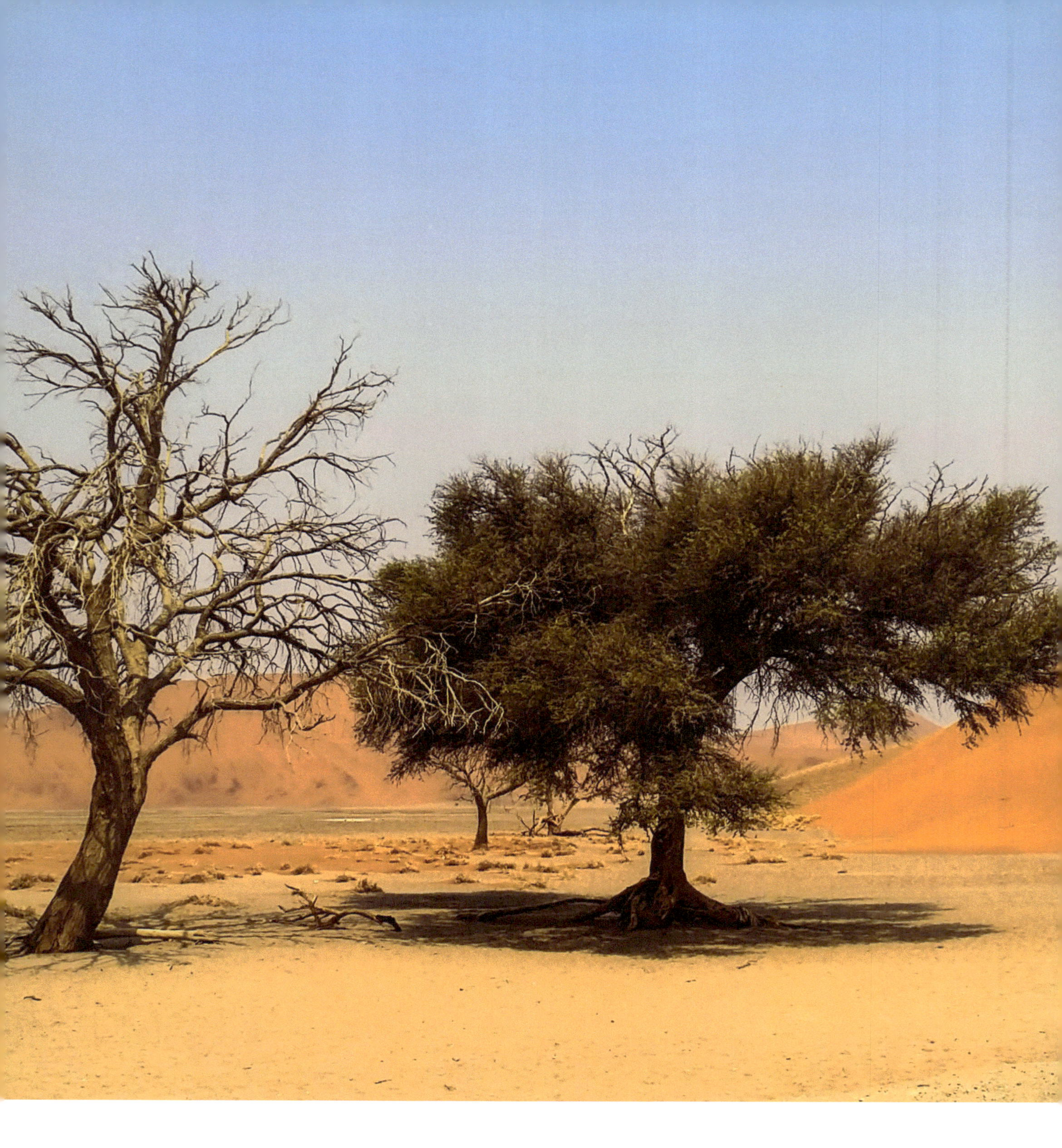

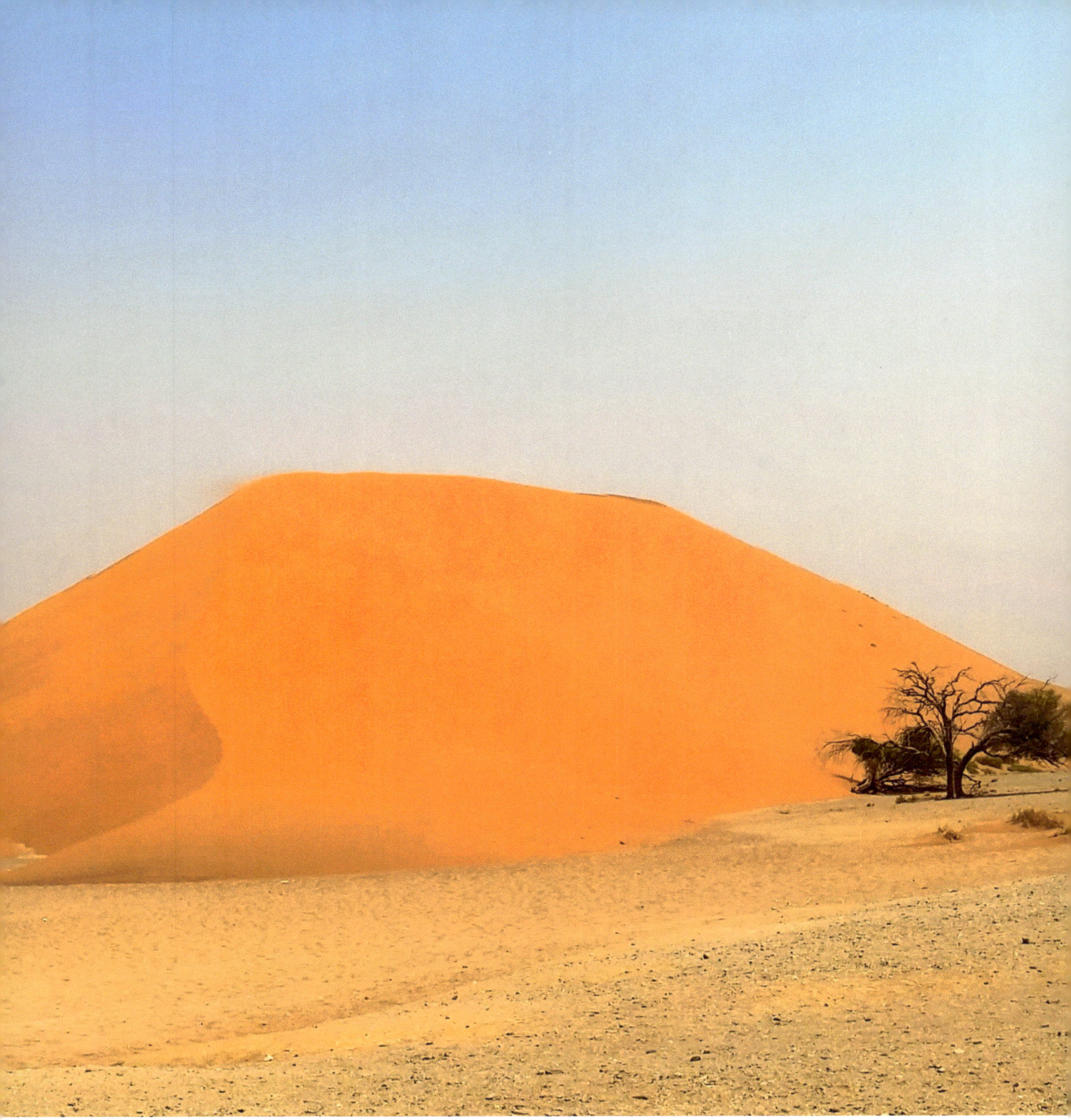

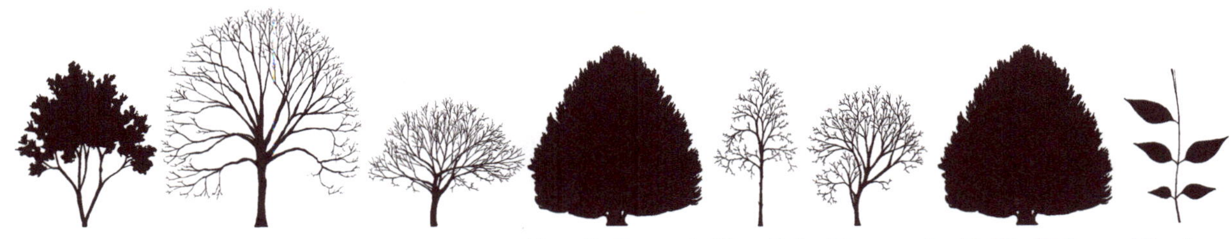

Namib Desert, Namibia / Image by Kolibri5 from Pixabay

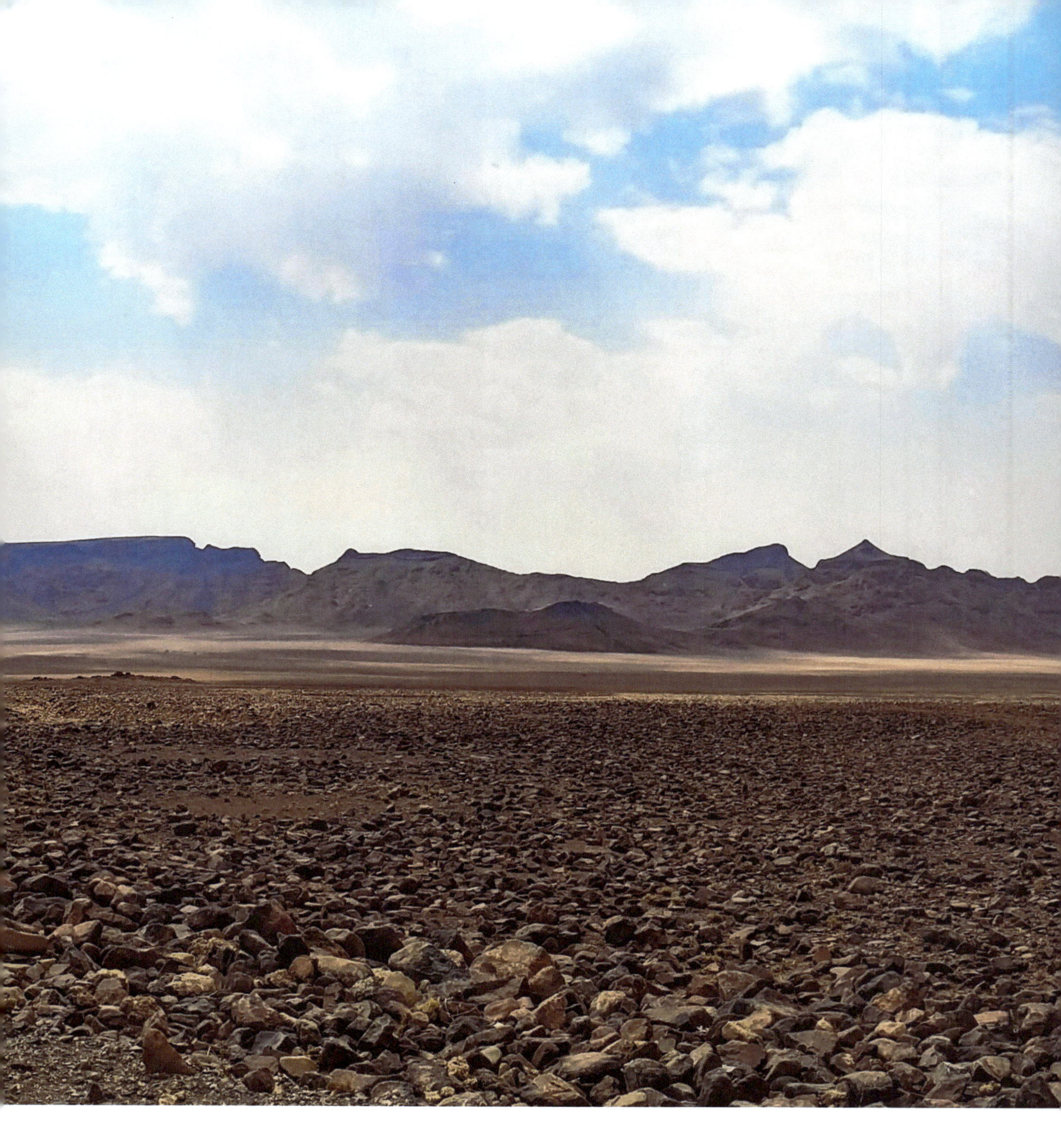

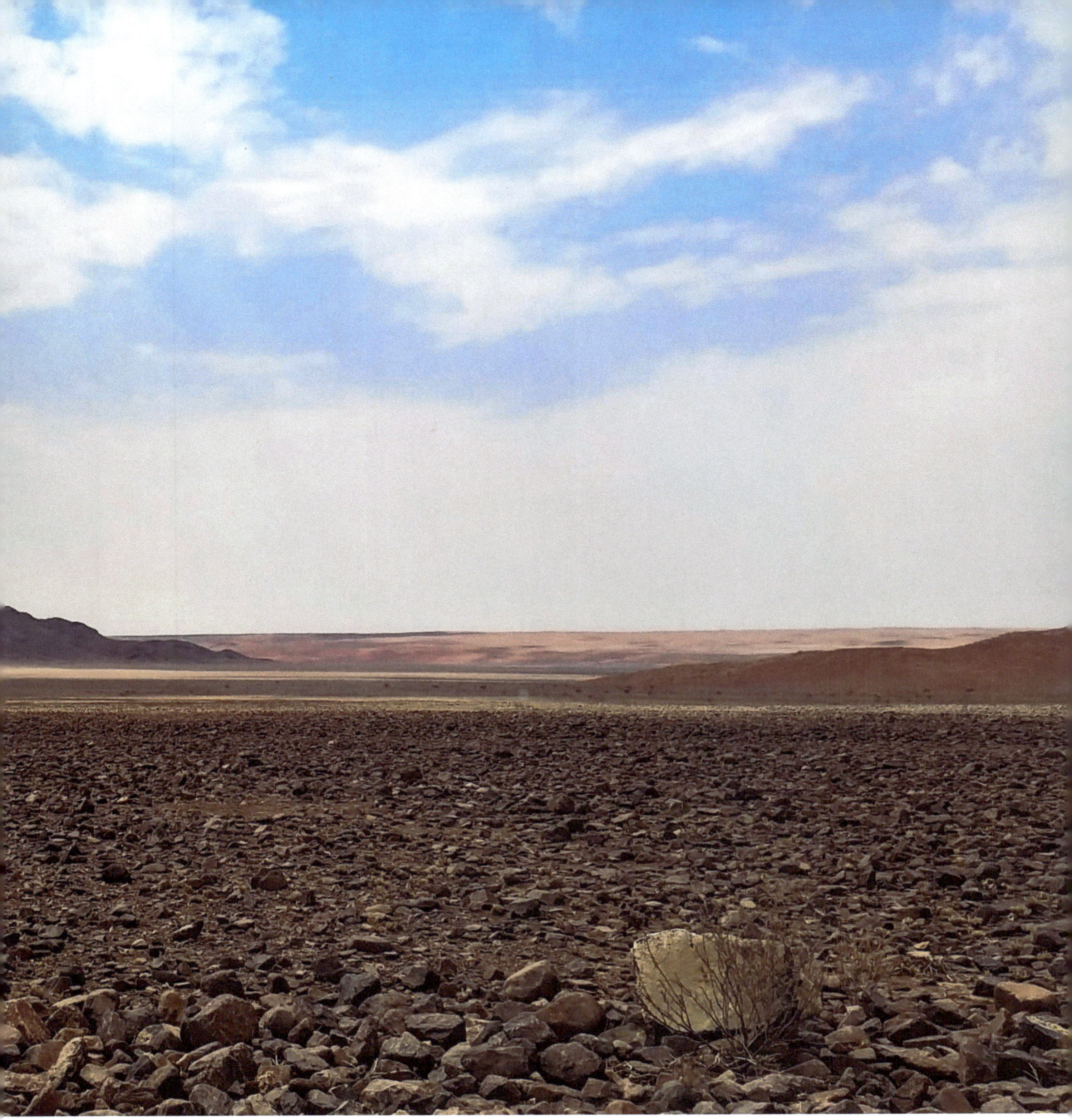

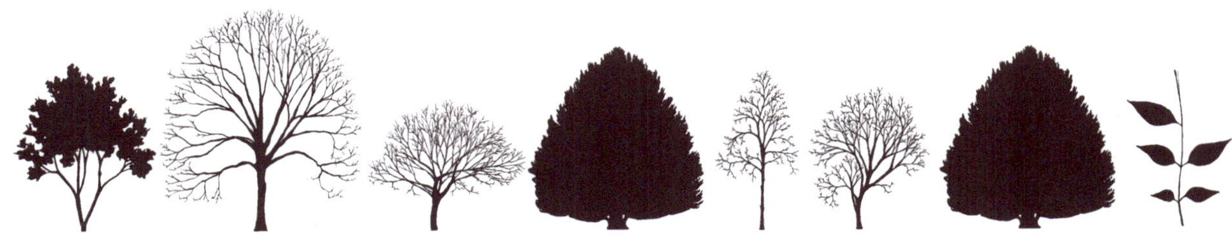

Namib Desert, Namibia / Image by Kolibri5 from Pixabay

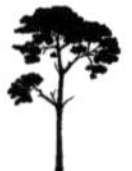

From the Desert to Prairie

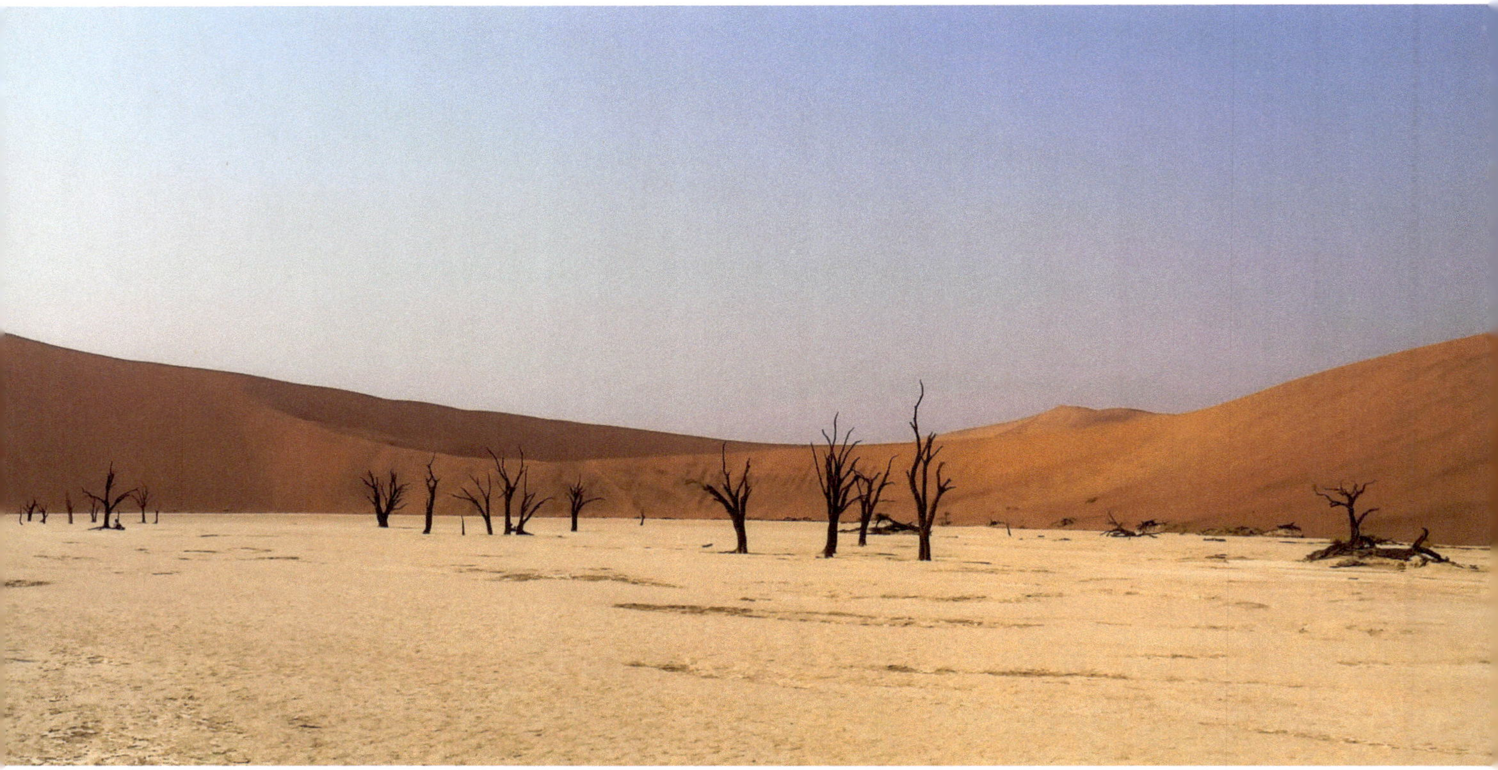

"Even if I knew that tomorrow the world would go to pieces,
I would still plant my apple tree."
— Martin Luther

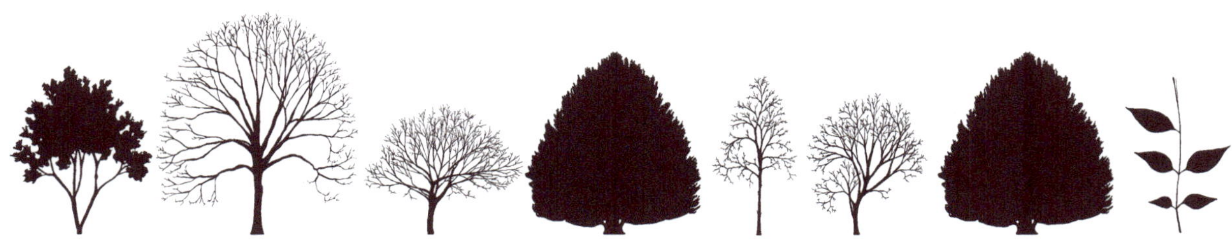

Namib Desert, Namibia / Image by Kolibri5 from Pixabay

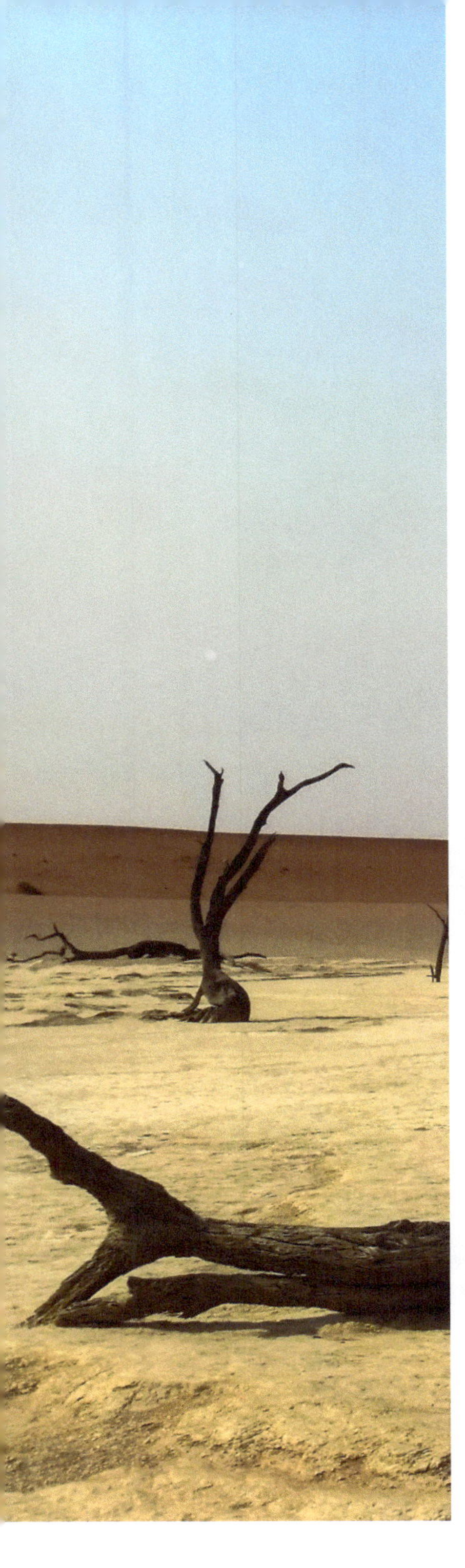
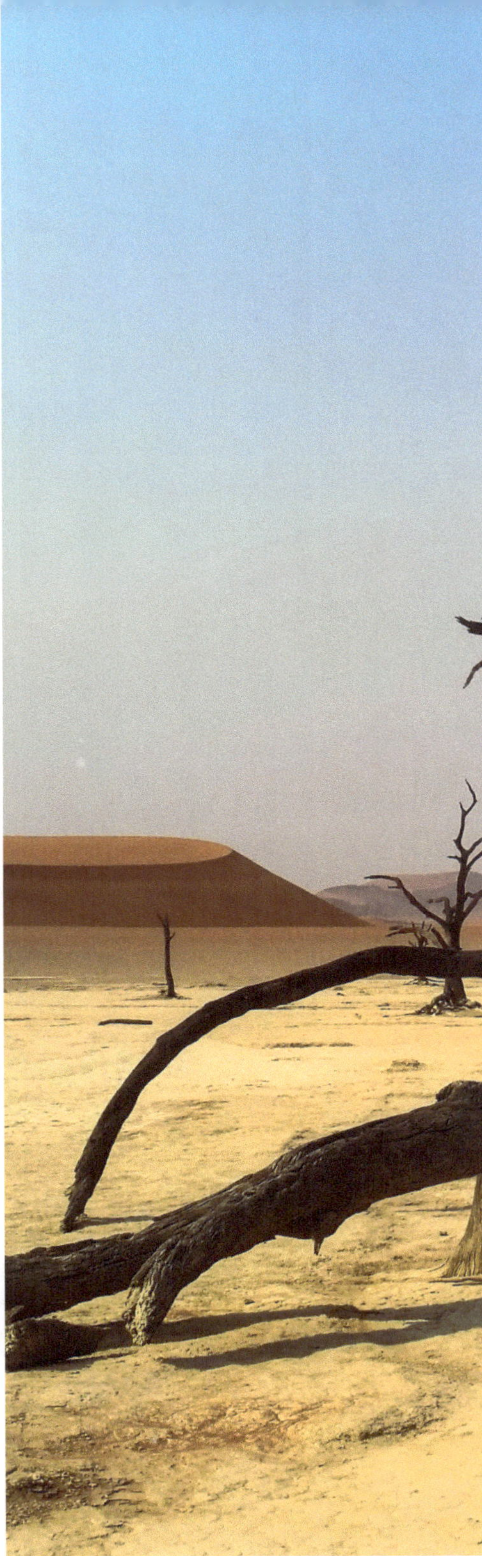
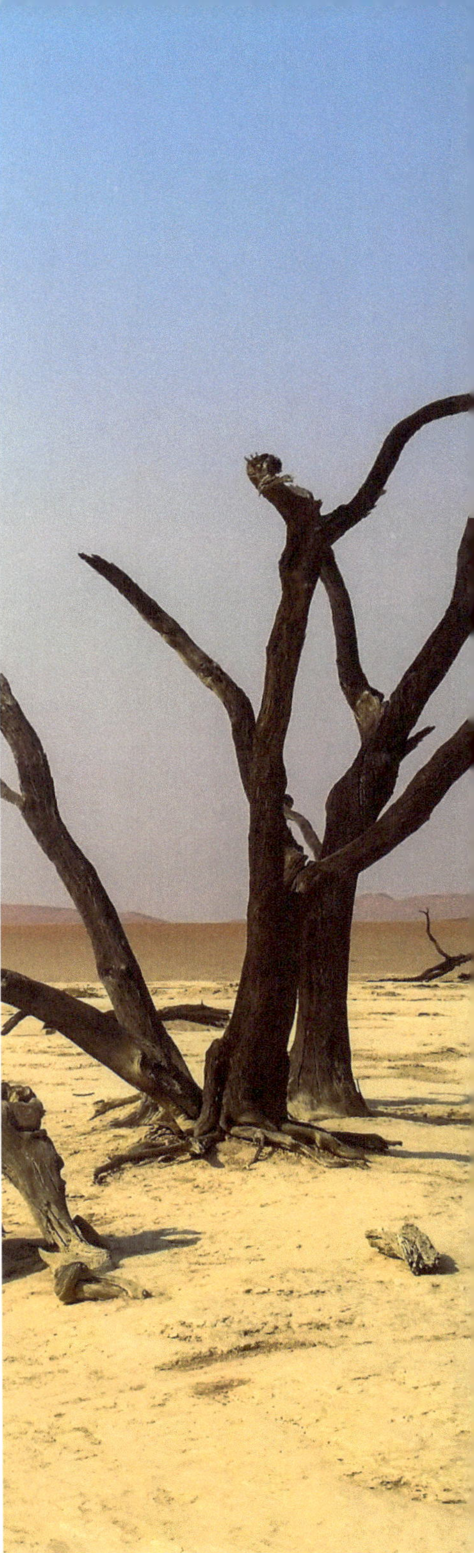
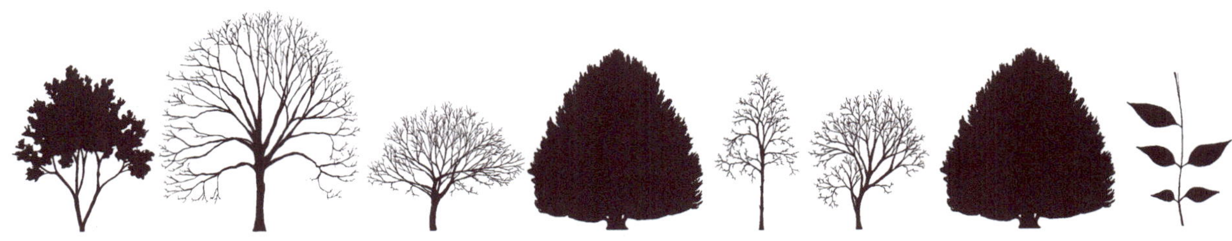

Namib Desert, Namibia / Image by Kolibri5 from Pixabay

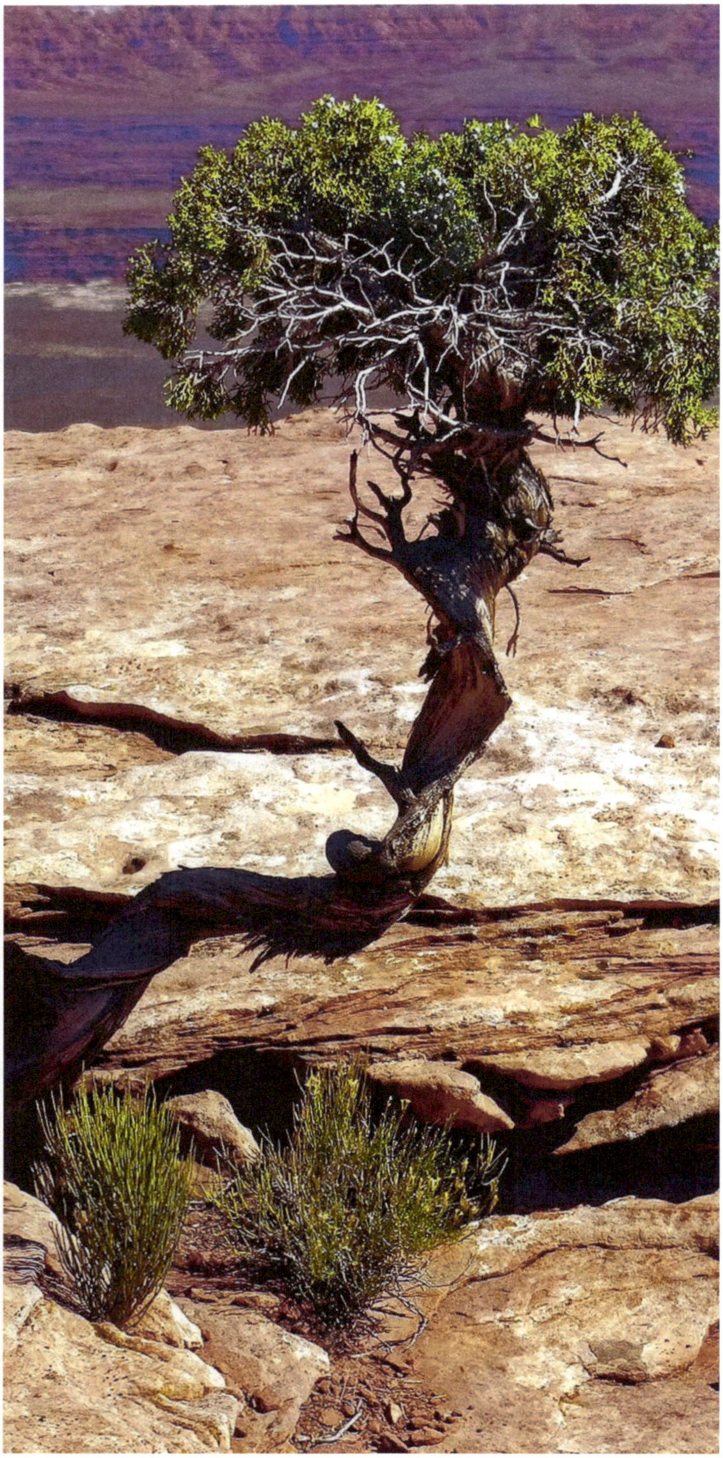

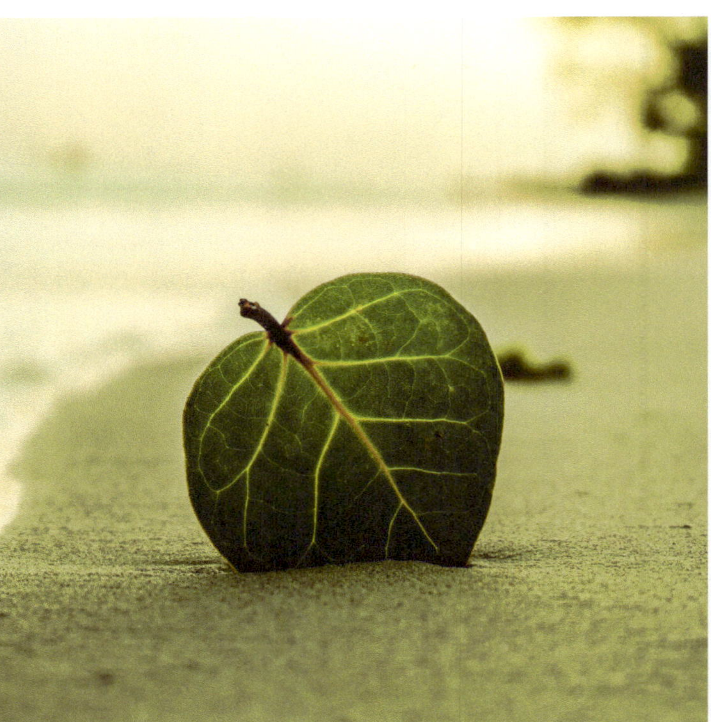

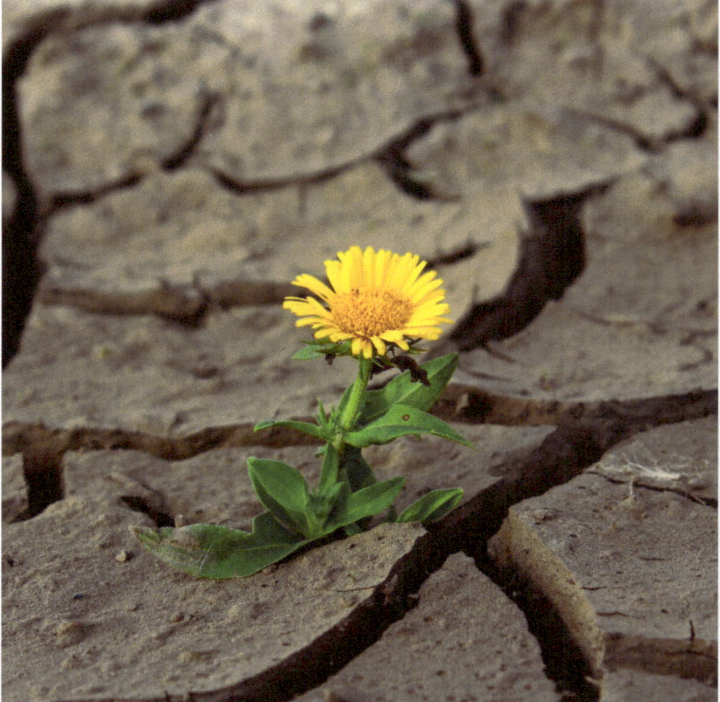

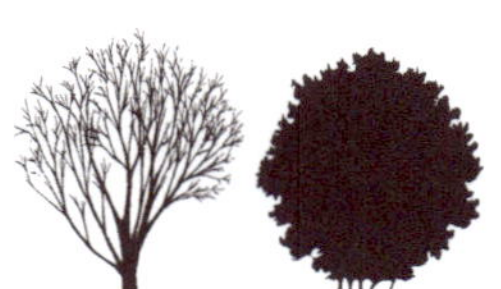

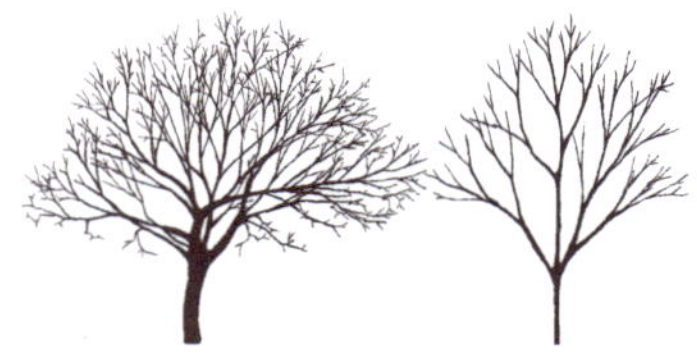

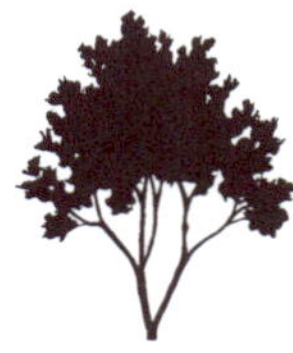

Images by Mike Goad (Tree), Leonardo Valente (Leaf), Klimkin (Flower) from Pixabay

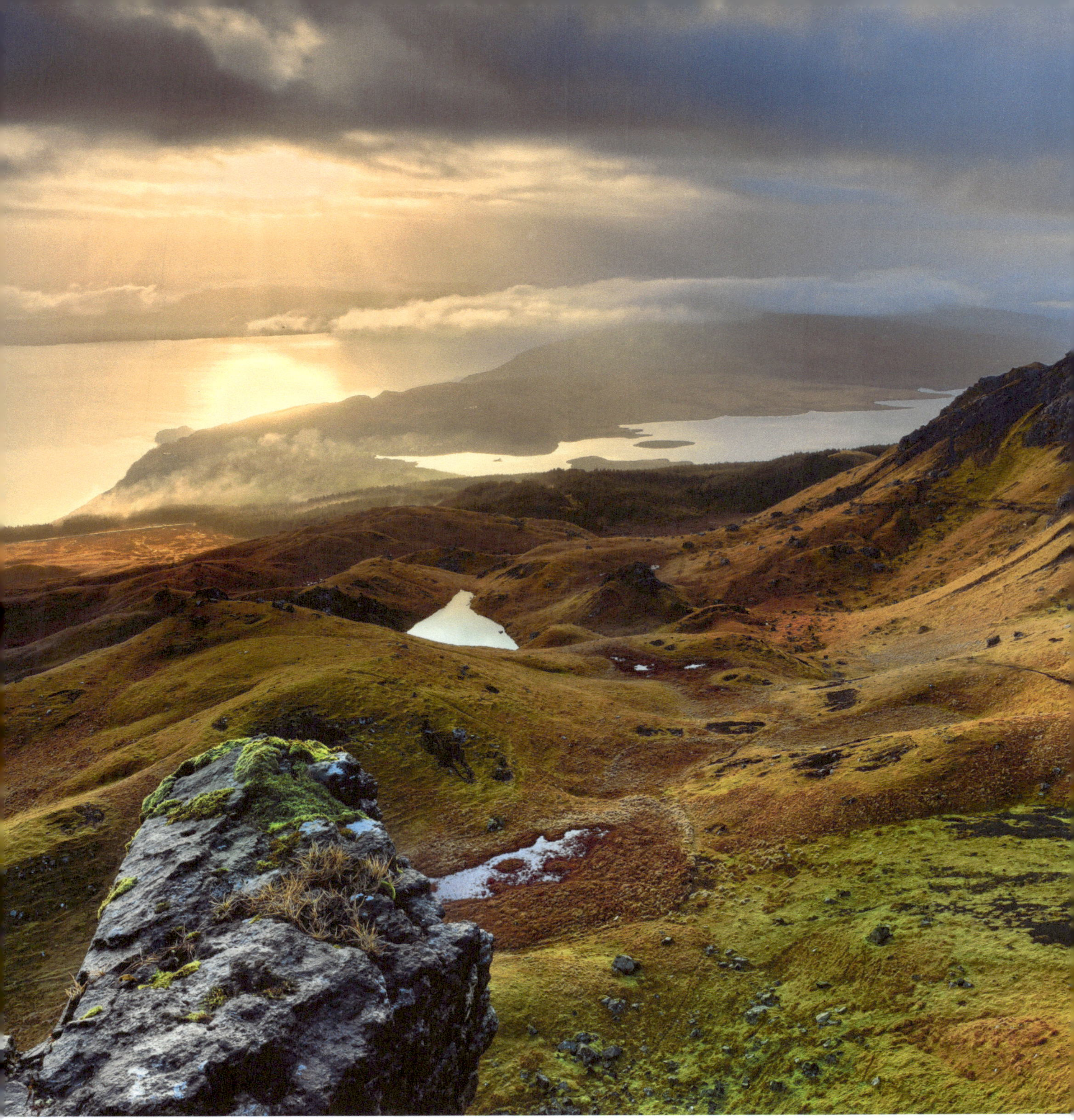

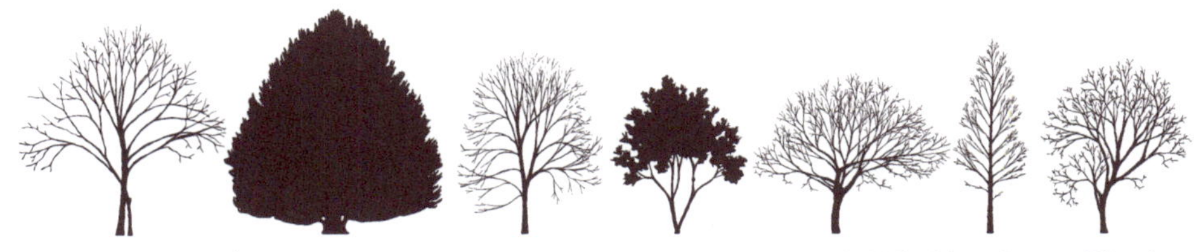

Quiraing (Meall na Suiramach), Isle of Skye, Scotland / Image by Frank Winkler from Pixabay

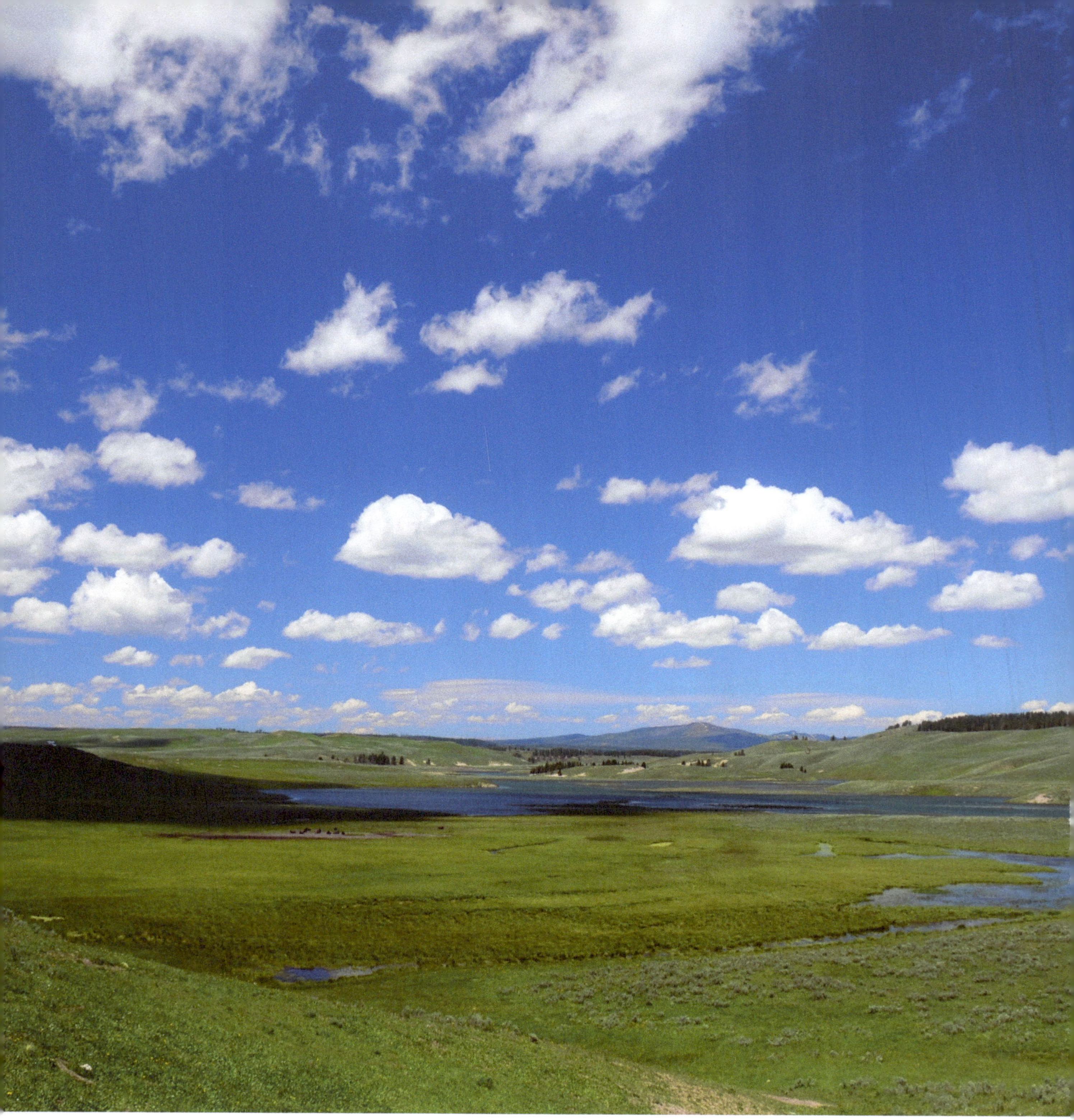

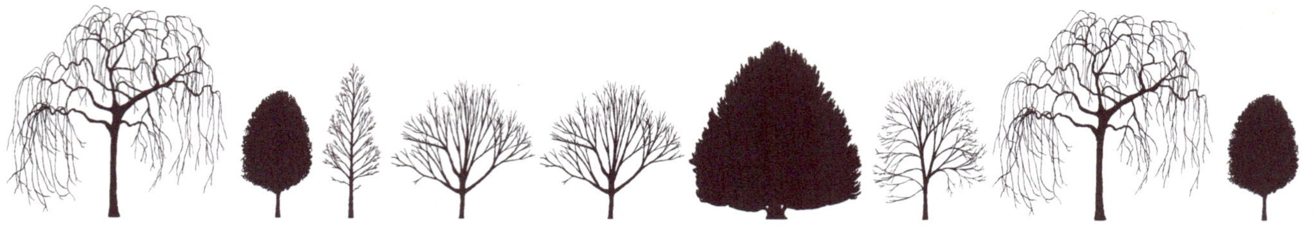

Image by Steppinstars from Pixabay

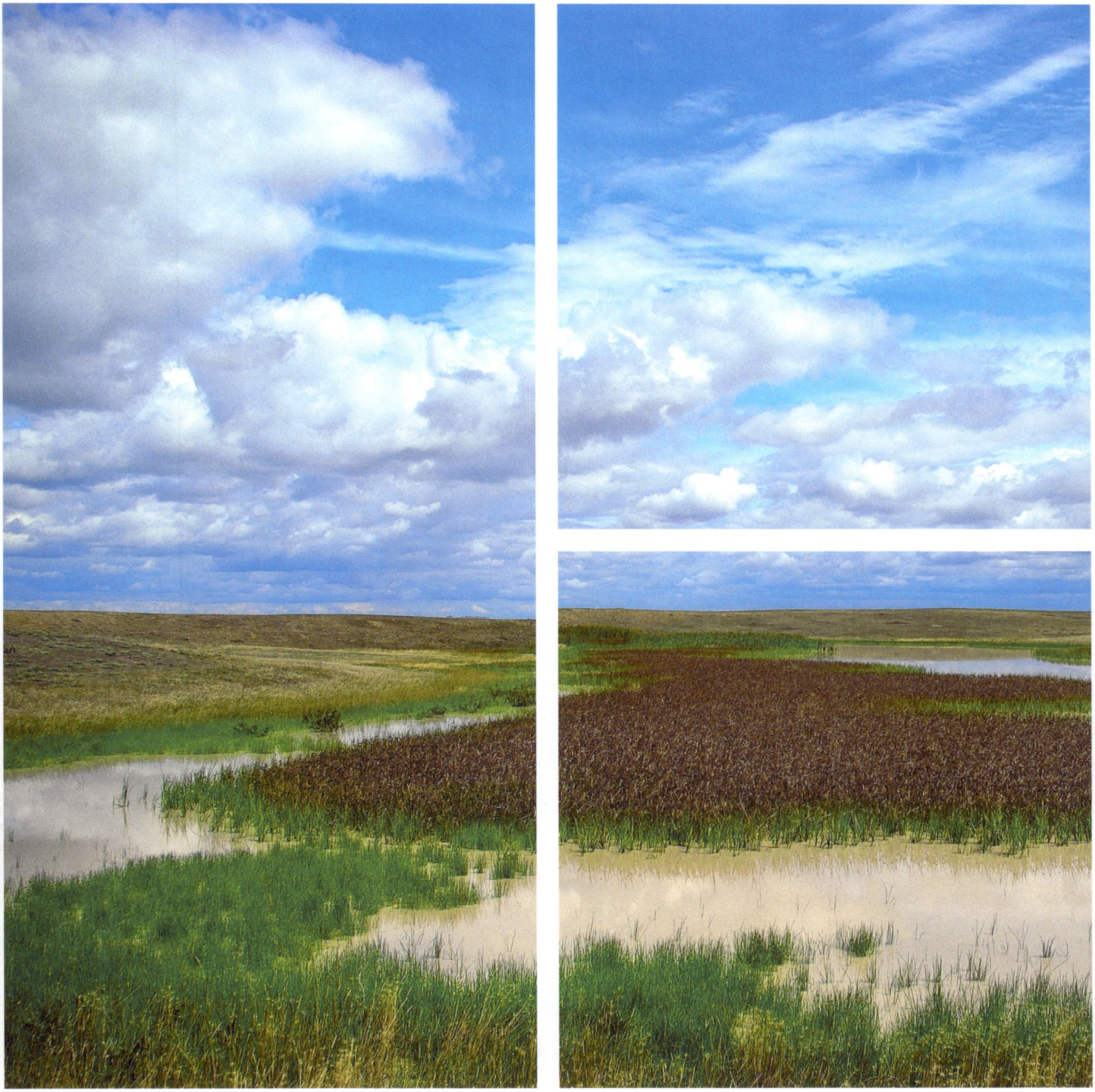

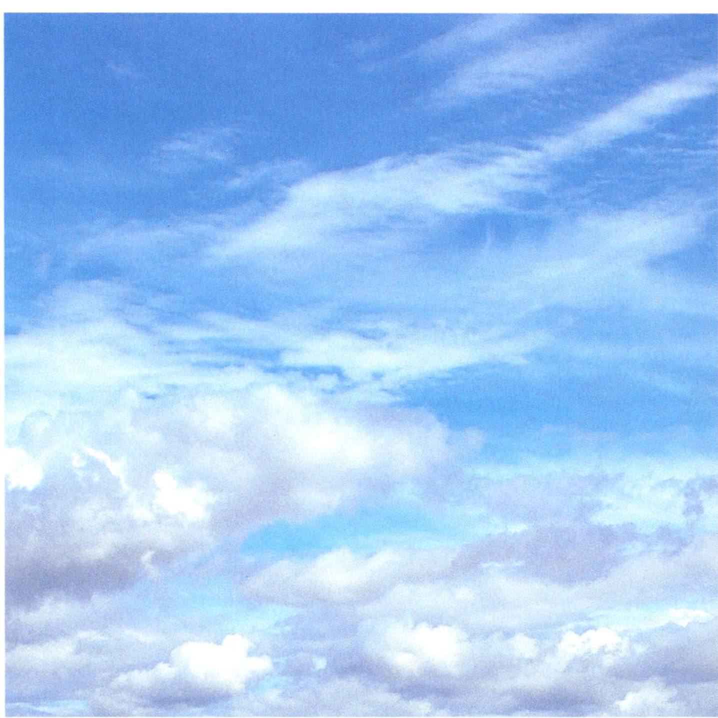
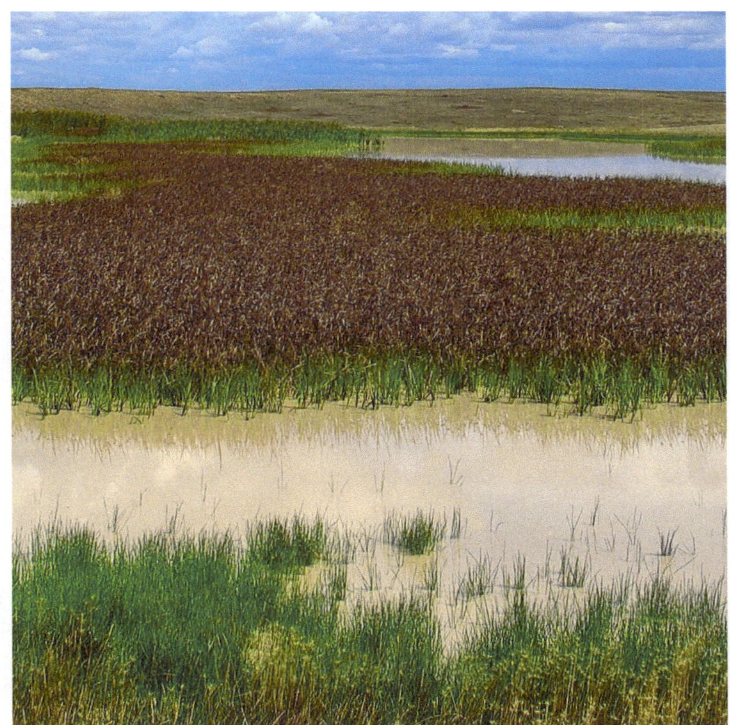
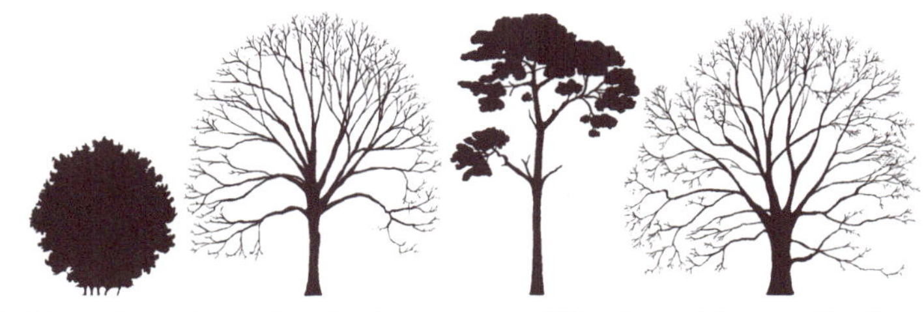

Buffalo Gap Grassland / Images by Mike Goad from Pixabay

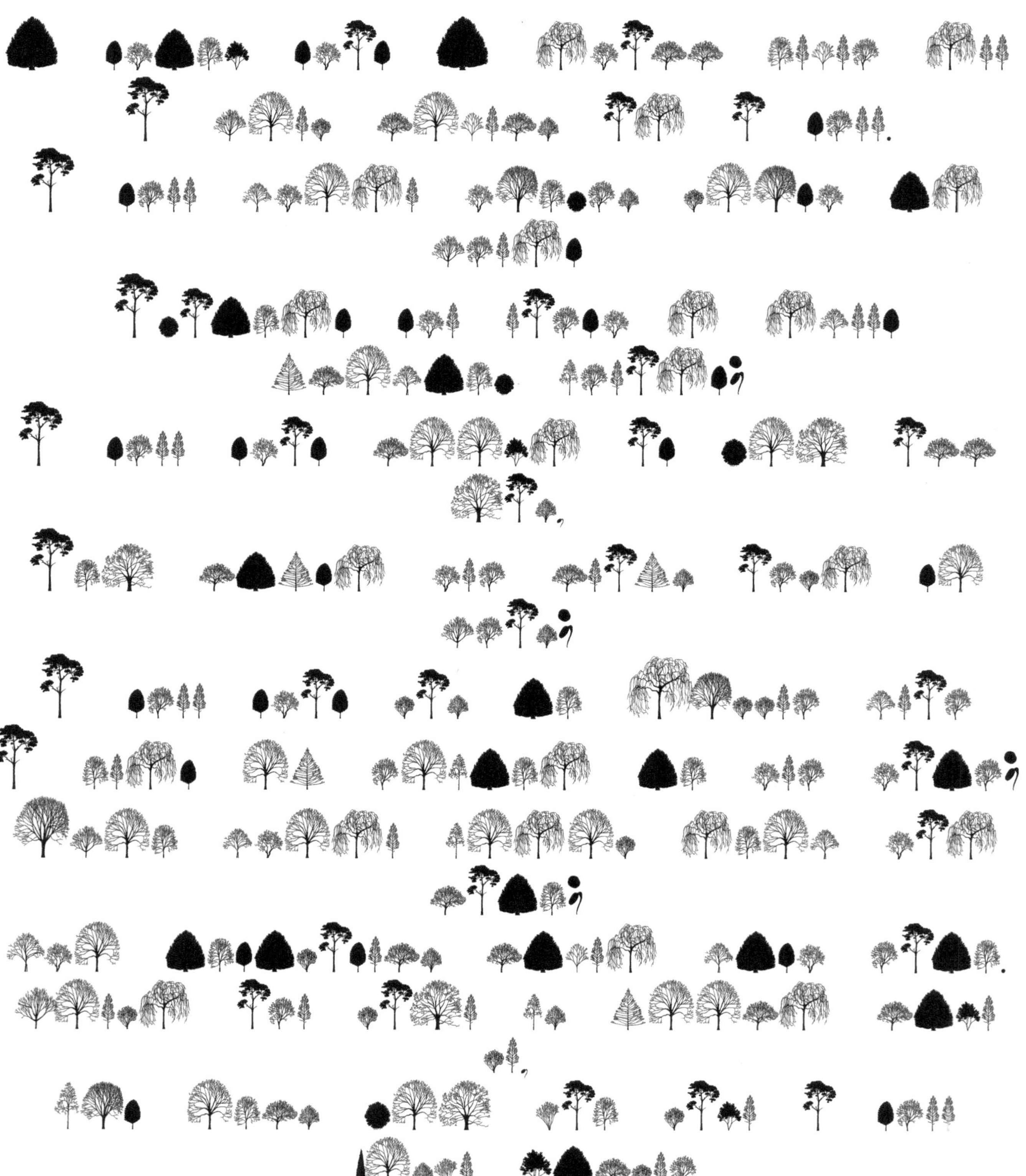

From the Prairie to Forest

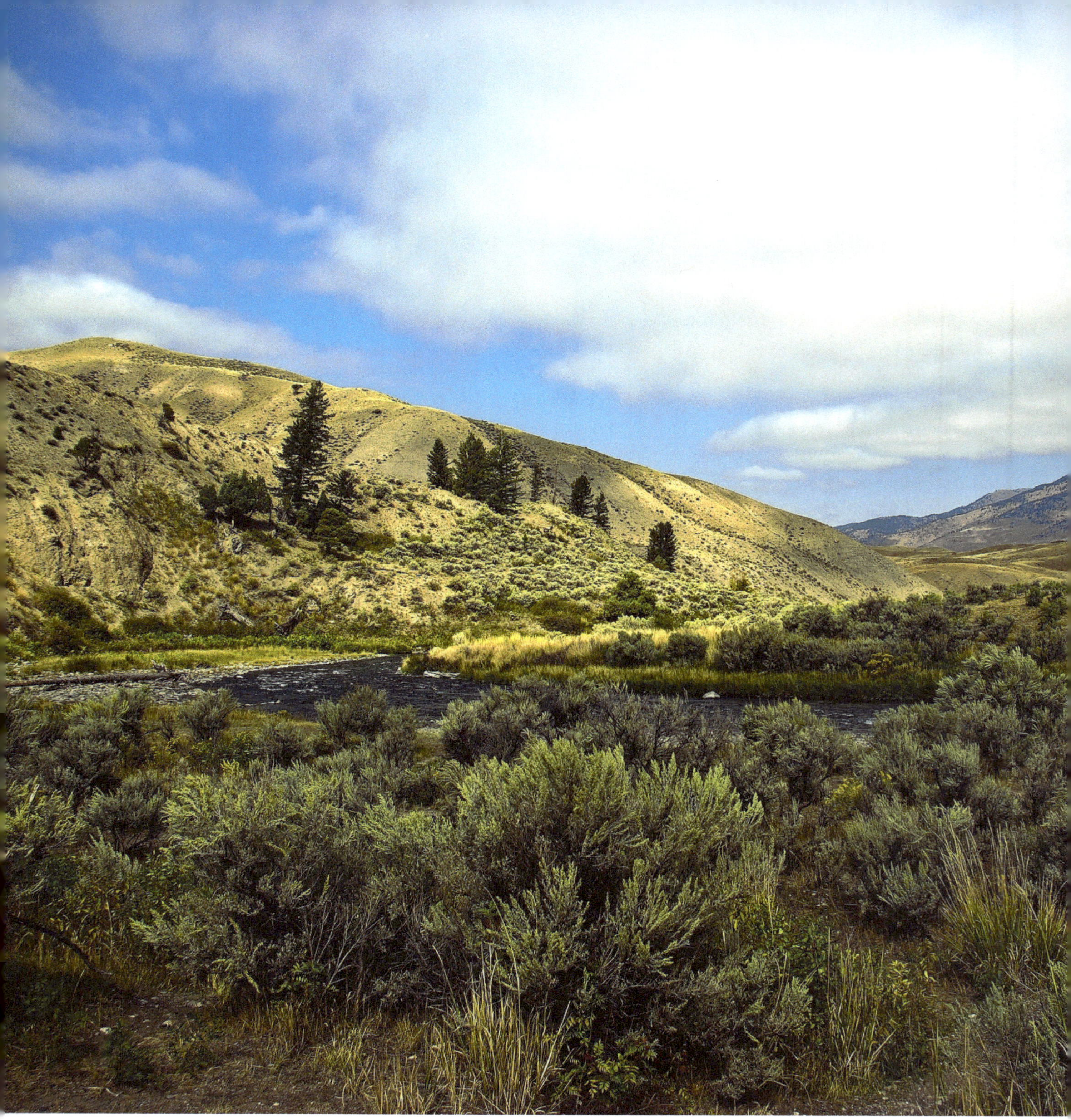

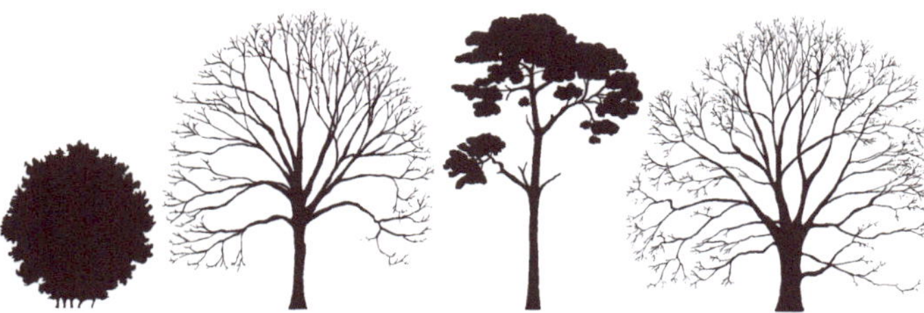

Gardner River Valley, Wyoming / Images by Mike Goad from Pixabay

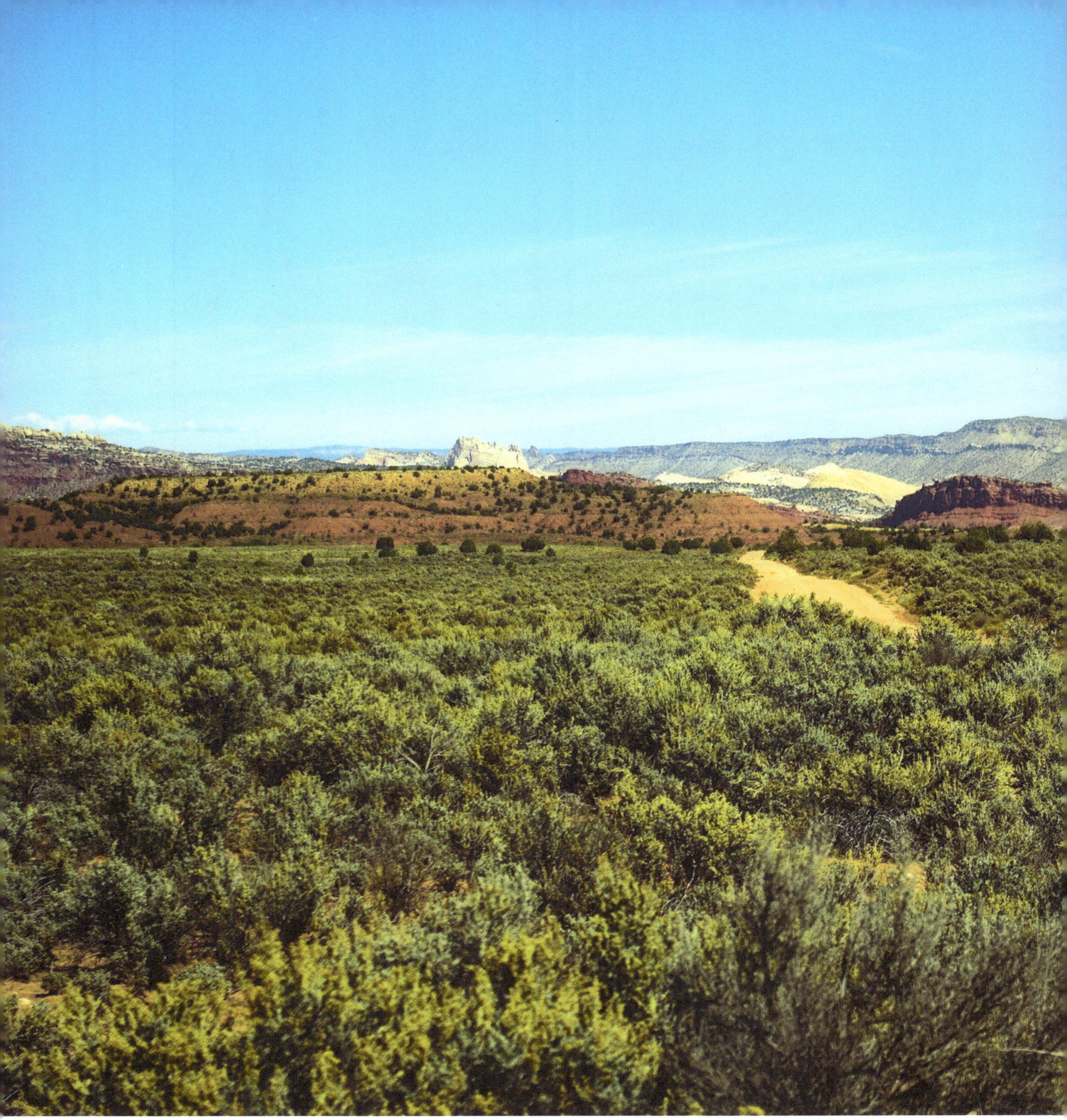

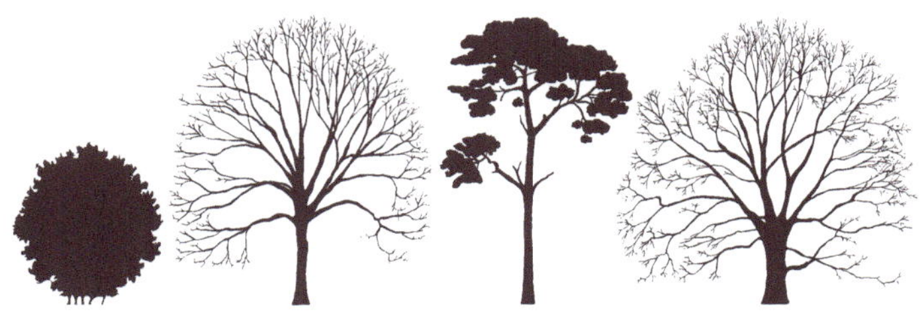

Paria Road, Utah / Images by Mike Goad from Pixabay

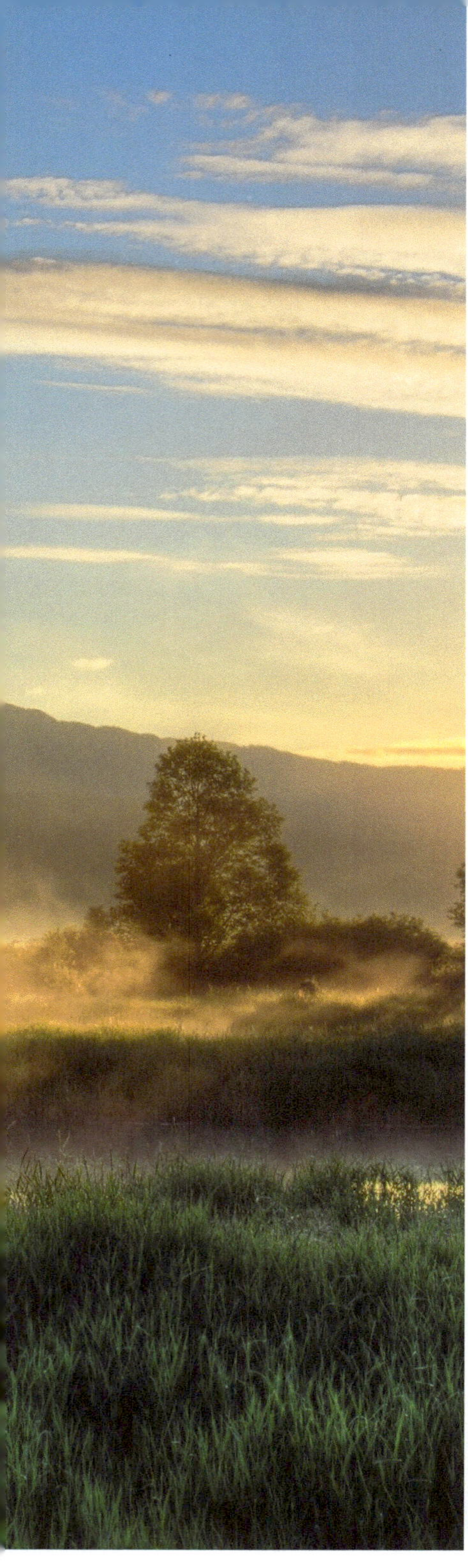
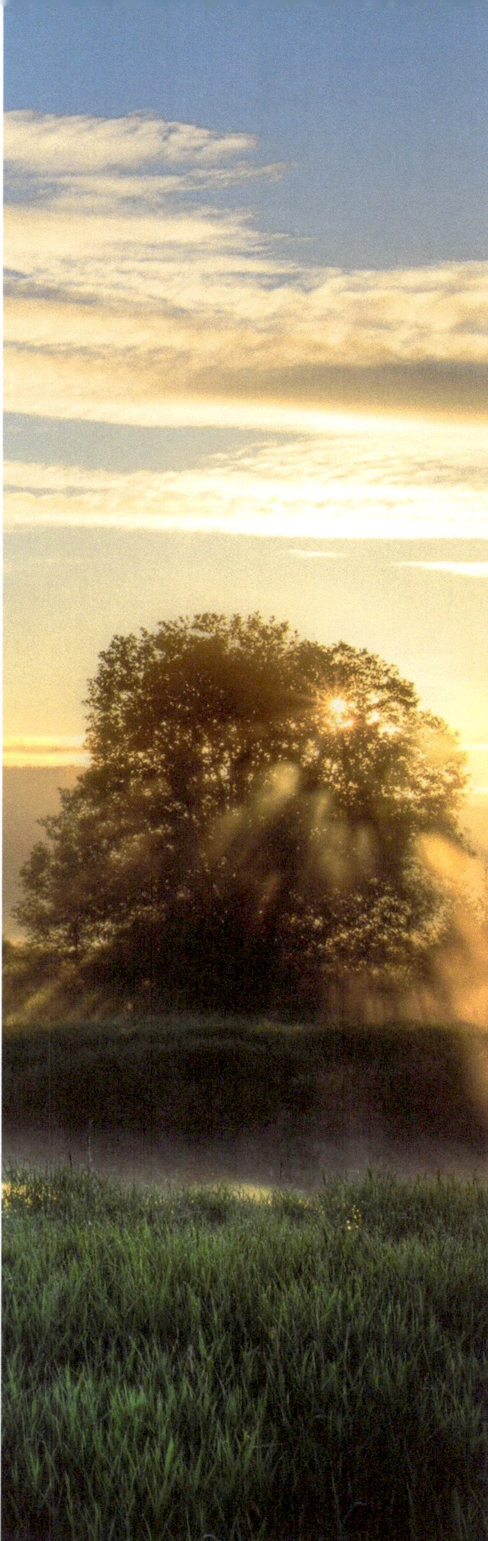
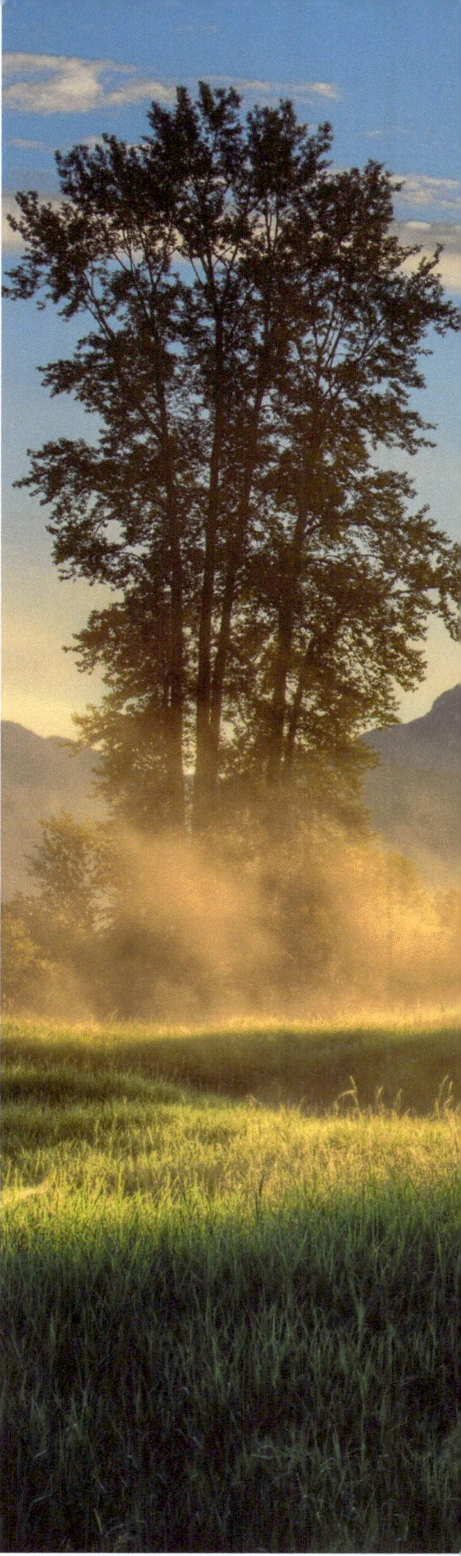
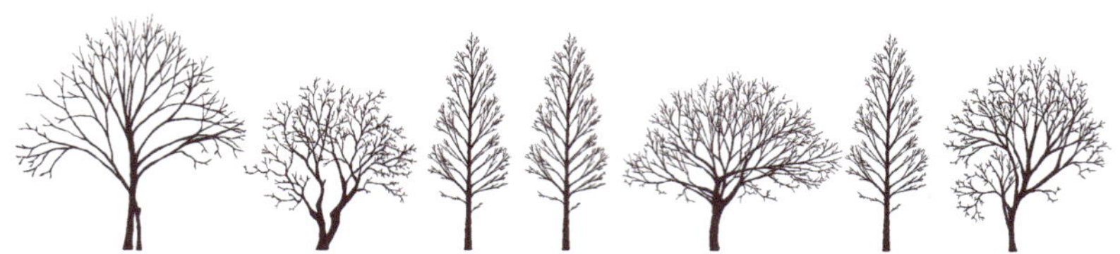

British Columbia, Canada / Image by James Wheeler from Pixabay

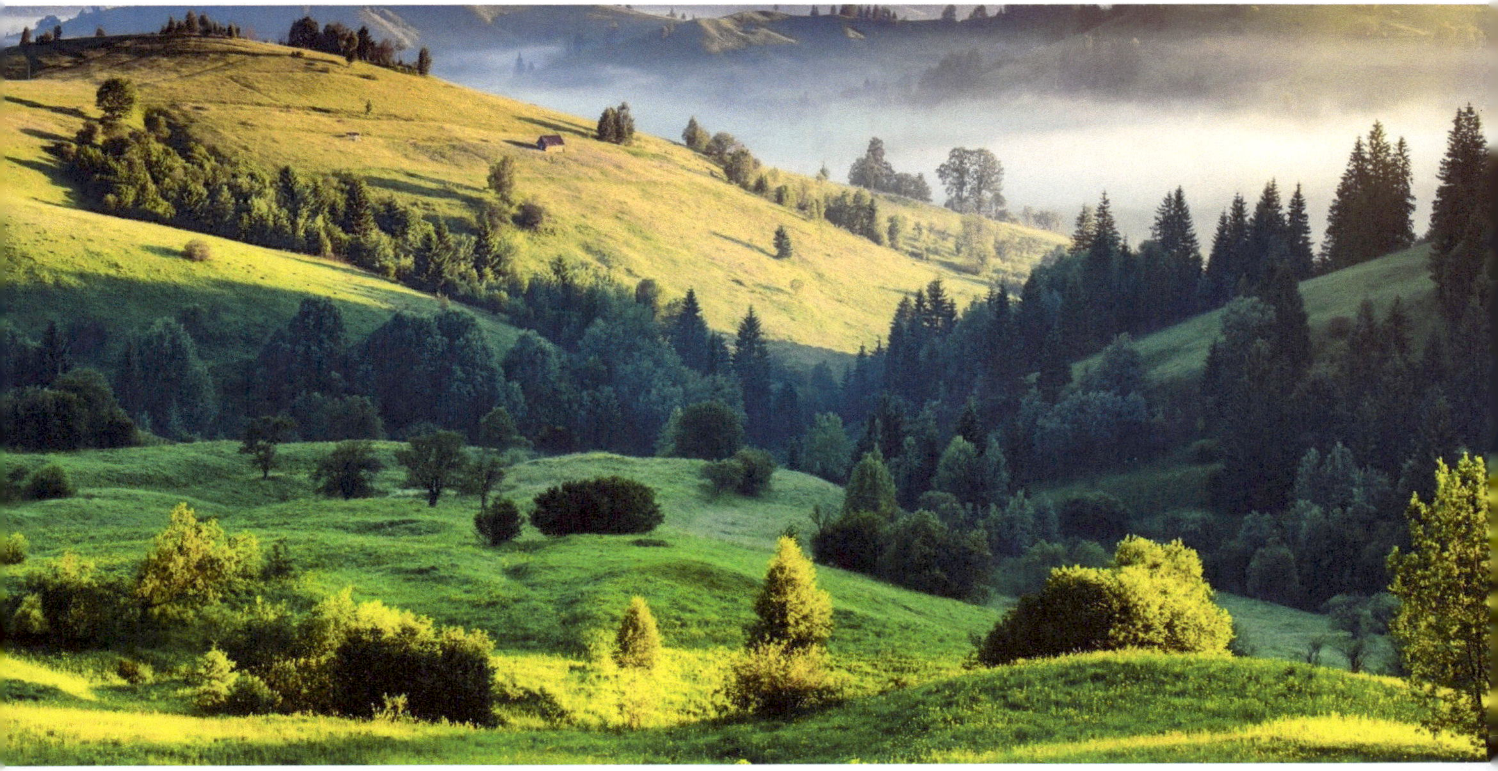

*"Trees are perhaps the only ones
who know the mystery of water thoroughly."*
—*Jules Renard*

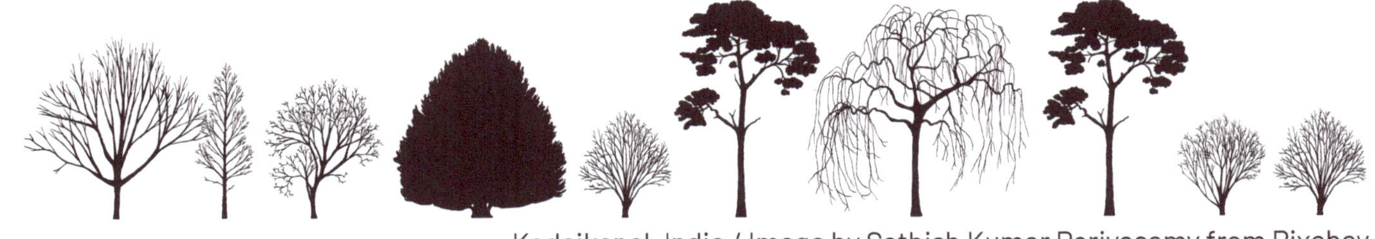

Kodaikanal, India / Image by Sathish Kumar Periyasamy from Pixabay

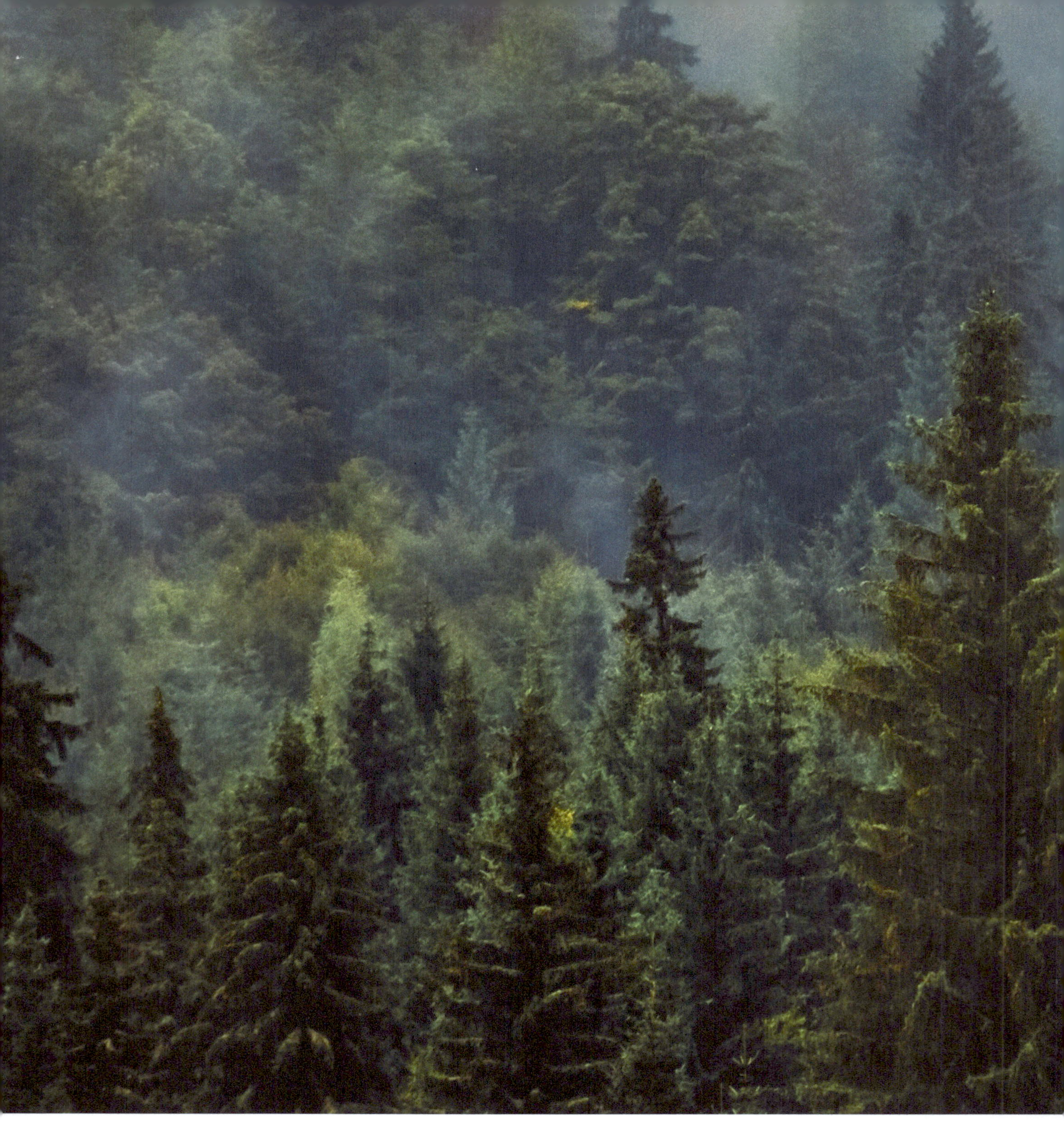

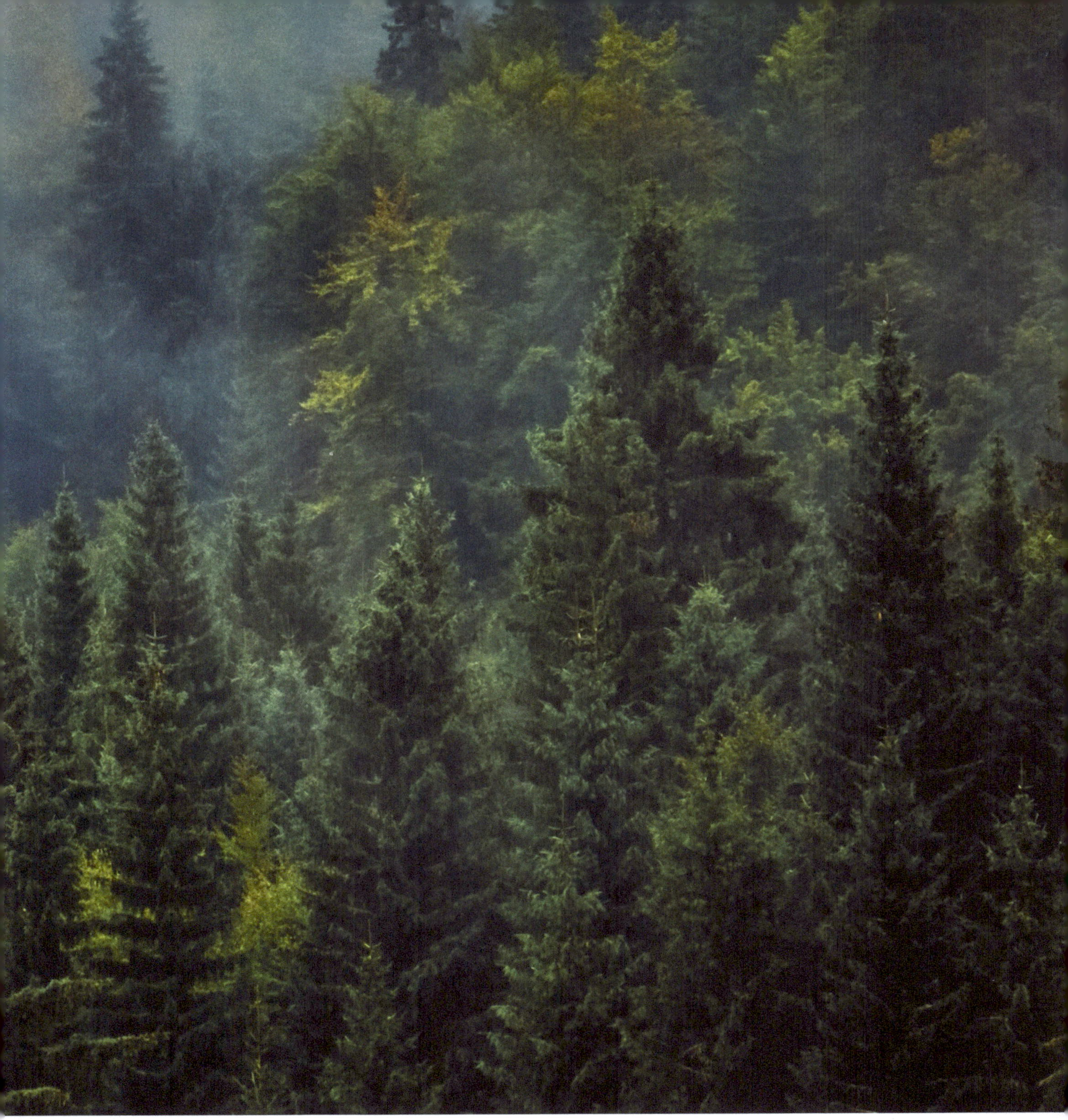

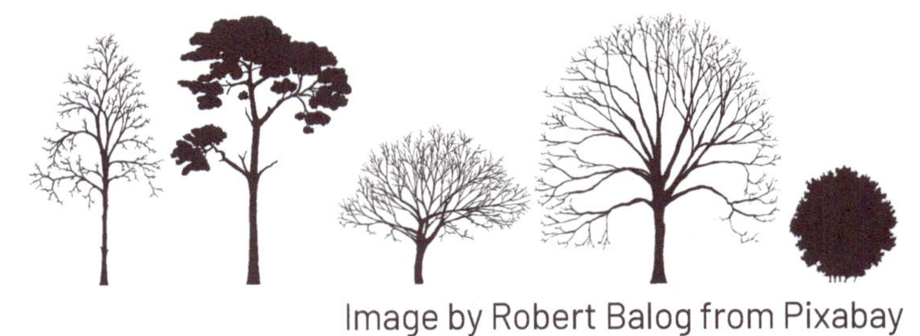

Image by Robert Balog from Pixabay

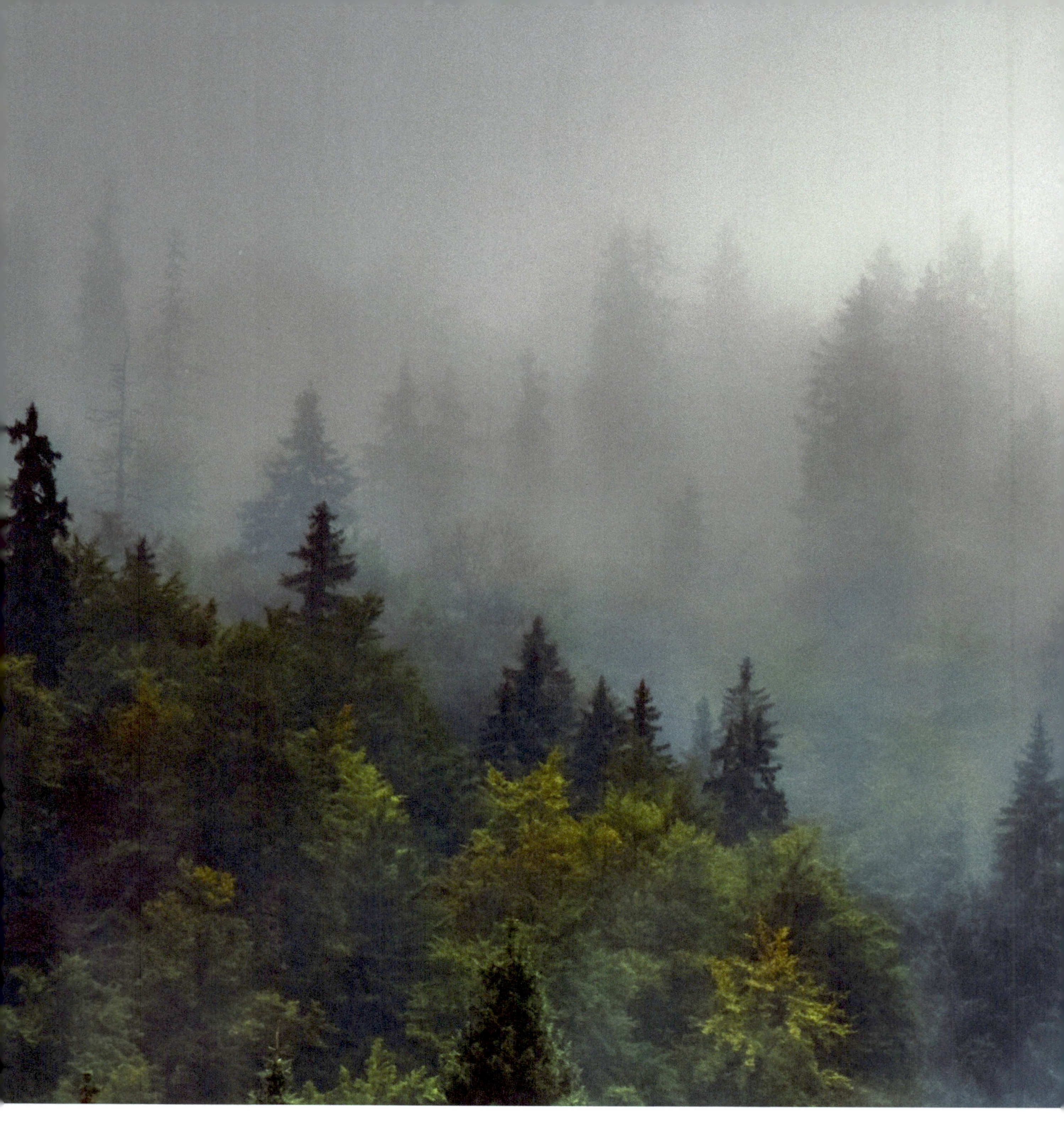

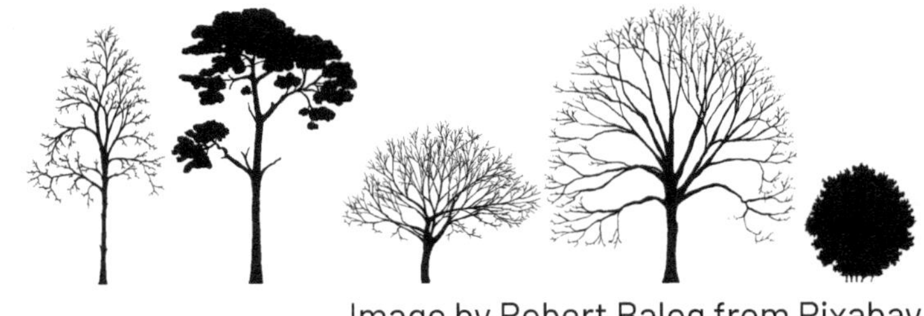

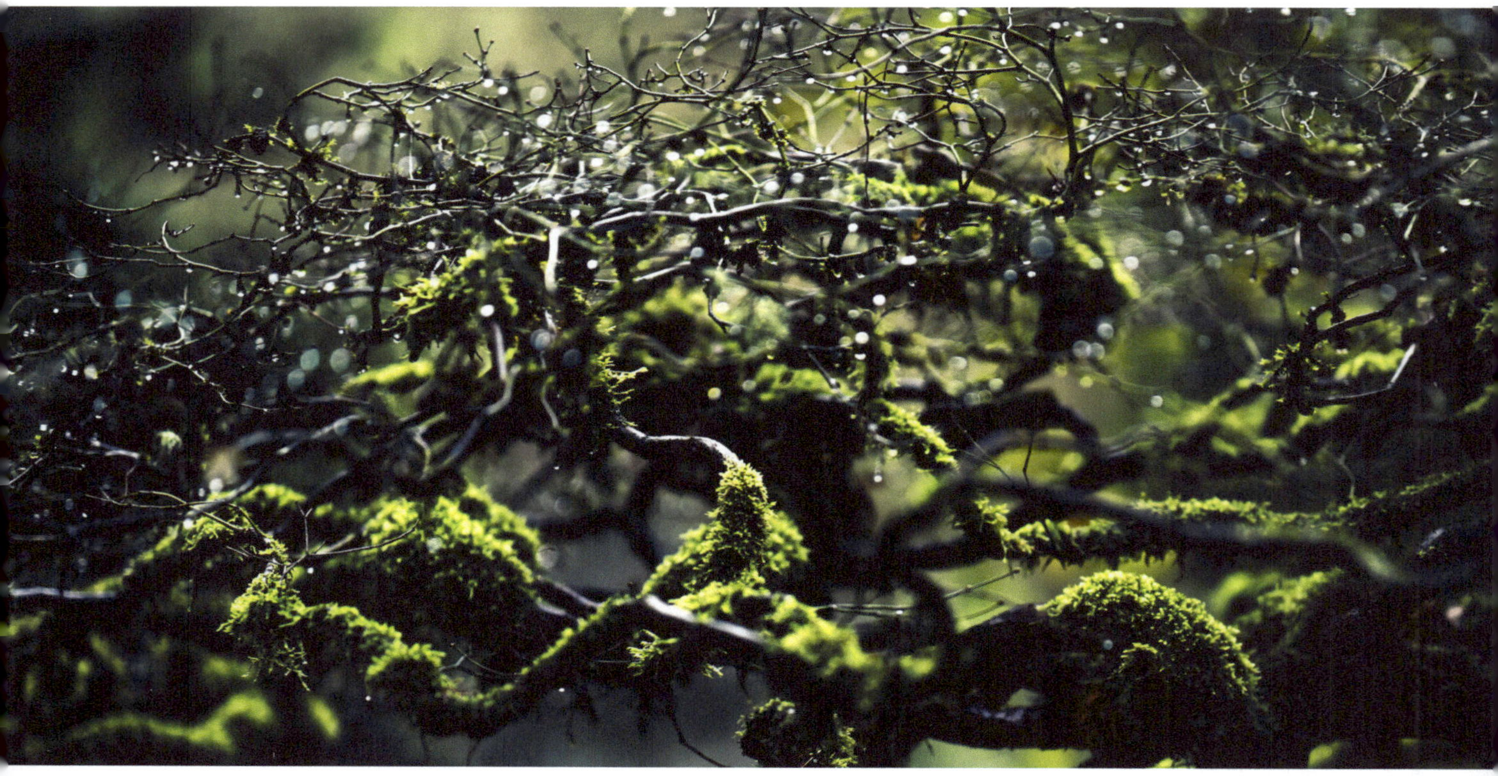

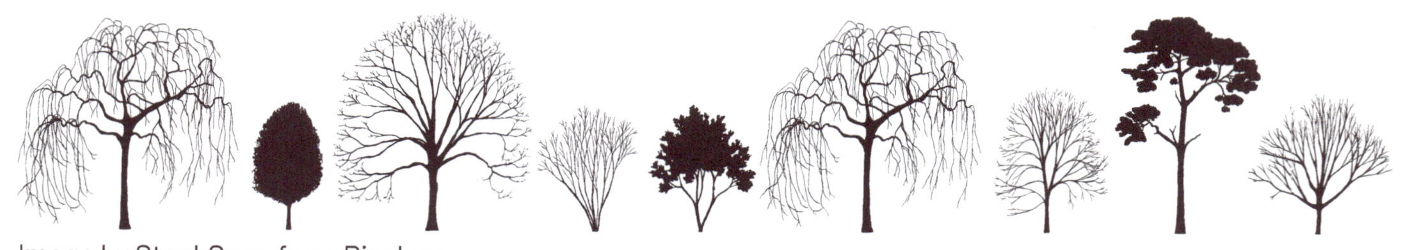

"Without forest, there is no water.
Without water, there is no bread.
Without bread, there is no life."
— Viktor Schauberger

Image by StockSnap from Pixabay

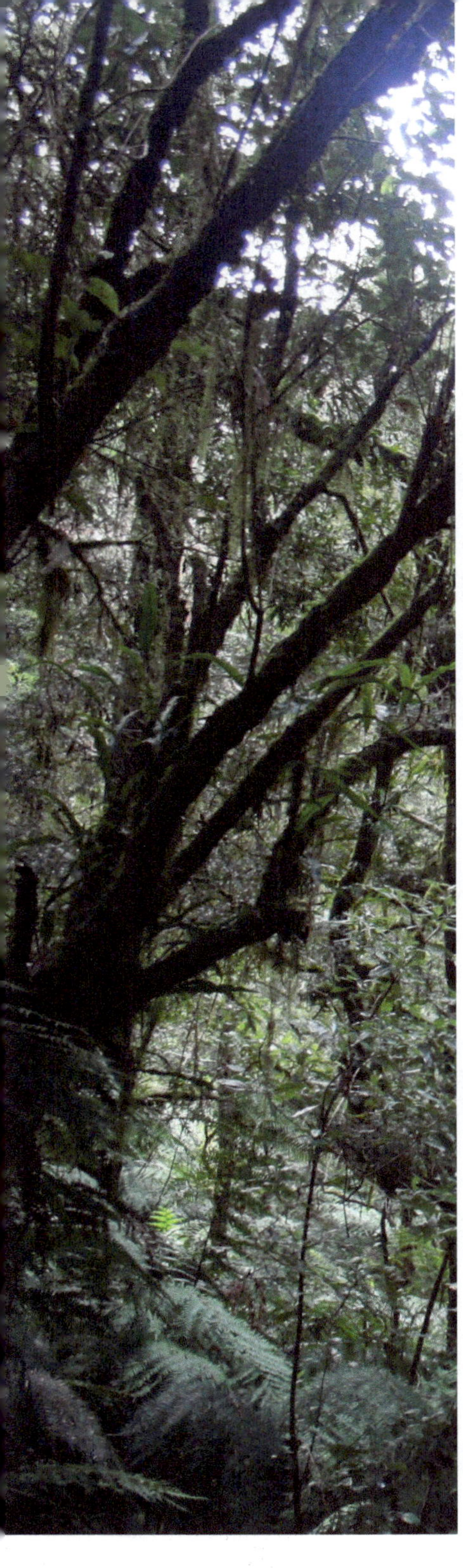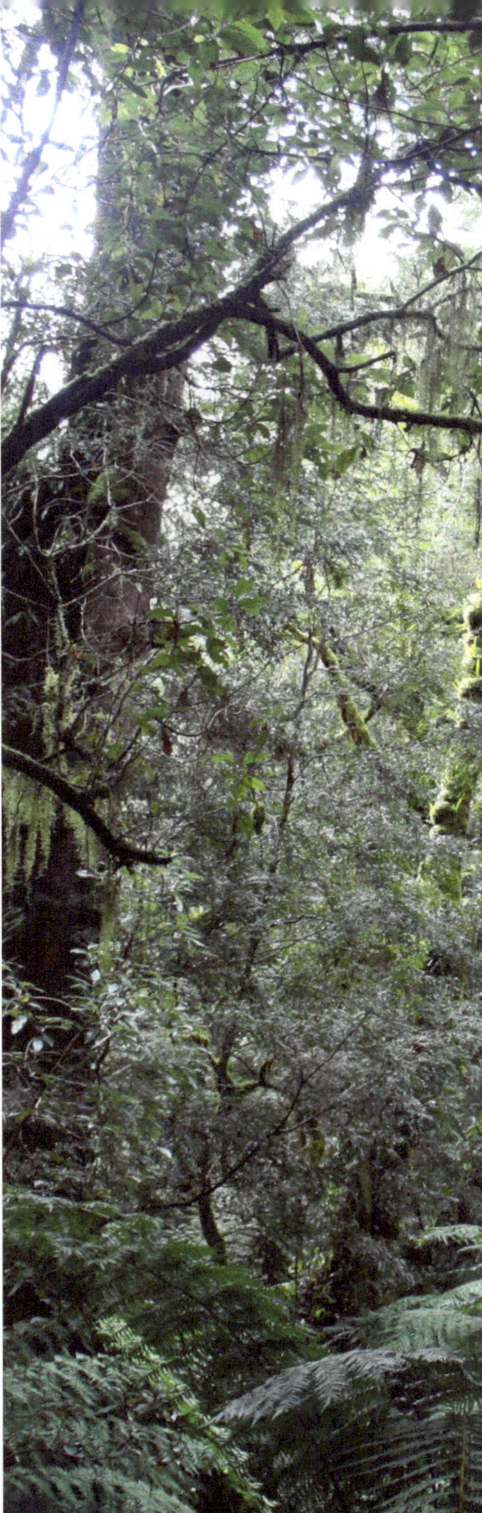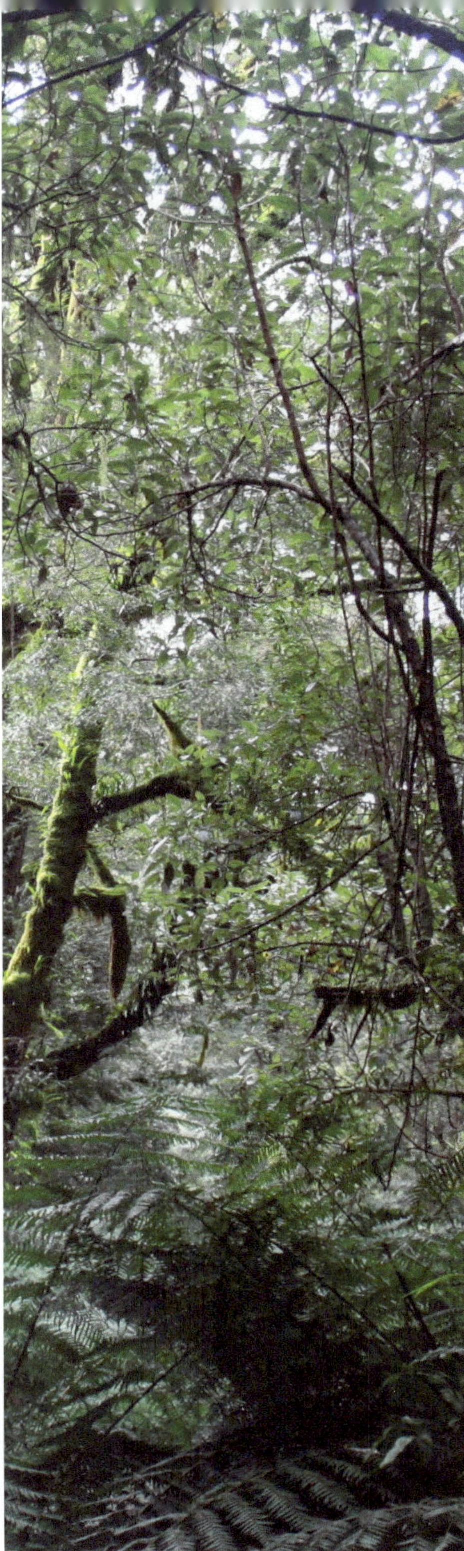

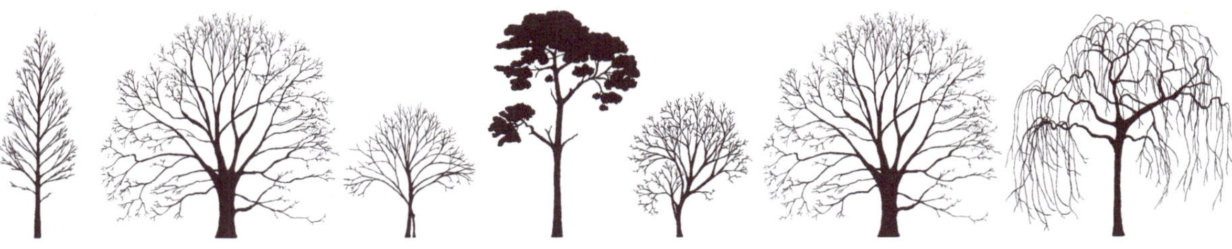

Image by Stephanie Edwards from Pixabay

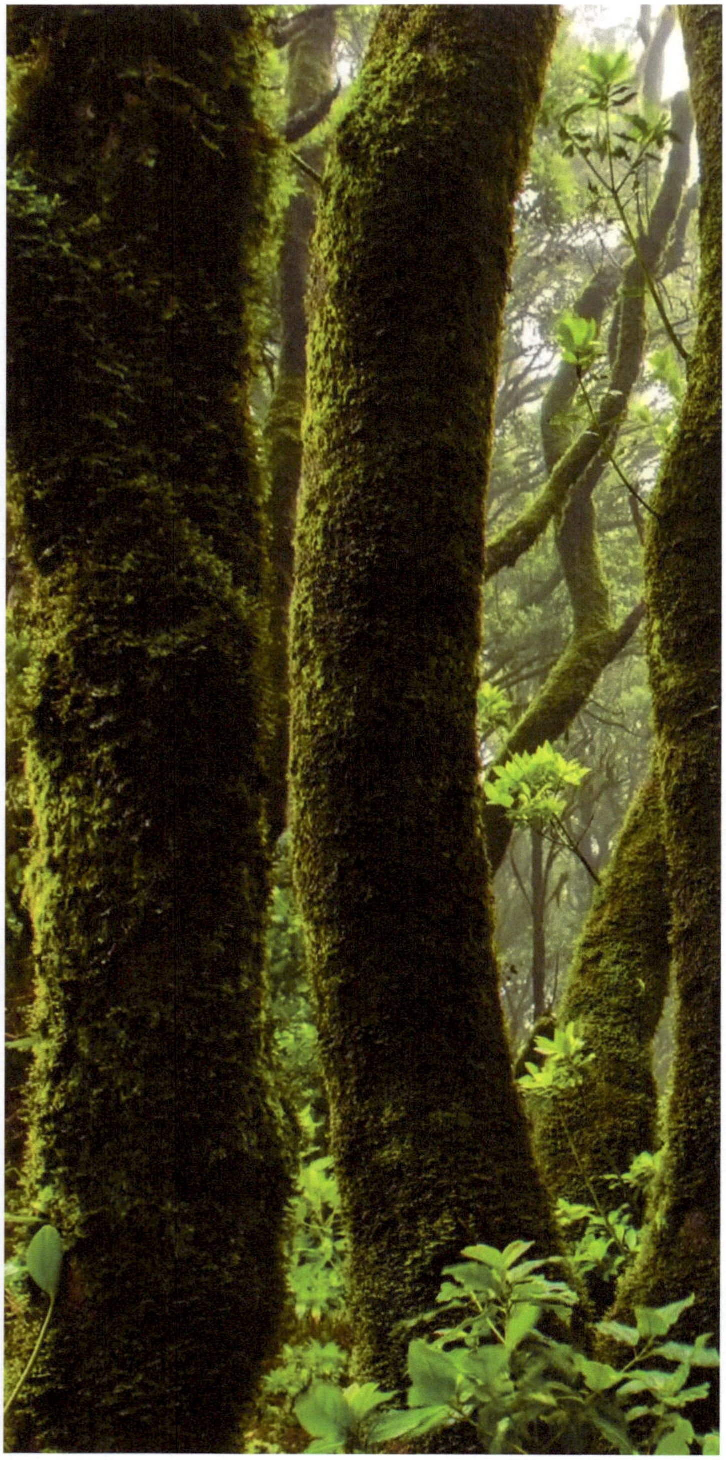

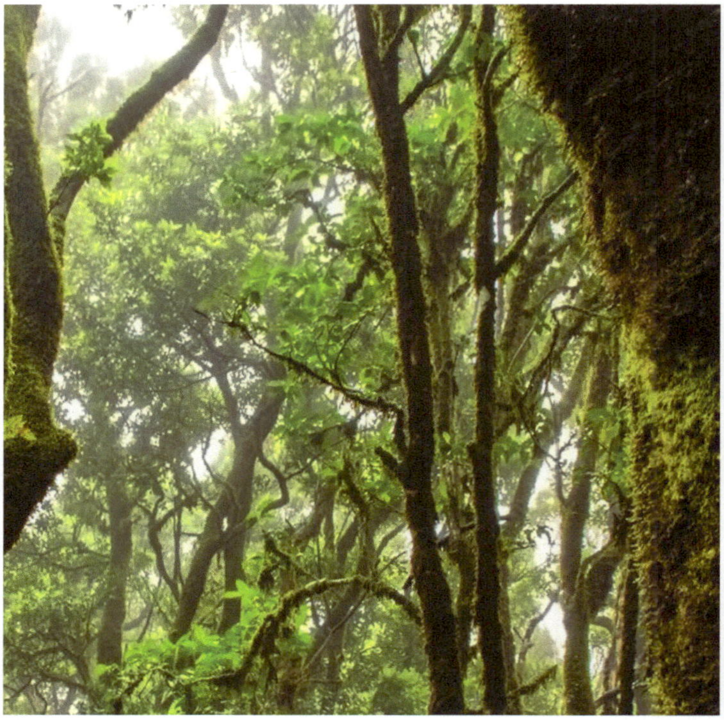

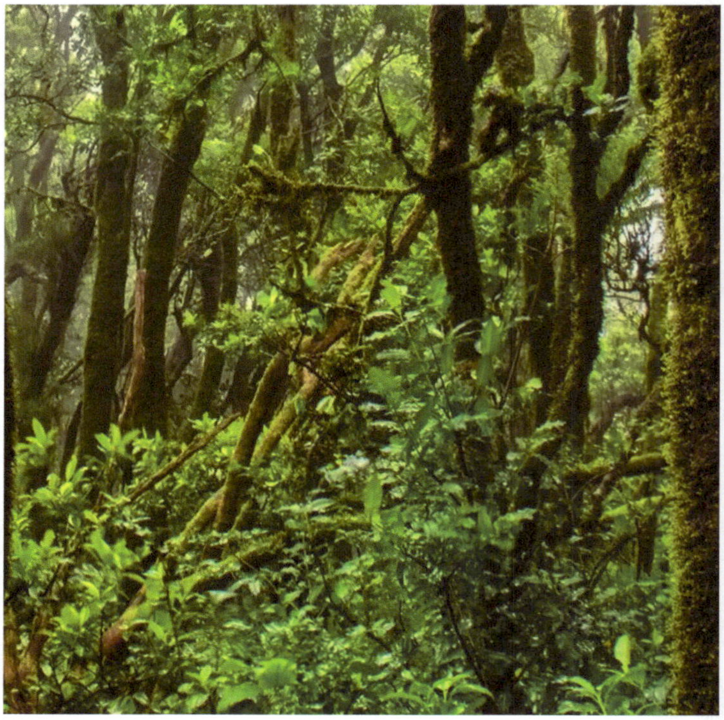

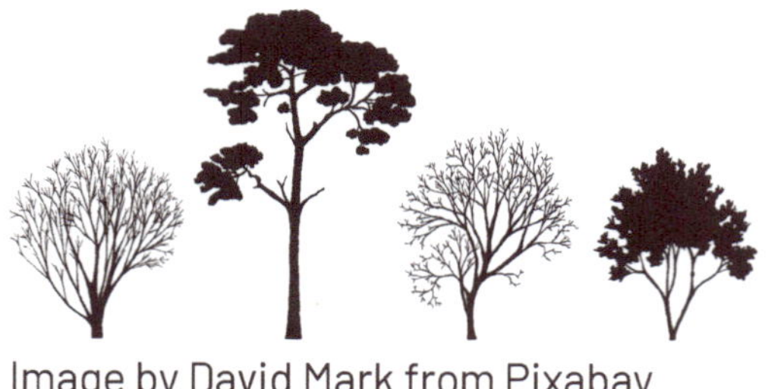

Image by David Mark from Pixabay

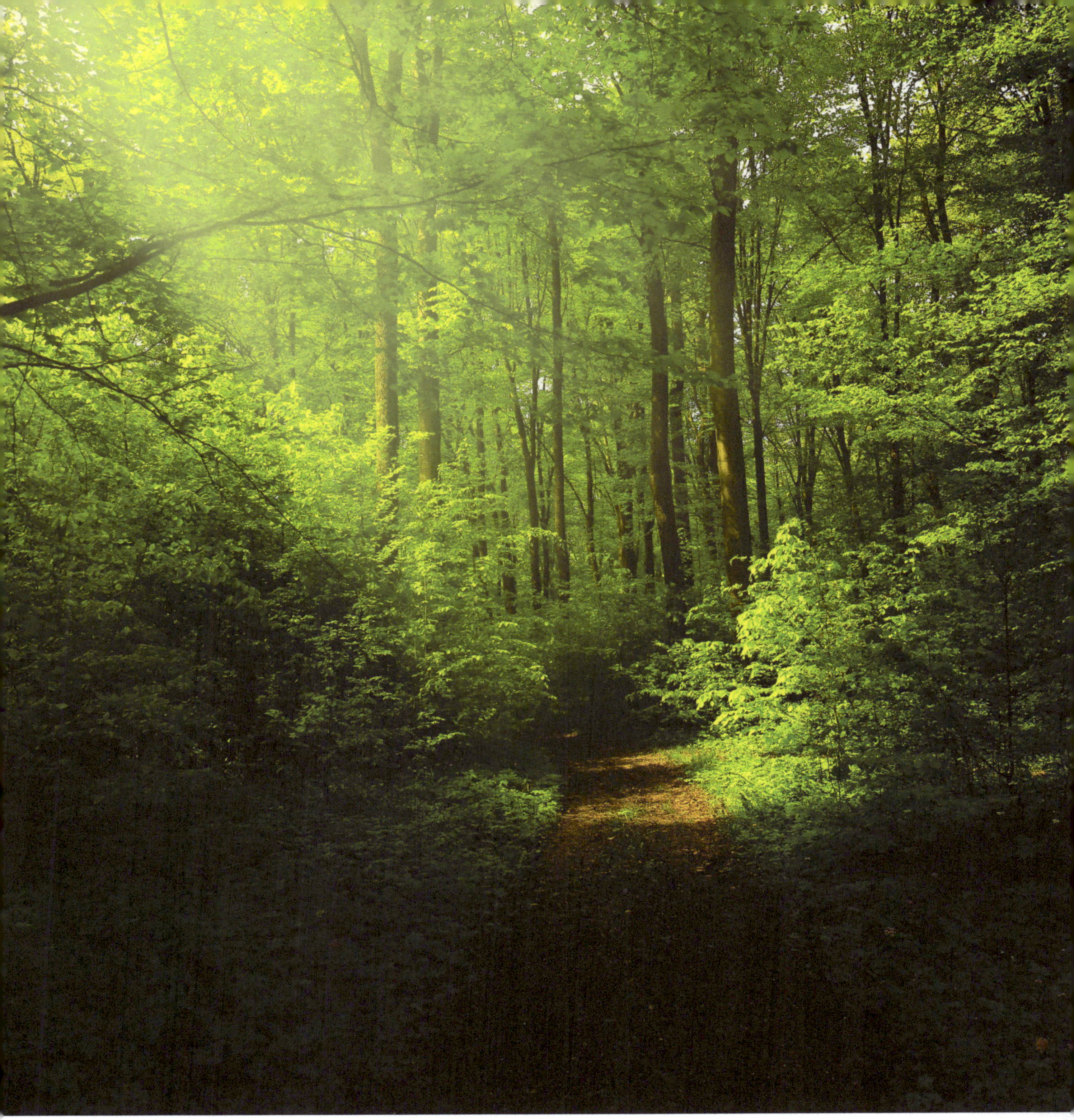

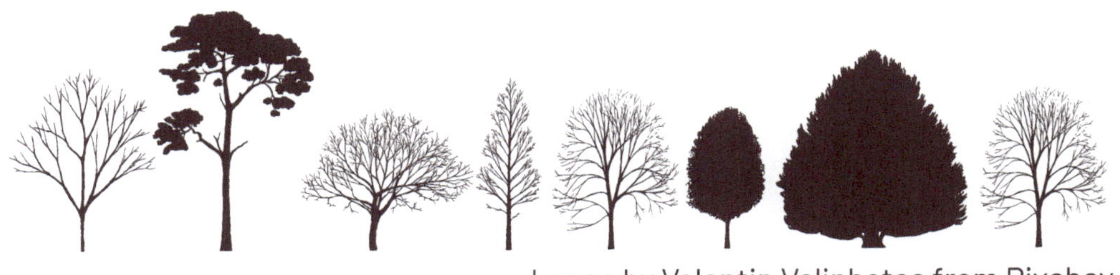

Image by Valentin Valiphotos from Pixabay

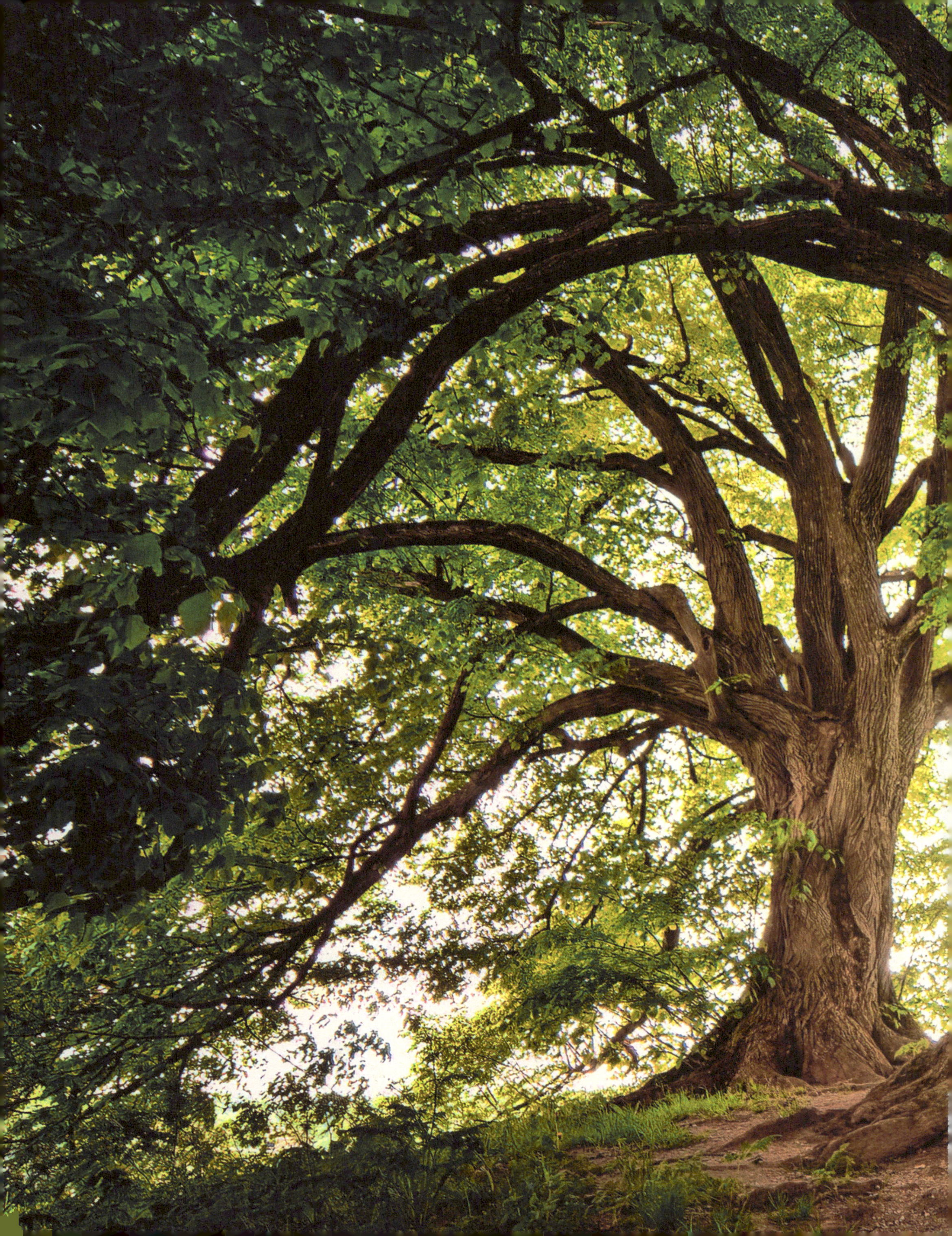

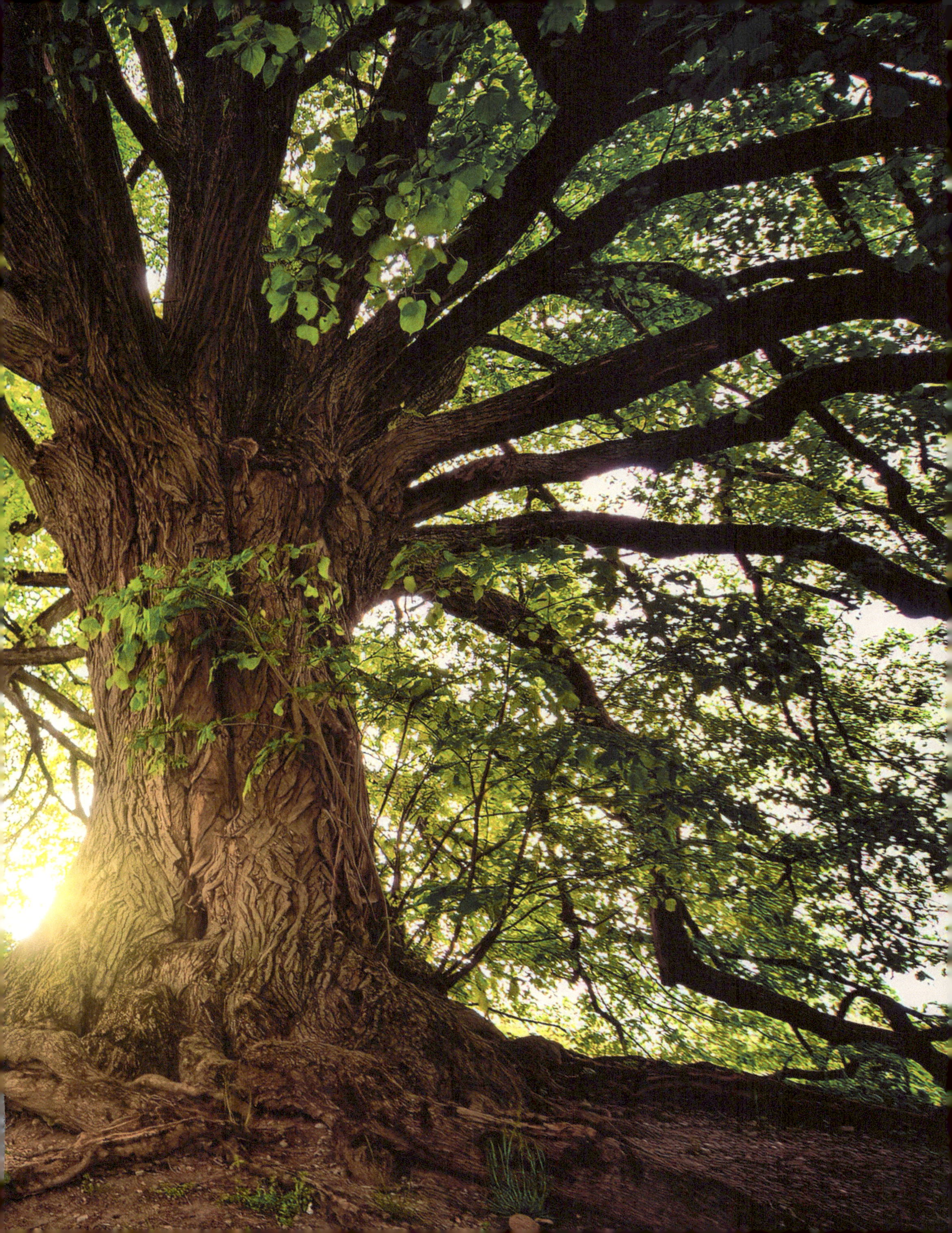

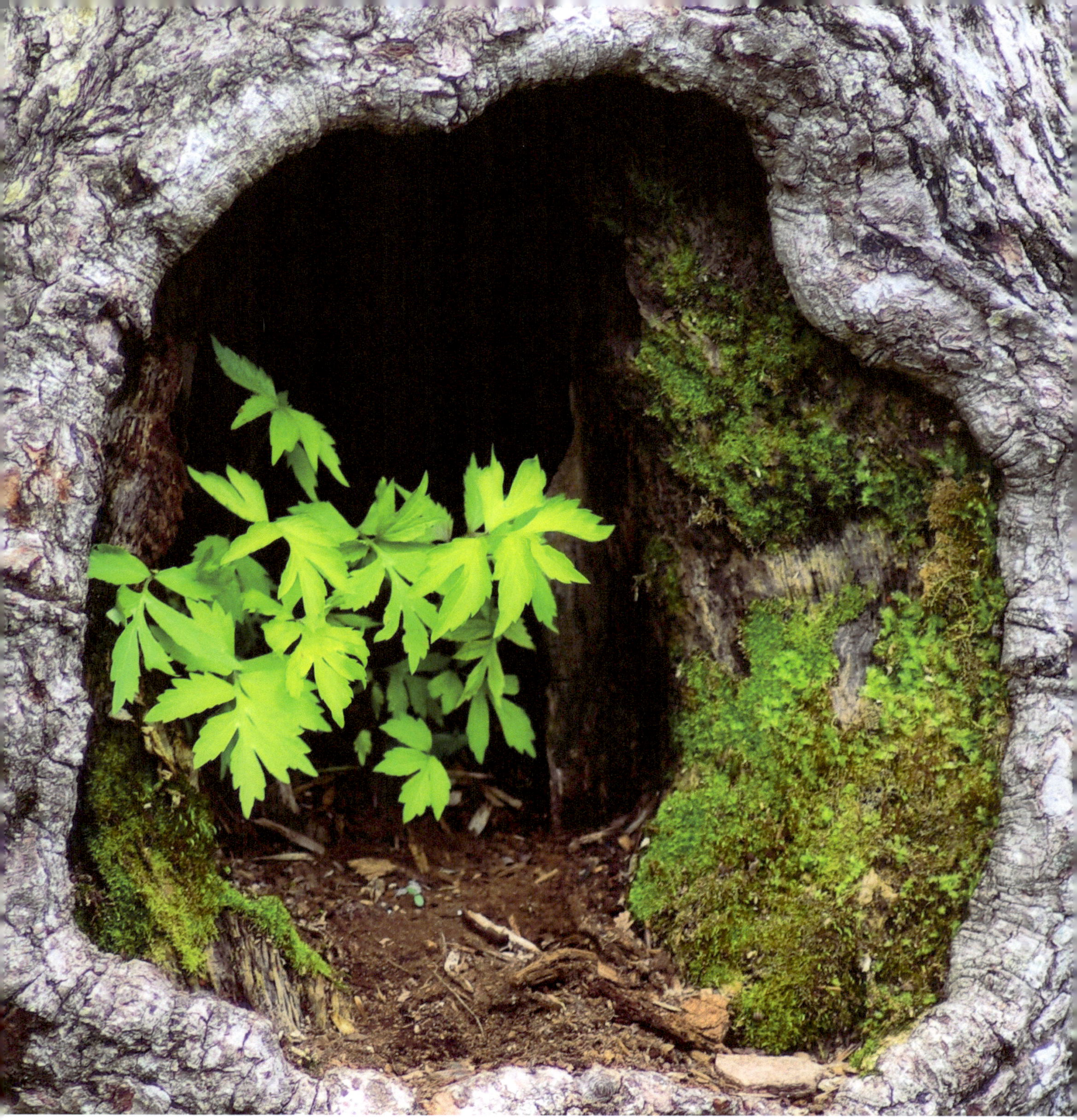

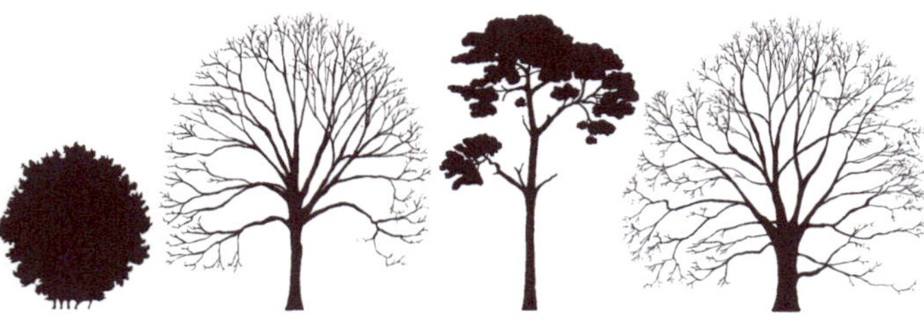

Image by Mike Goad from Pixabay

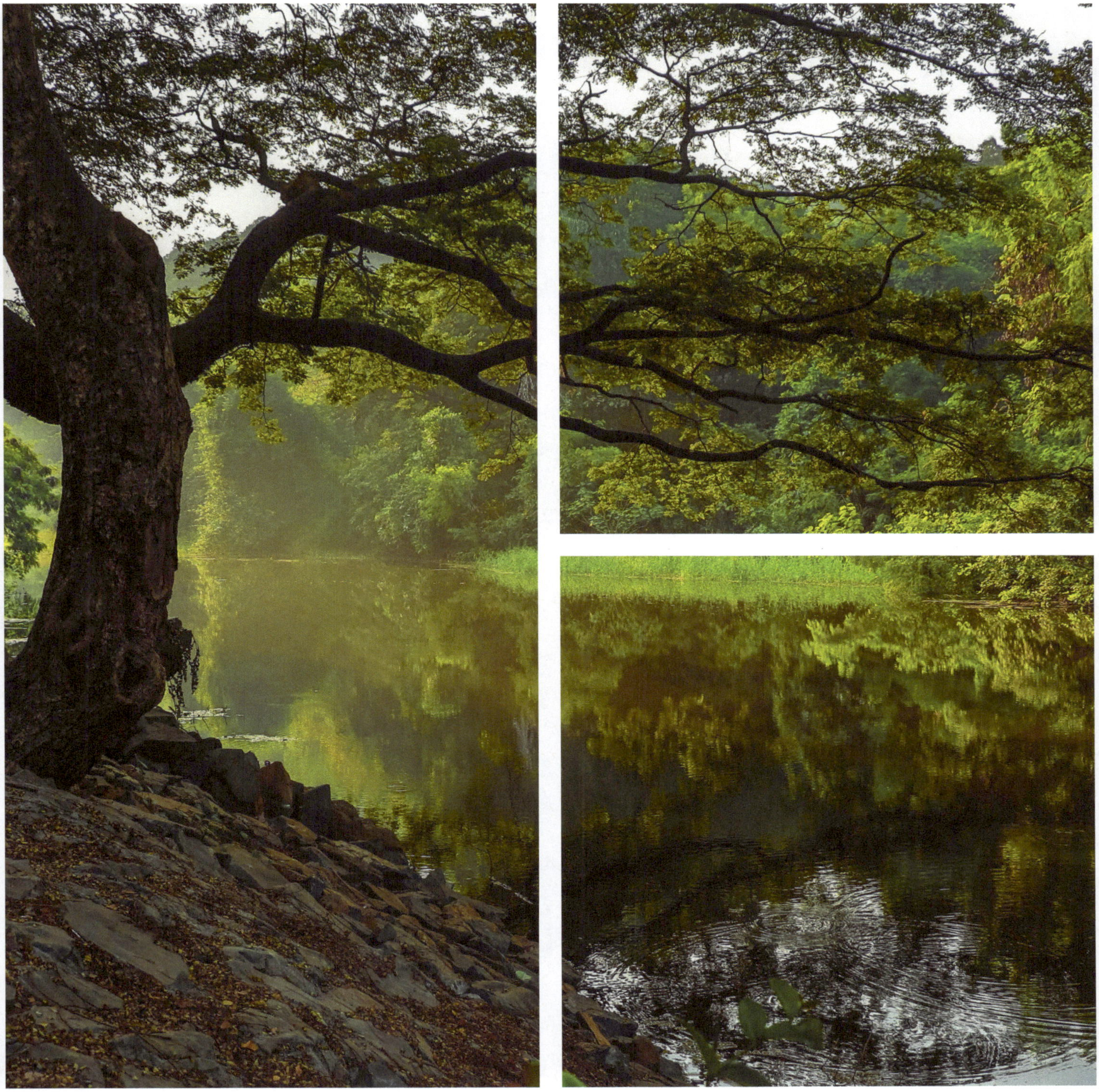

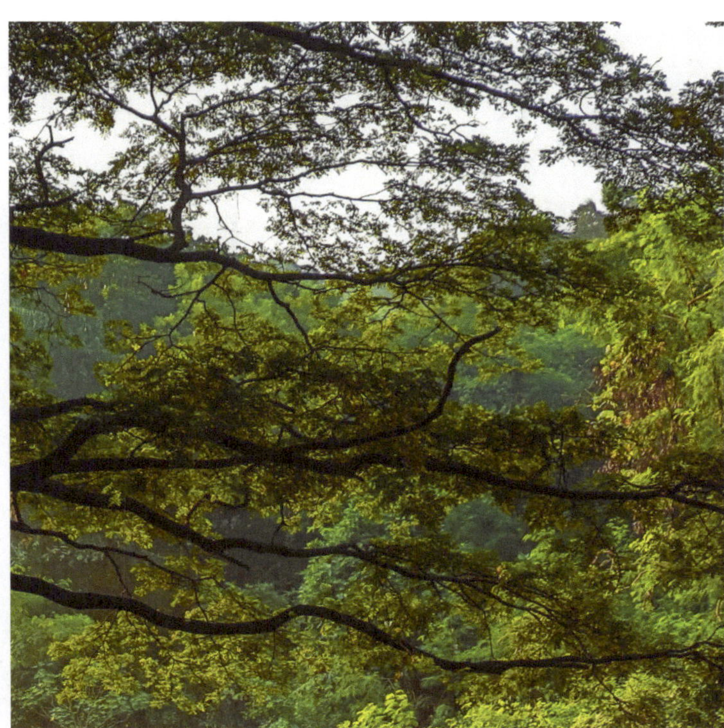

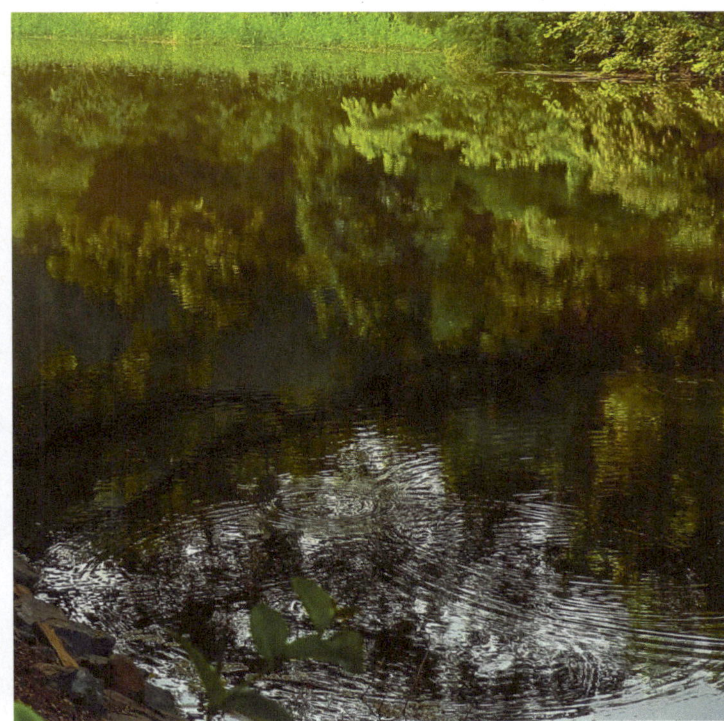

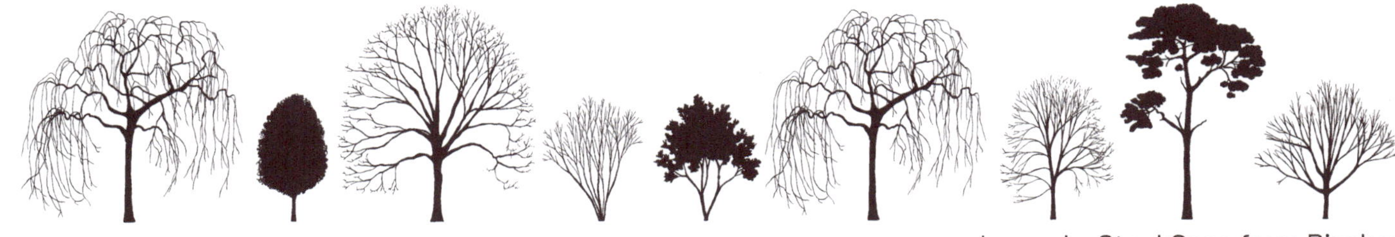

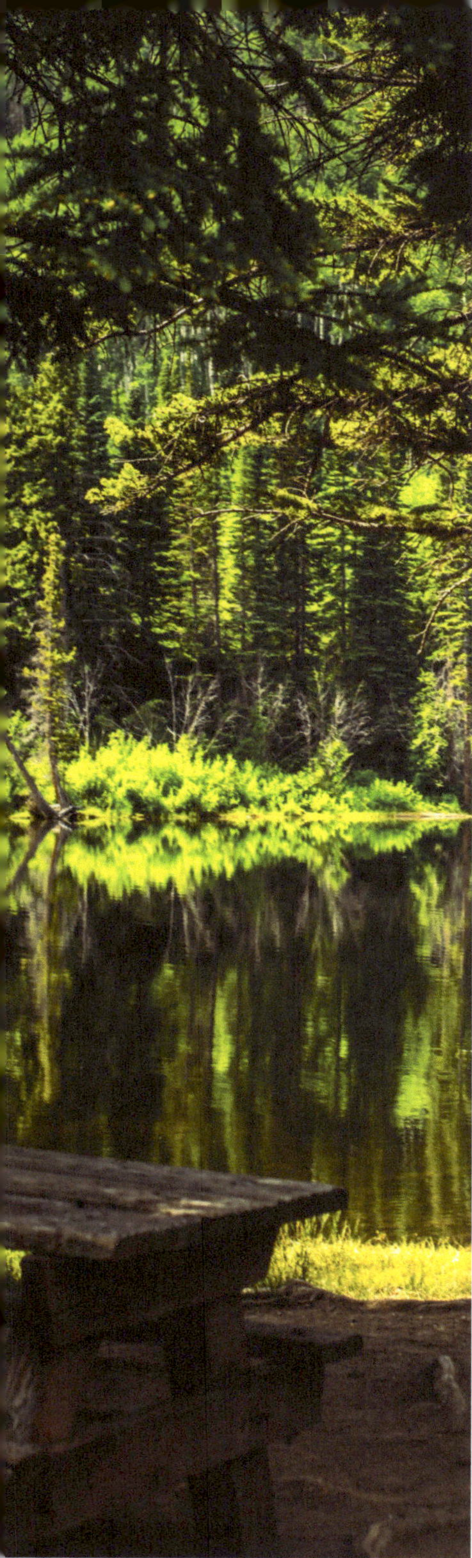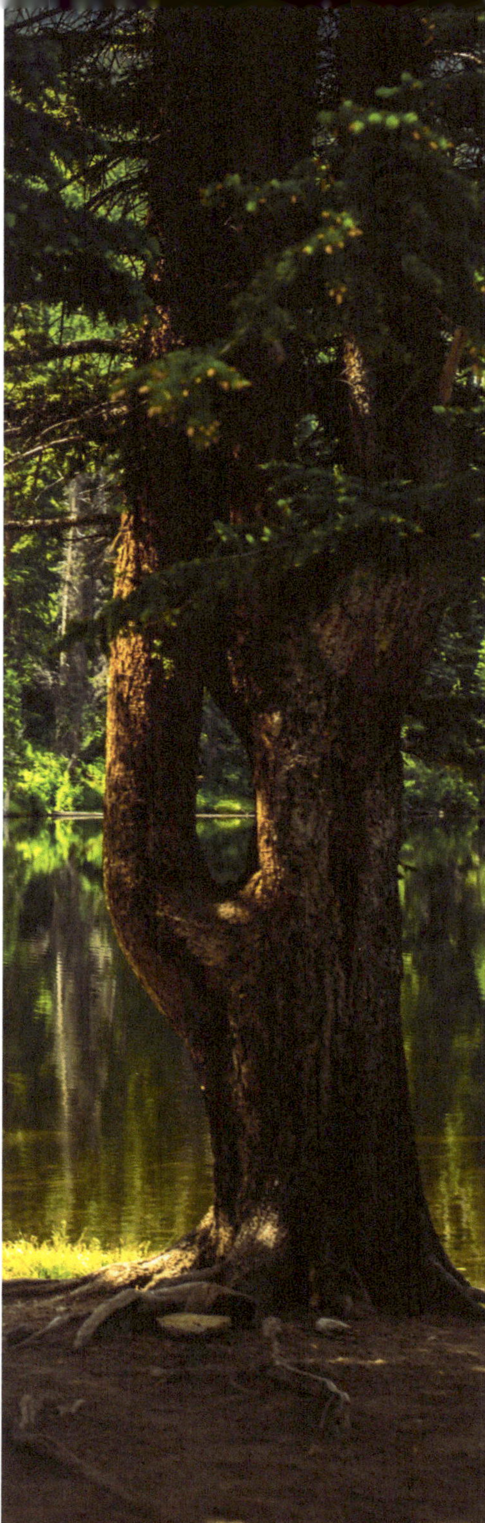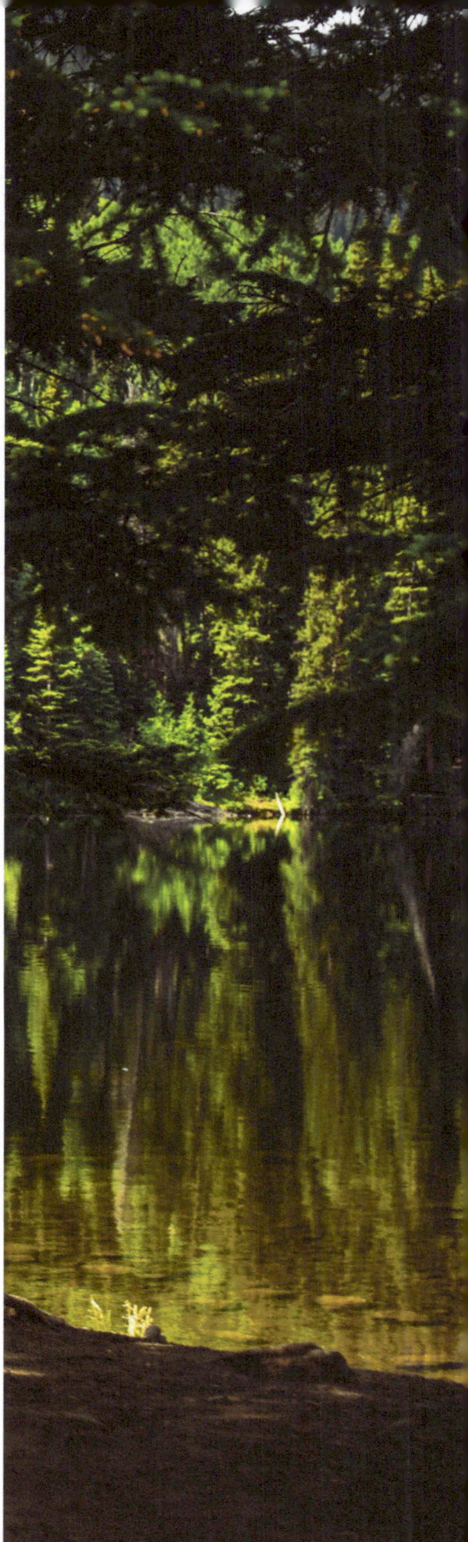

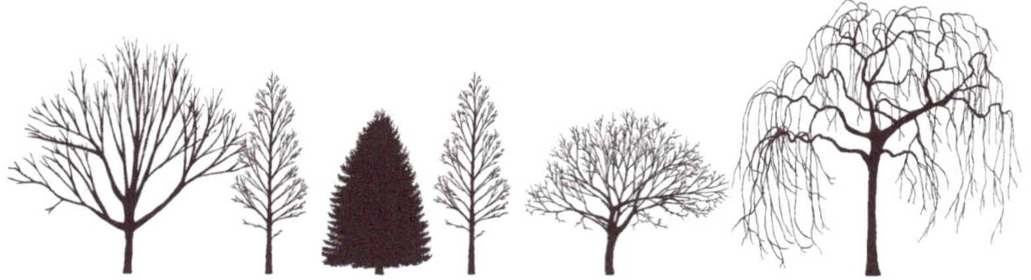

Image by Pexels from Pixabay

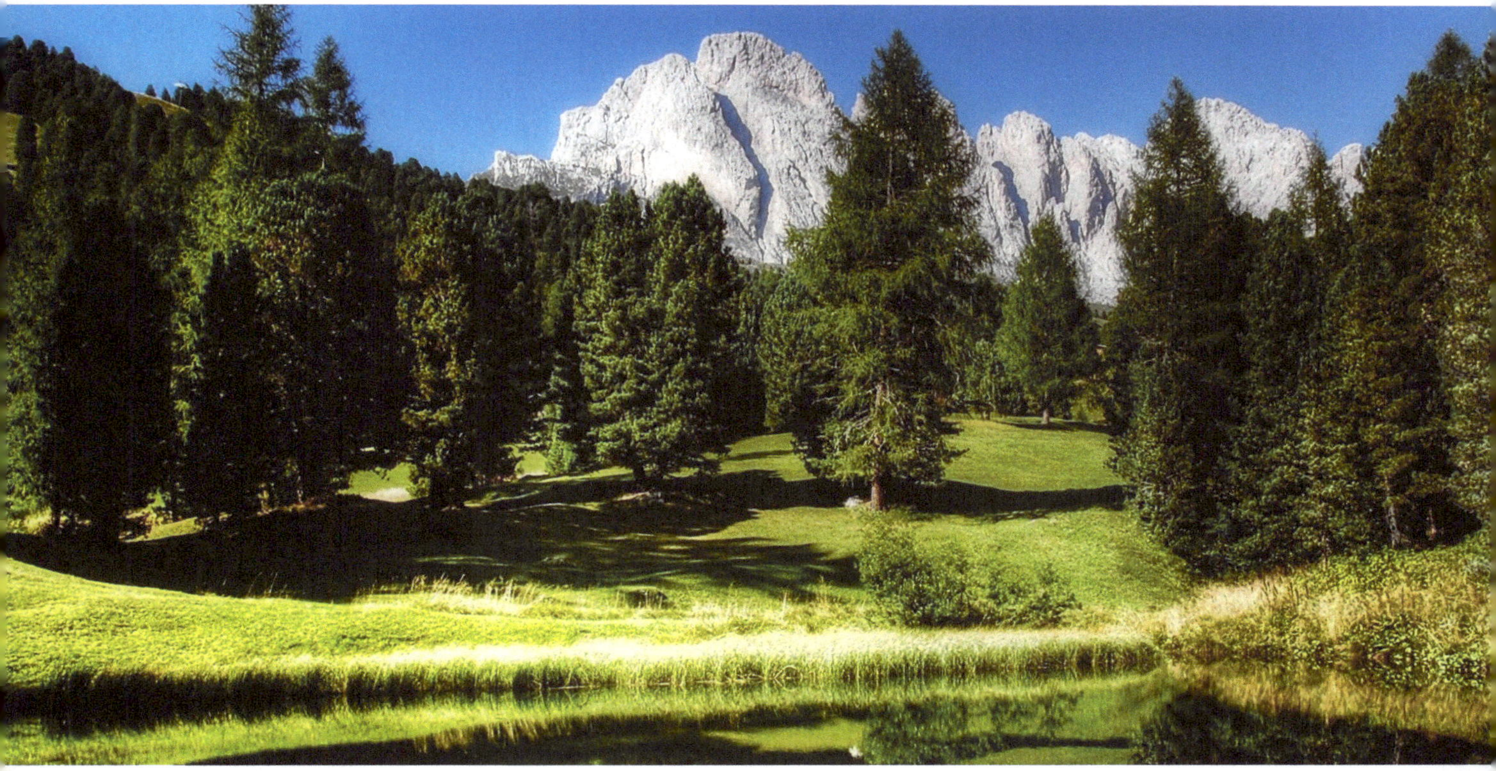

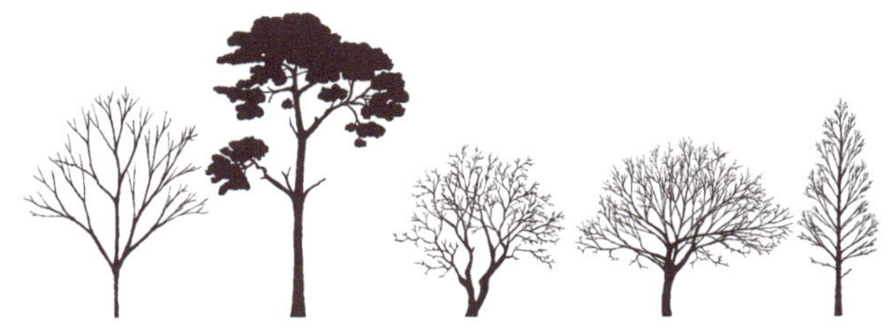

"Why are there trees I never walk under
but large and melodious thoughts descend upon me?"
— Walt Whitman

Dolomites Mountains, South Tyrol, Italy / Image by Kordula Vahle from Pixabay

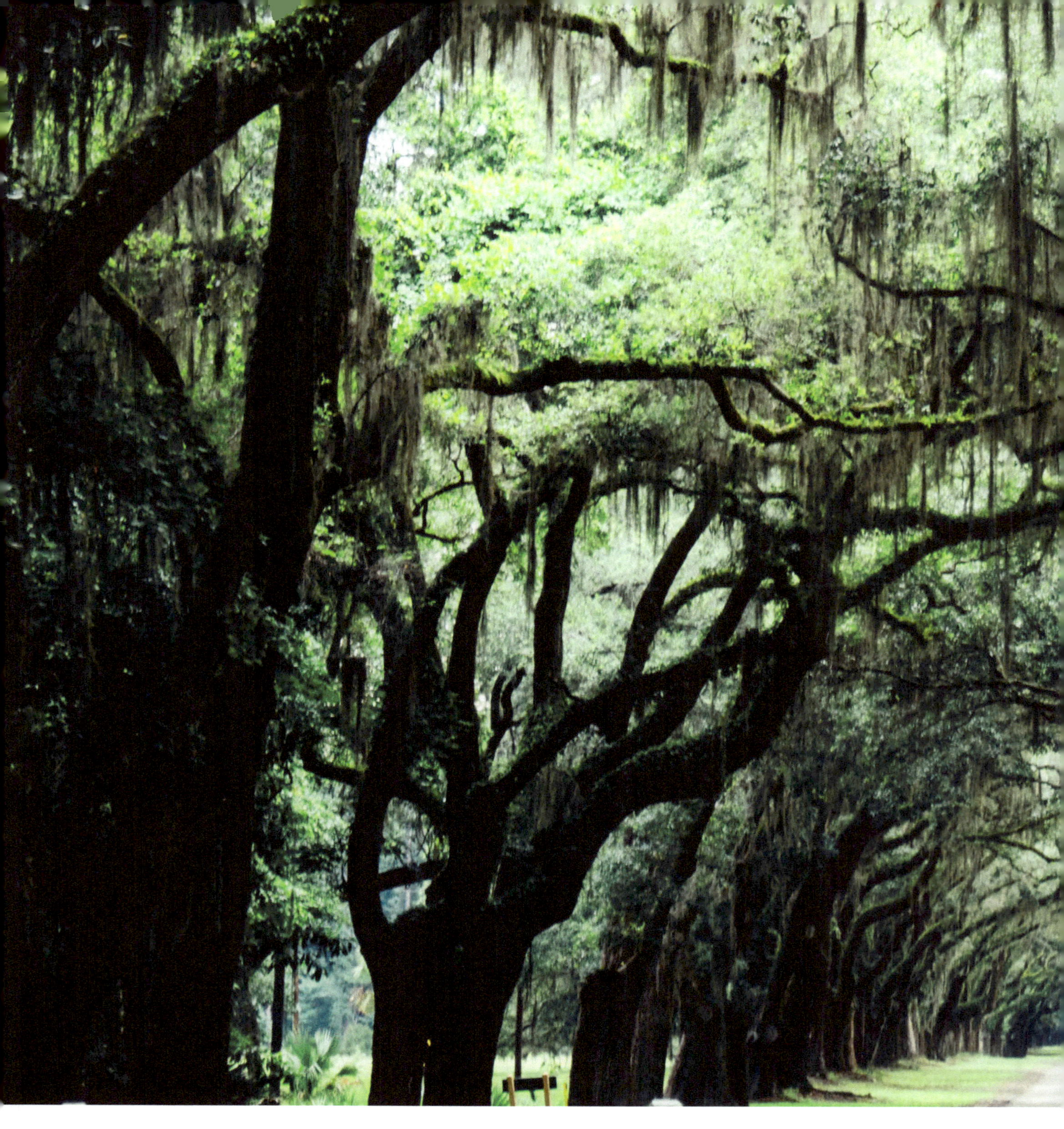

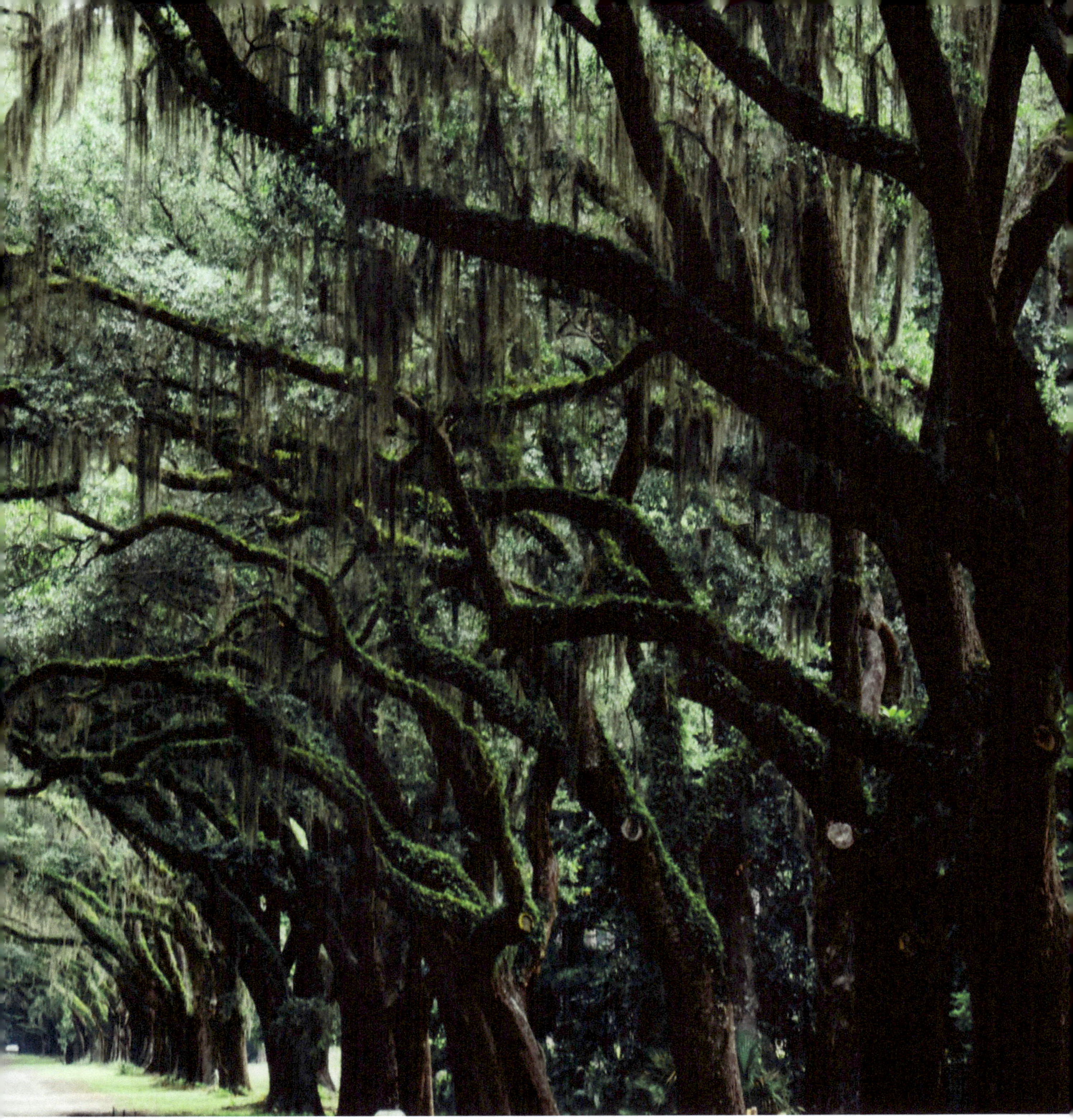

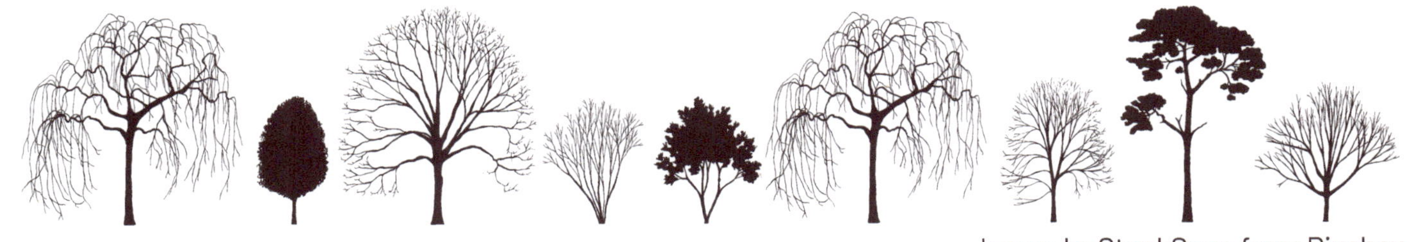

Image by StockSnap from Pixabay

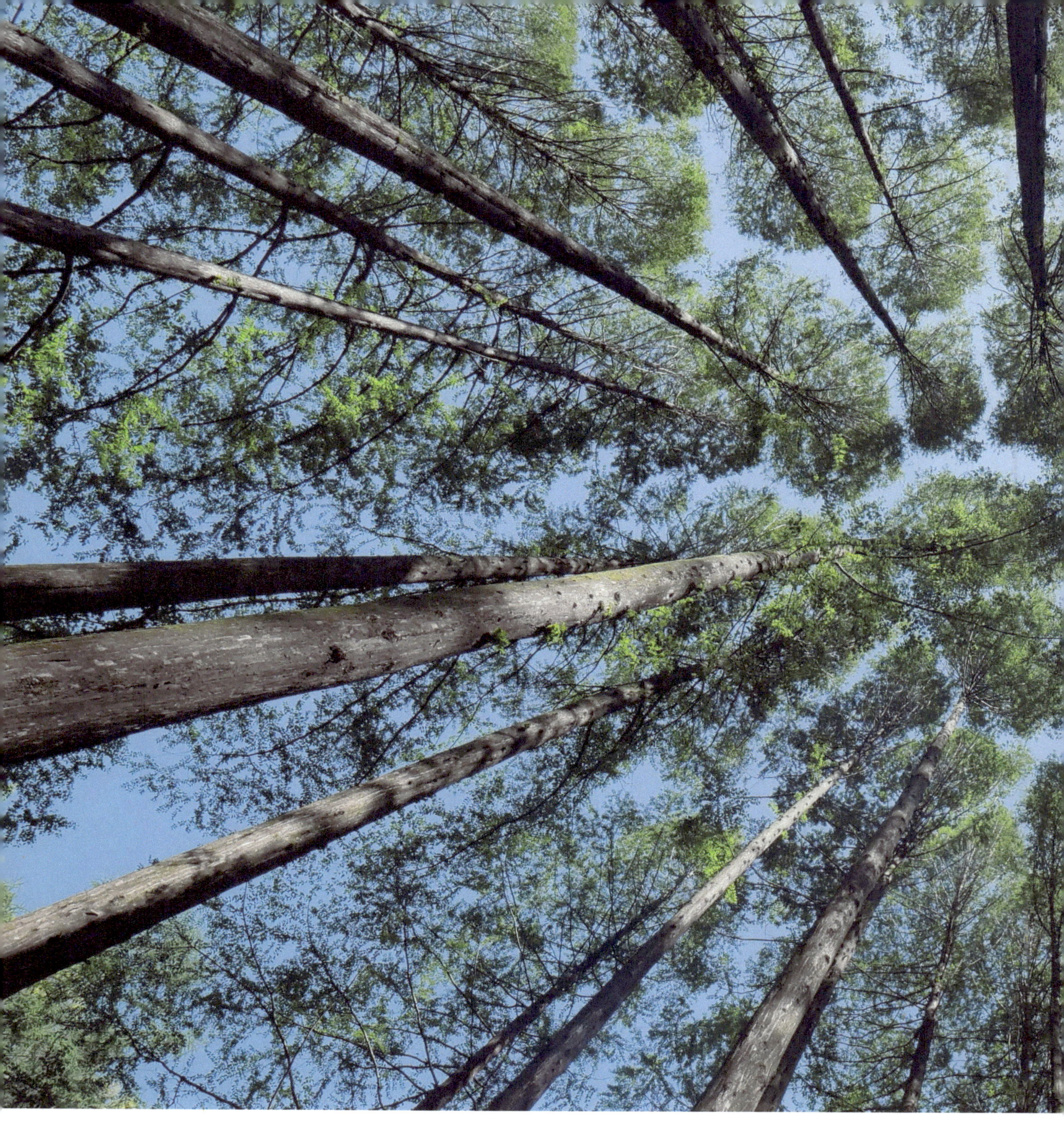

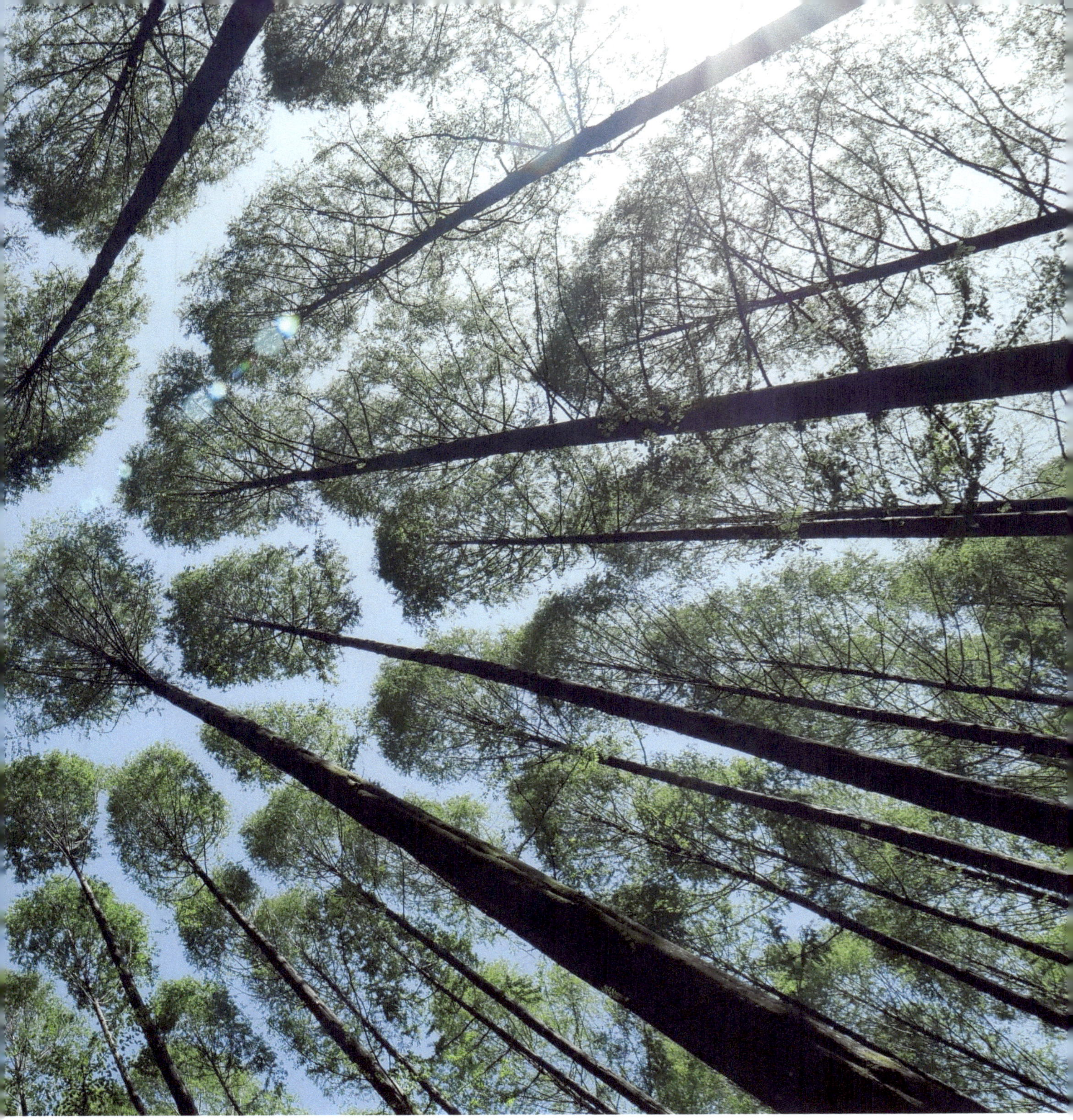

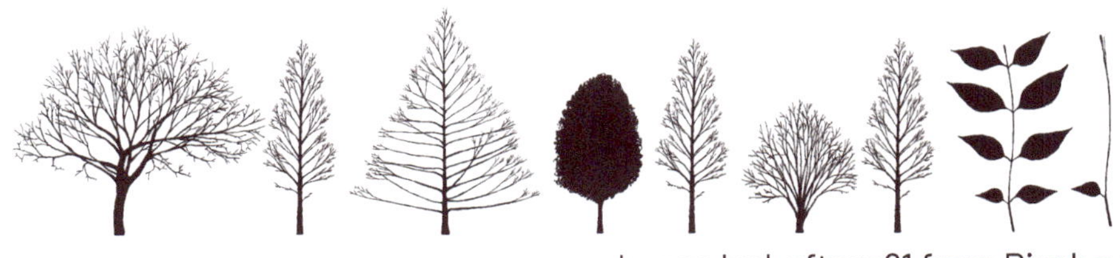

Image by Lefteye81 from Pixabay

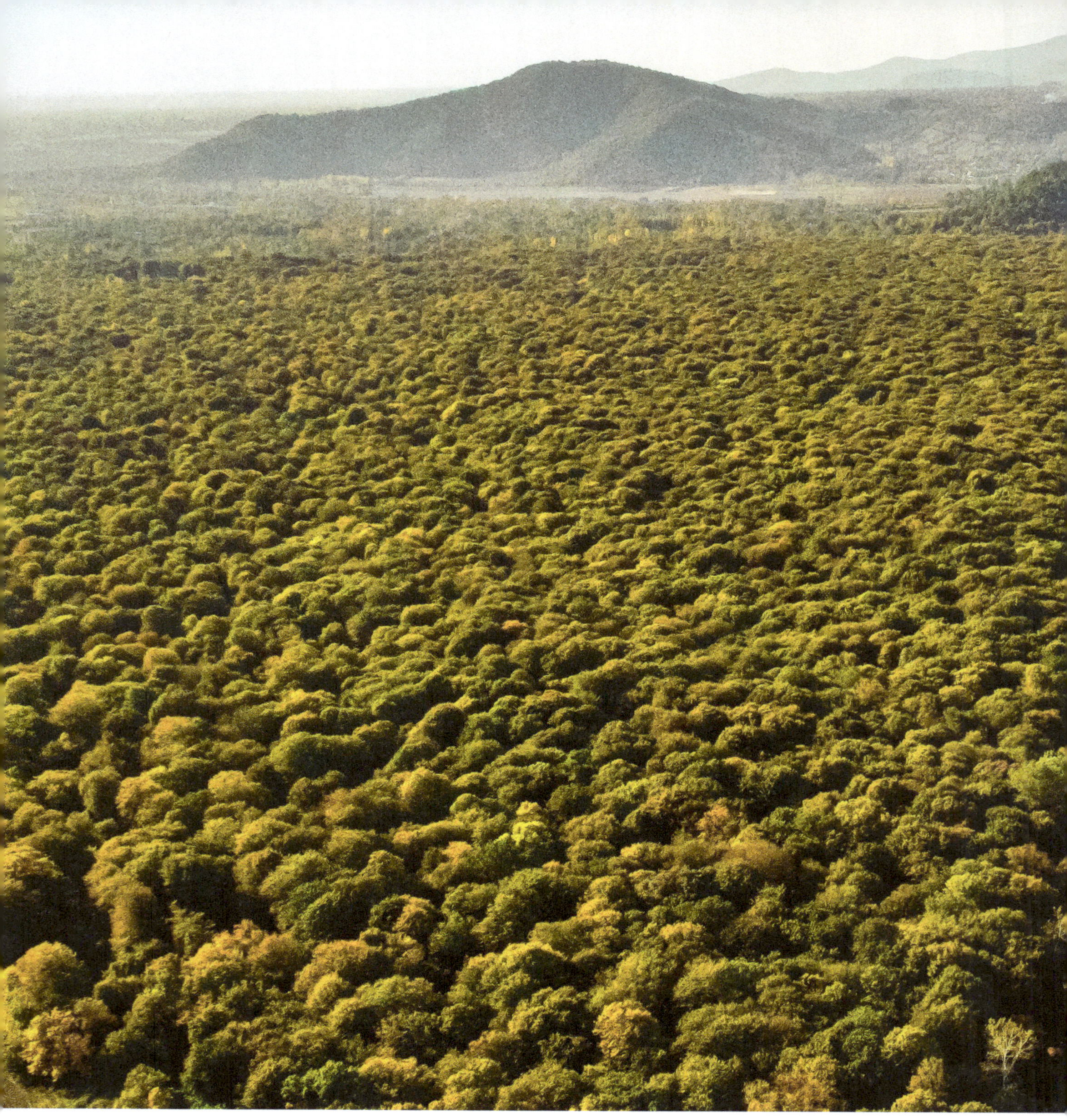

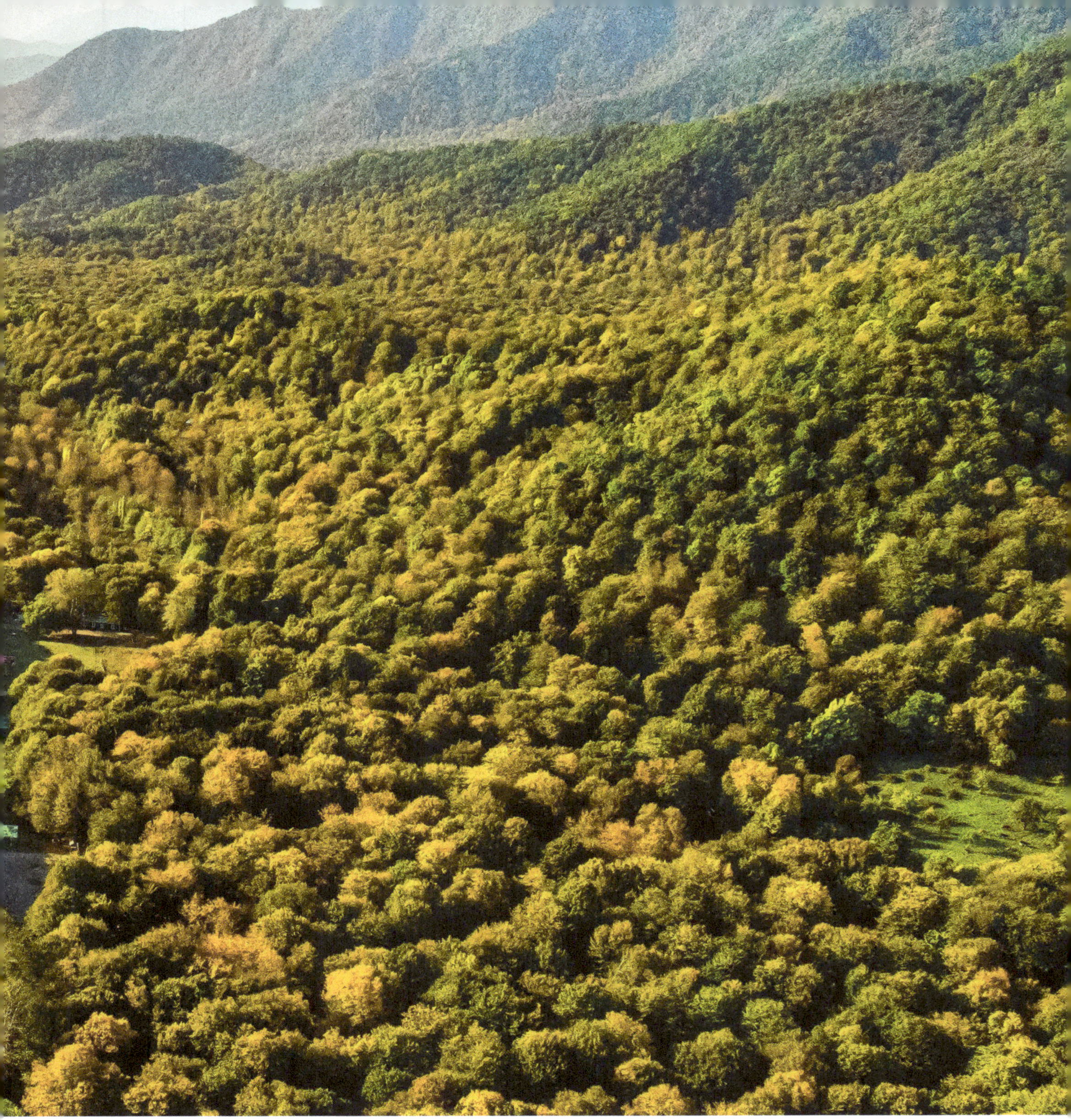

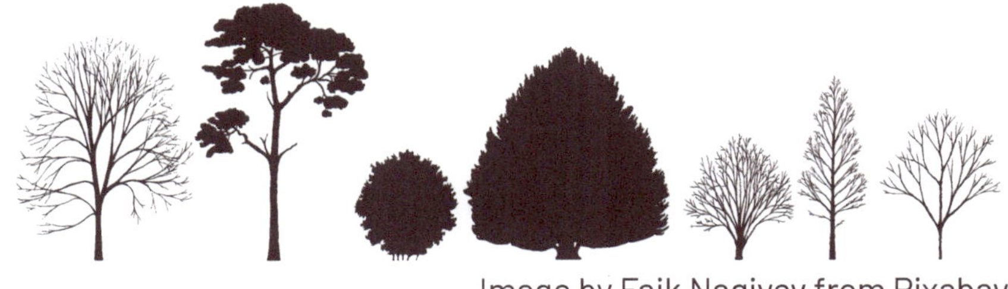

Image by Faik Nagiyev from Pixabay

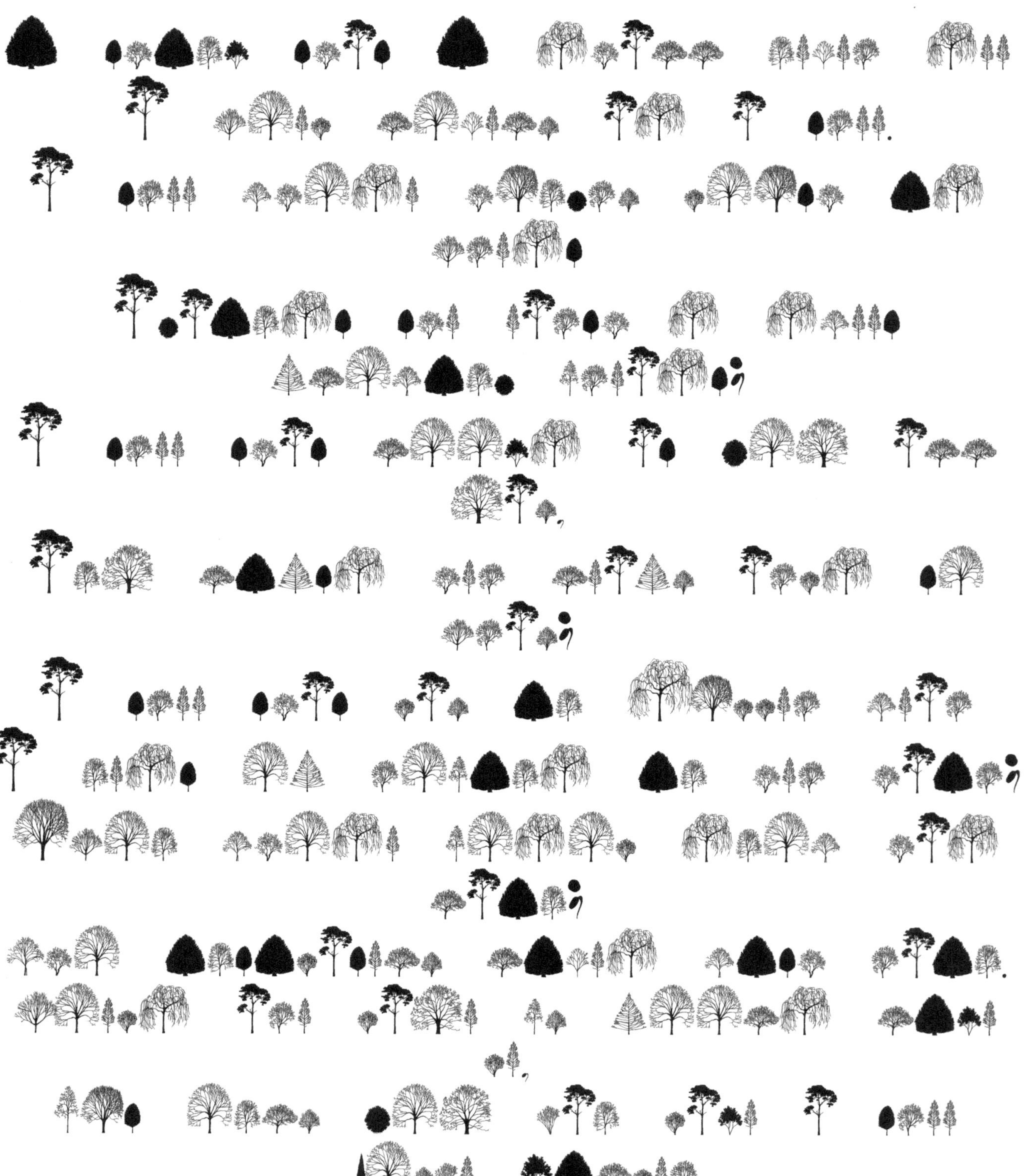

From the Forest

to Desert?

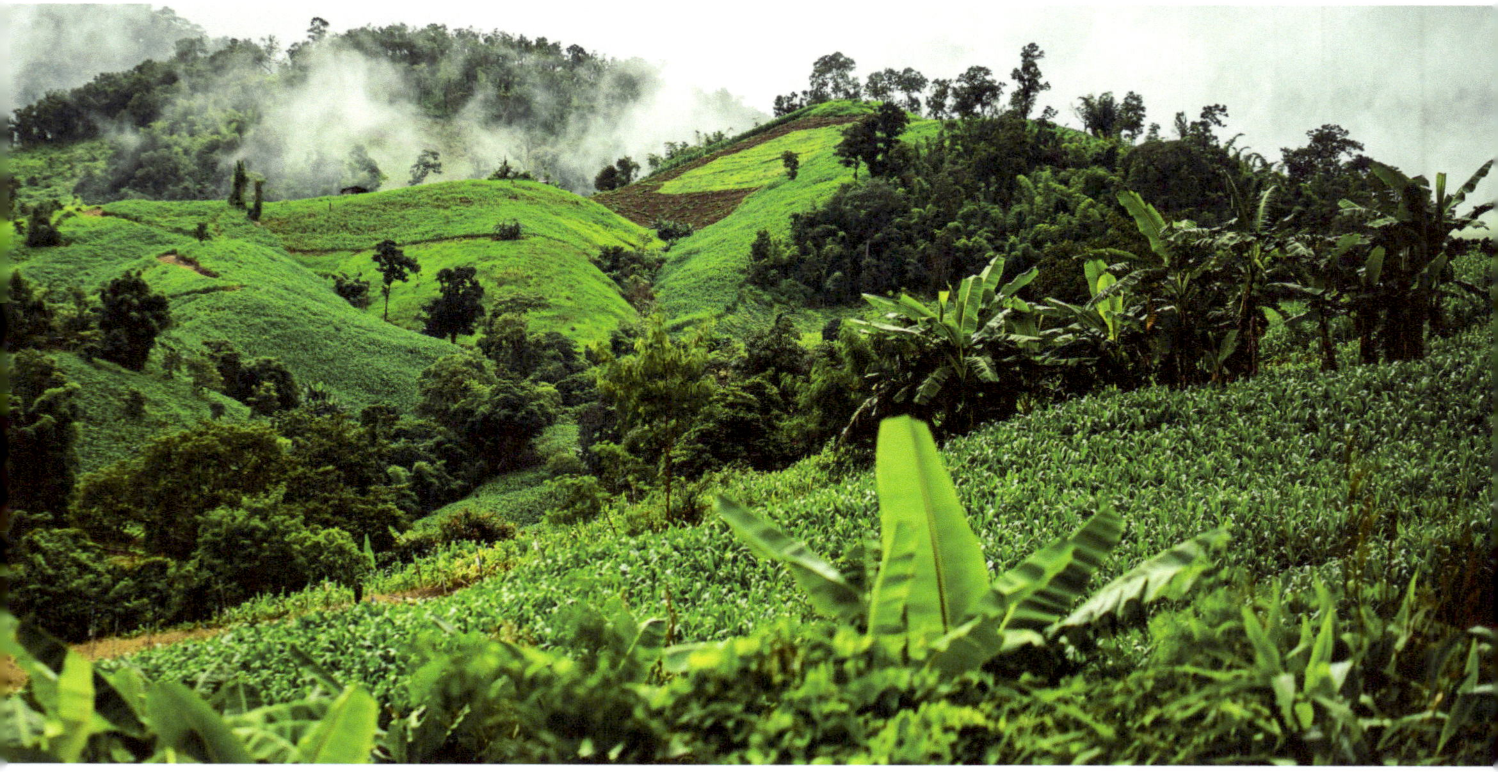

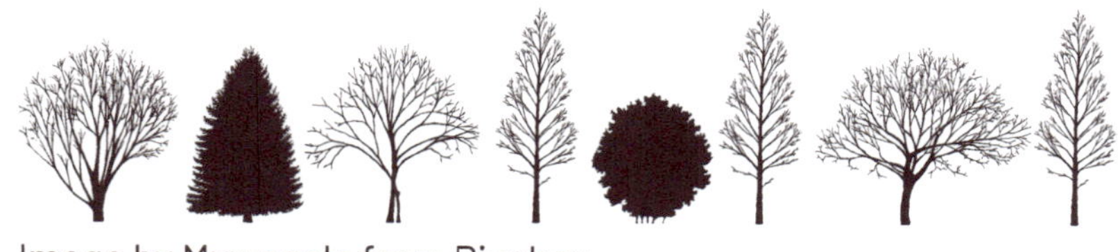

"He plants trees,
which will be of use to another age."
— Caecilius Statius

Image by Mxwegele from Pixabay

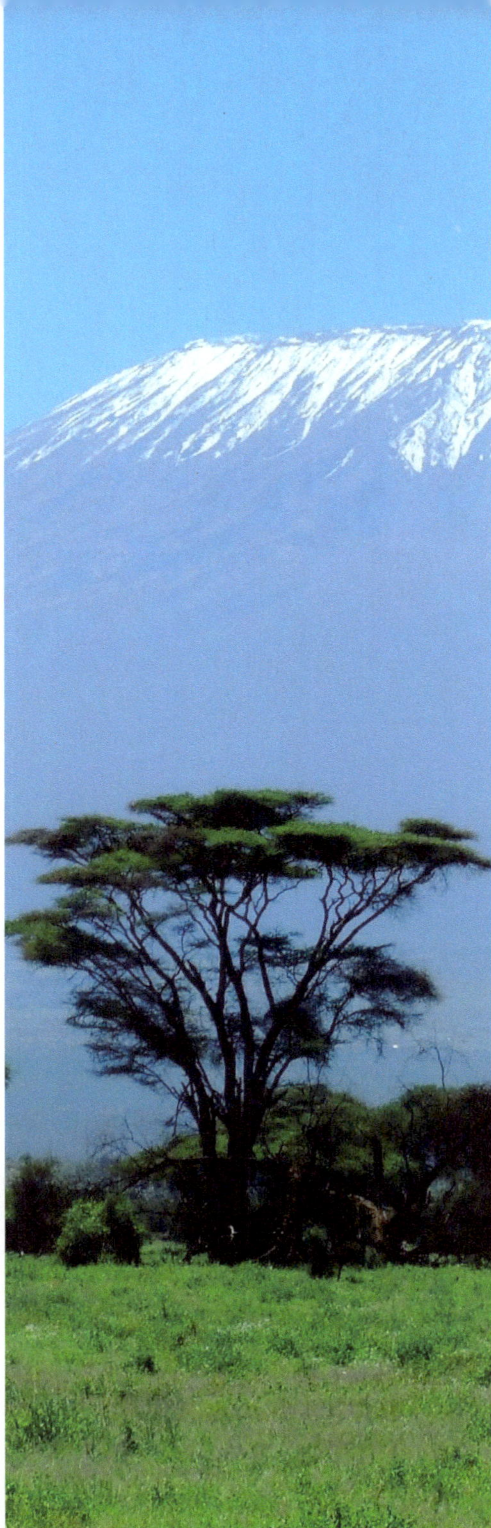
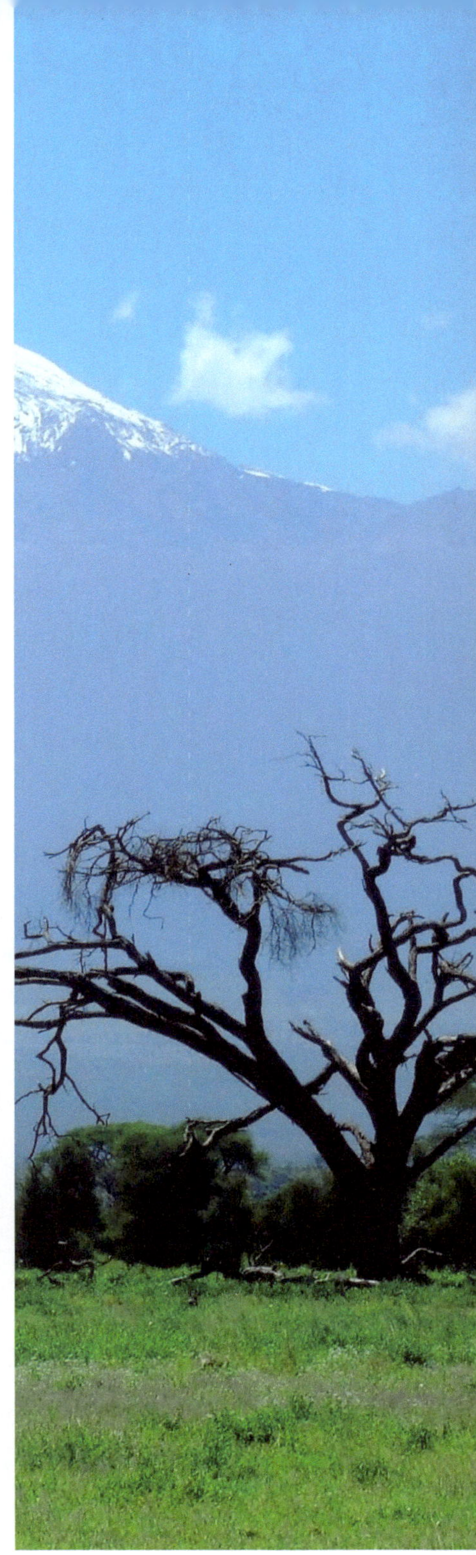
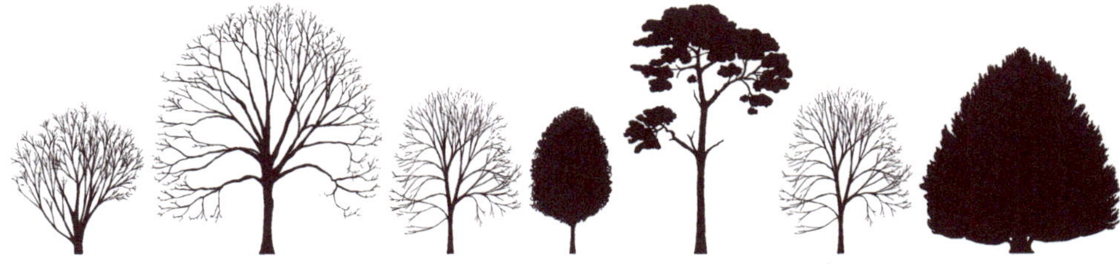

Mount Kilimanjaro is in the background, Amboseli, Kenya / Image by Greg Montani from Pixabay

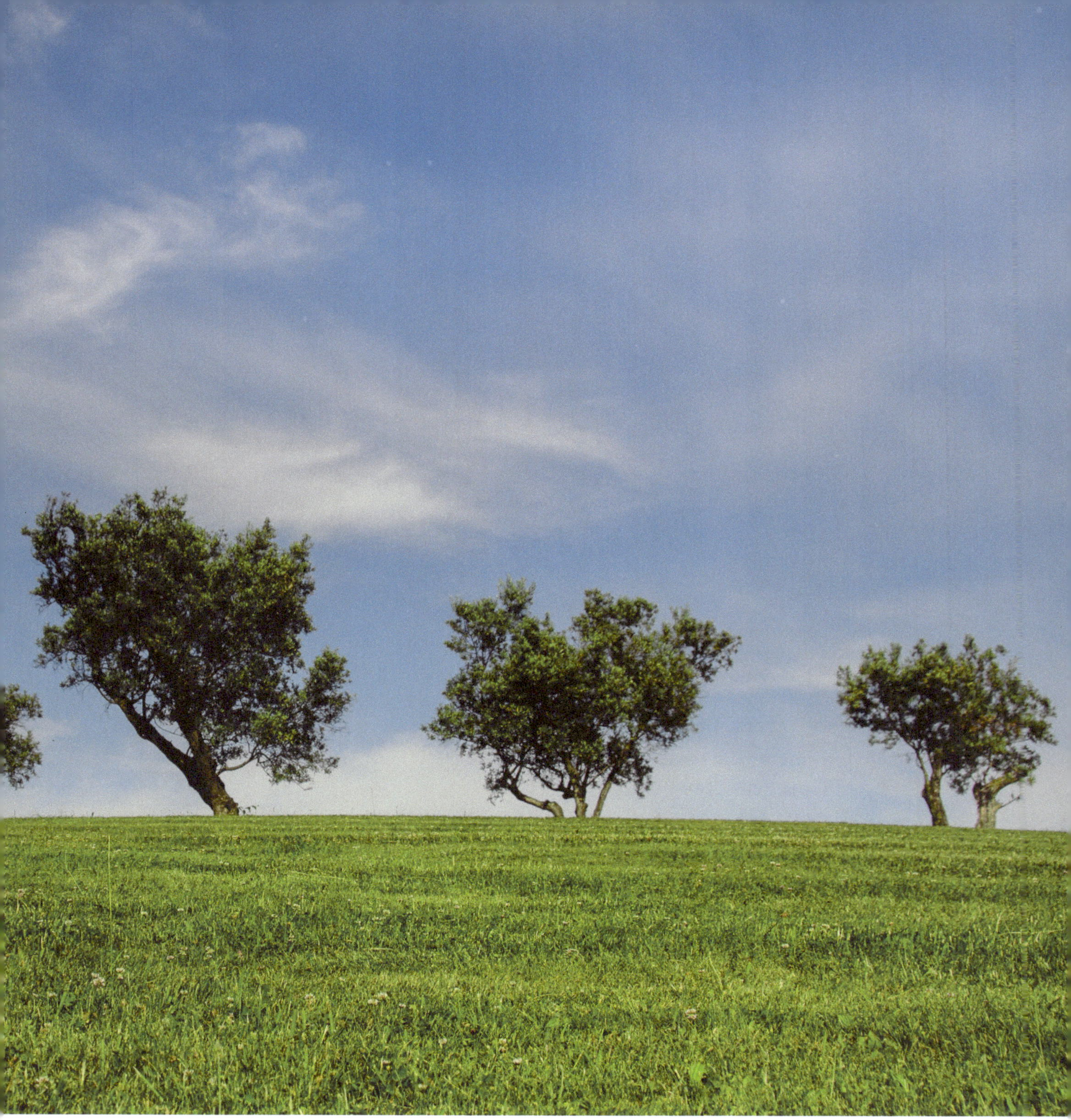

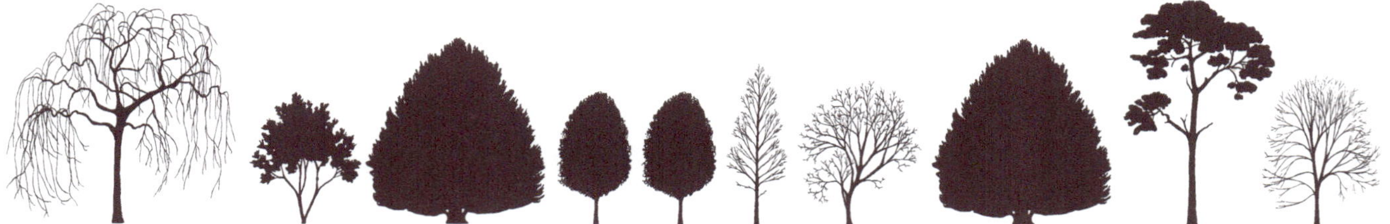

Image by Rudy and Peter Skitterians from Pixabay

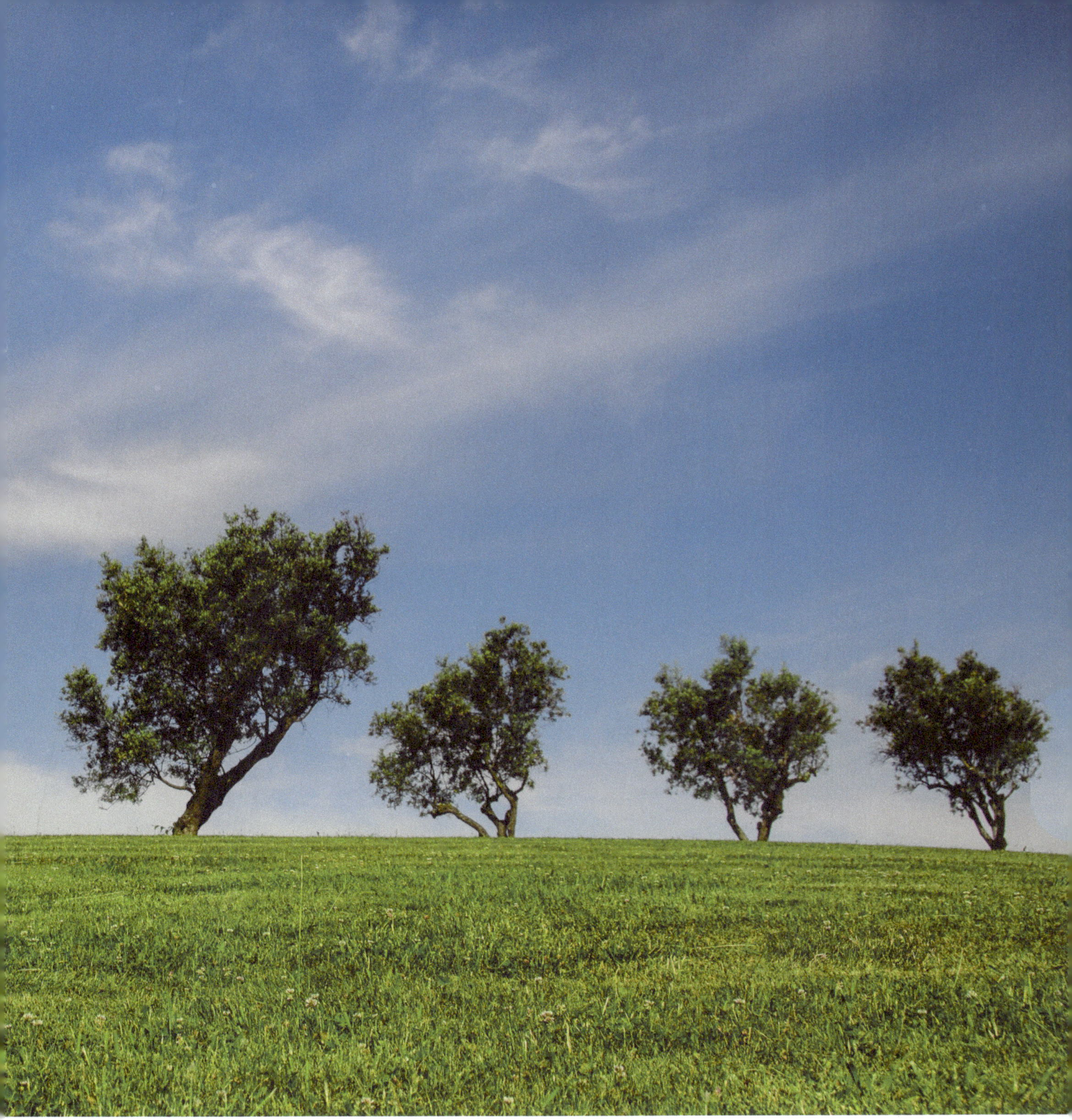

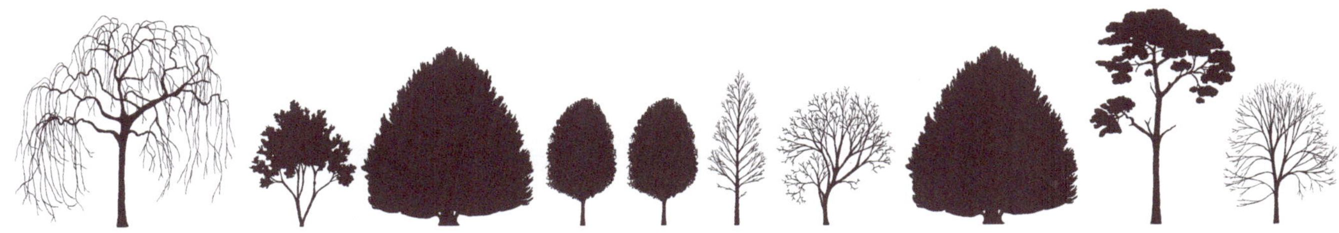

Image by Rudy and Peter Skitterians from Pixabay

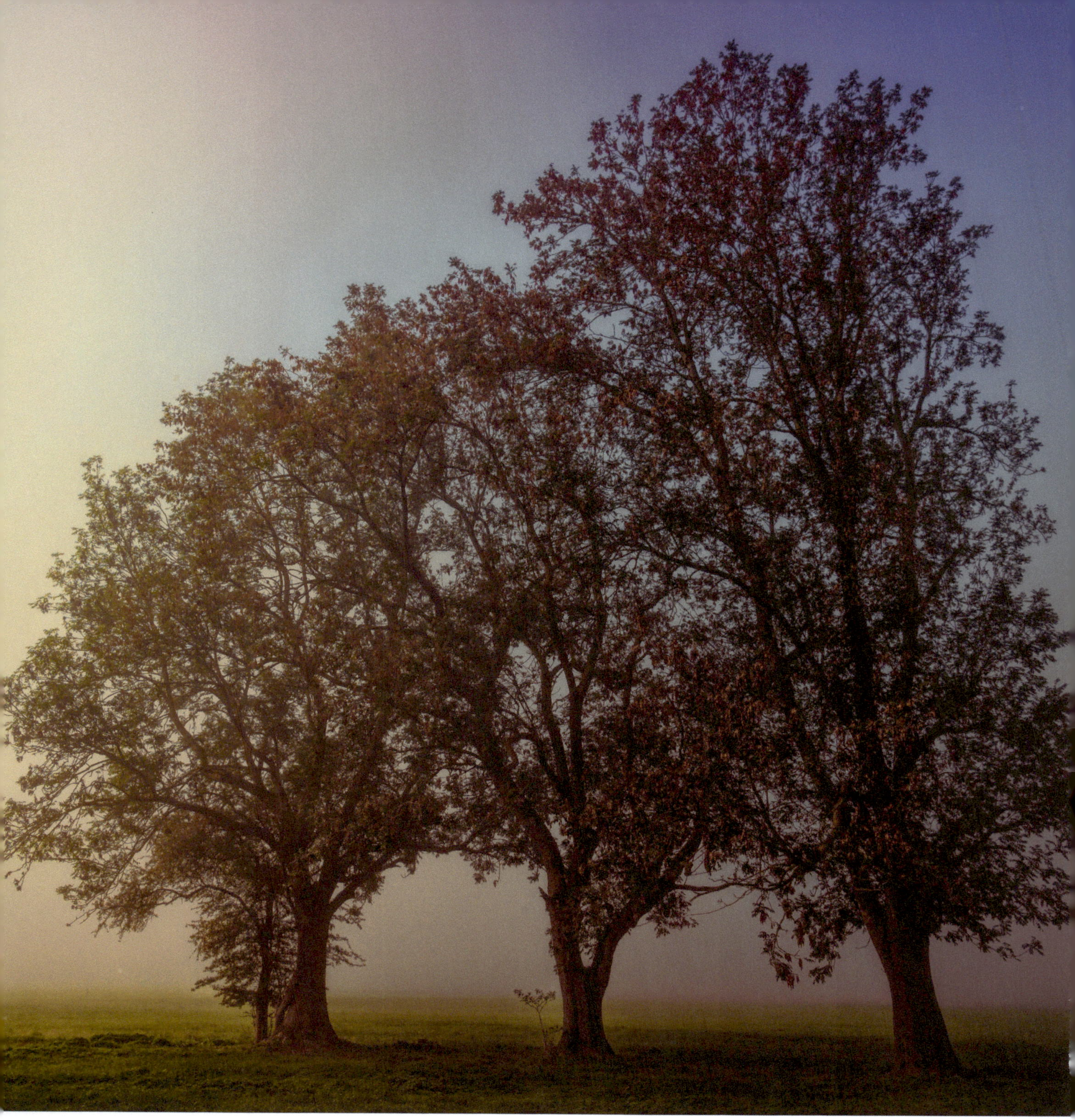

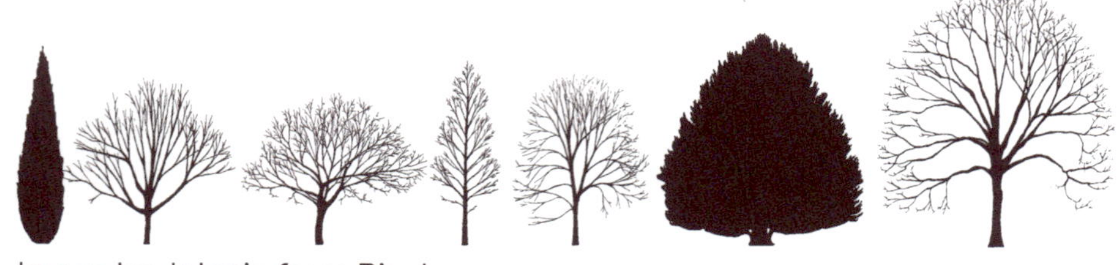

Image by Jplenio from Pixabay

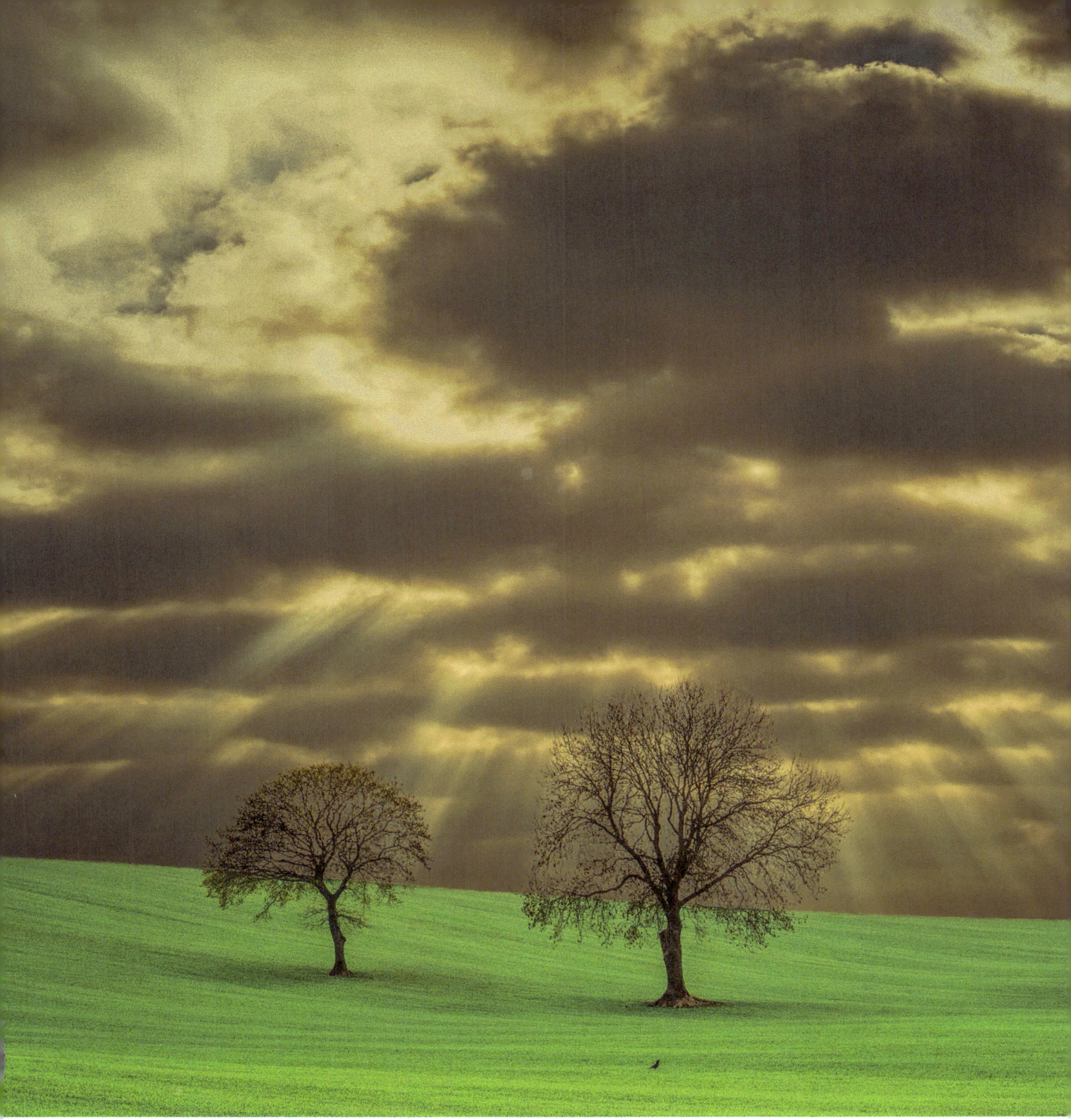

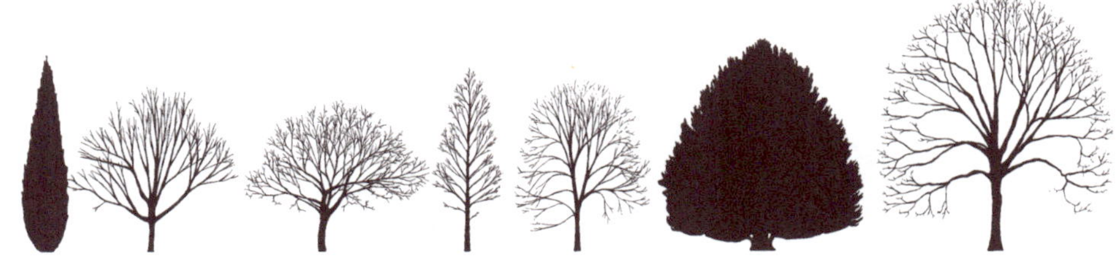

Image by Jplenio from Pixabay

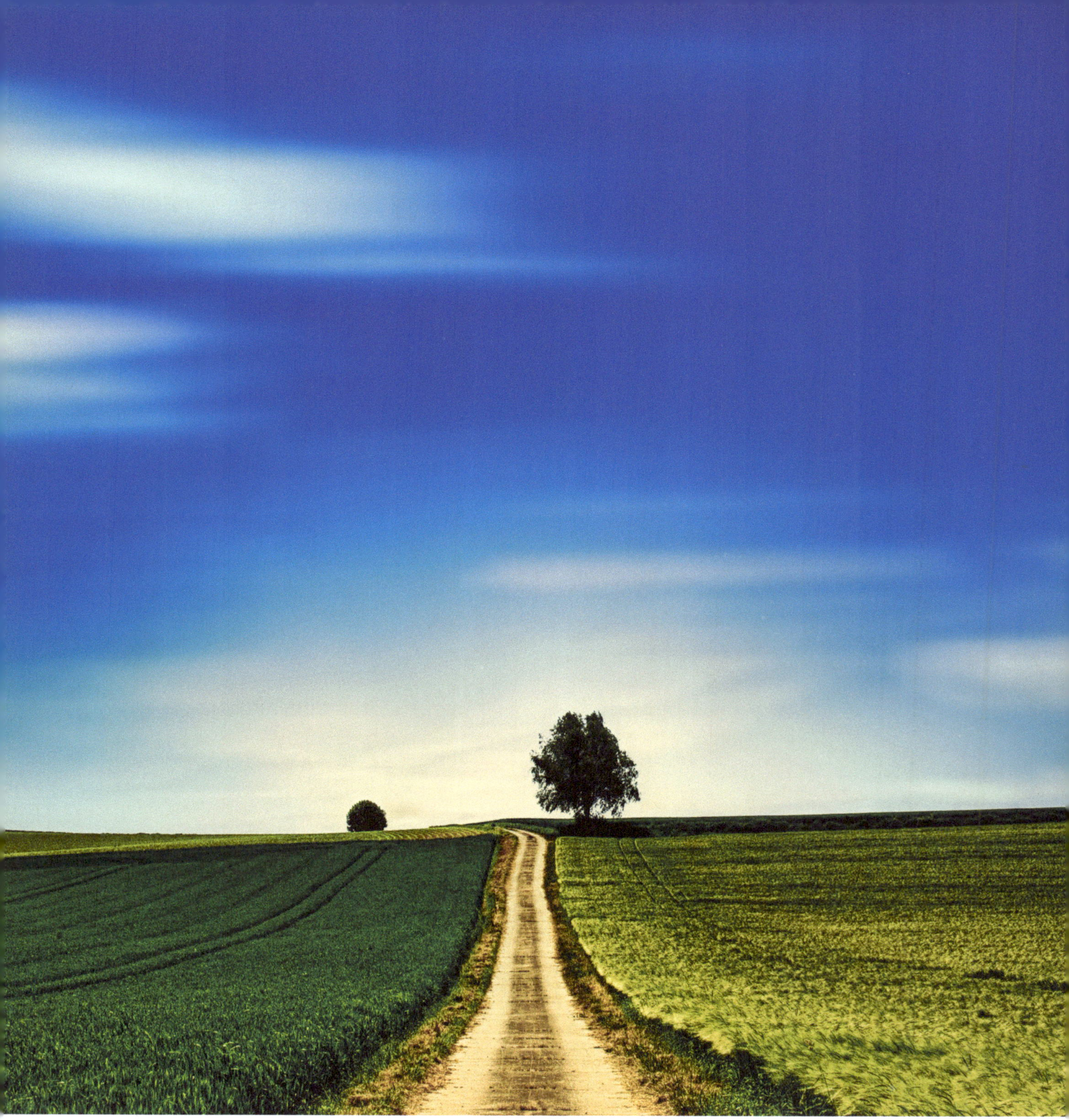

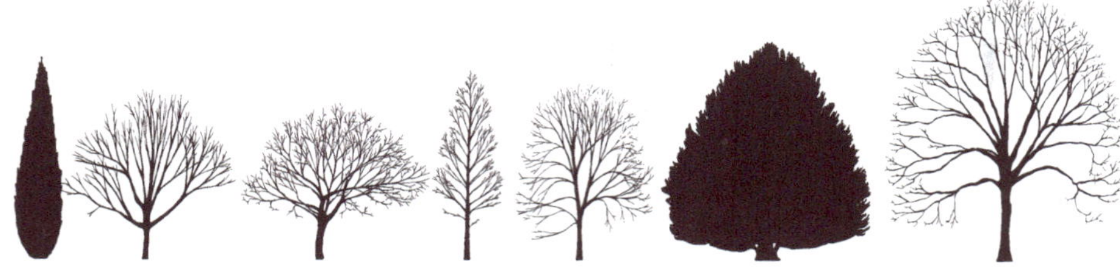

Image by Jplenio from Pixabay

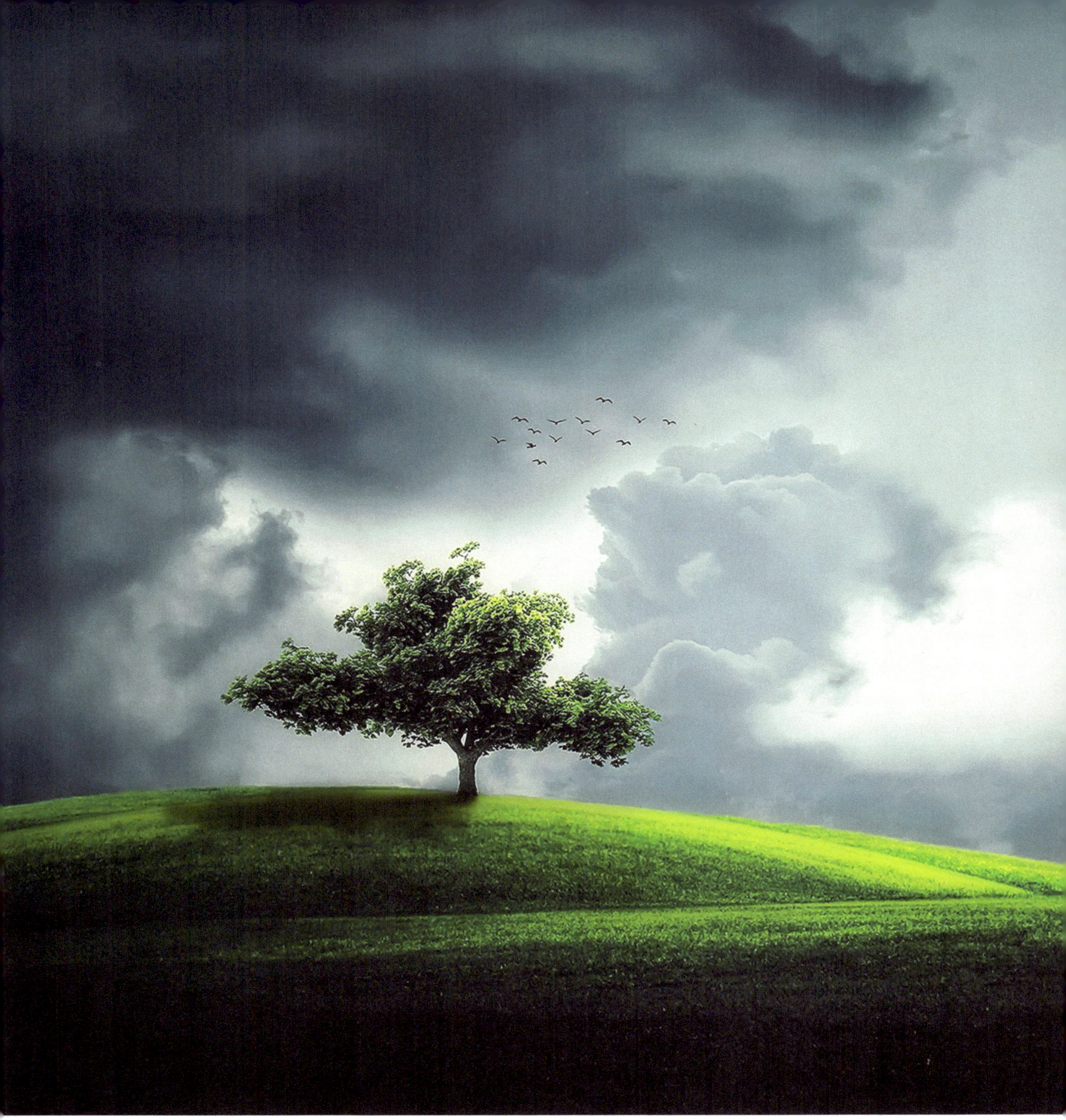

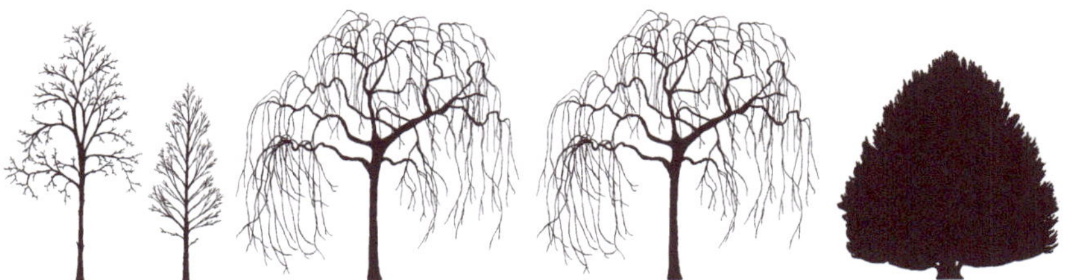

Image by Bessi from Pixabay

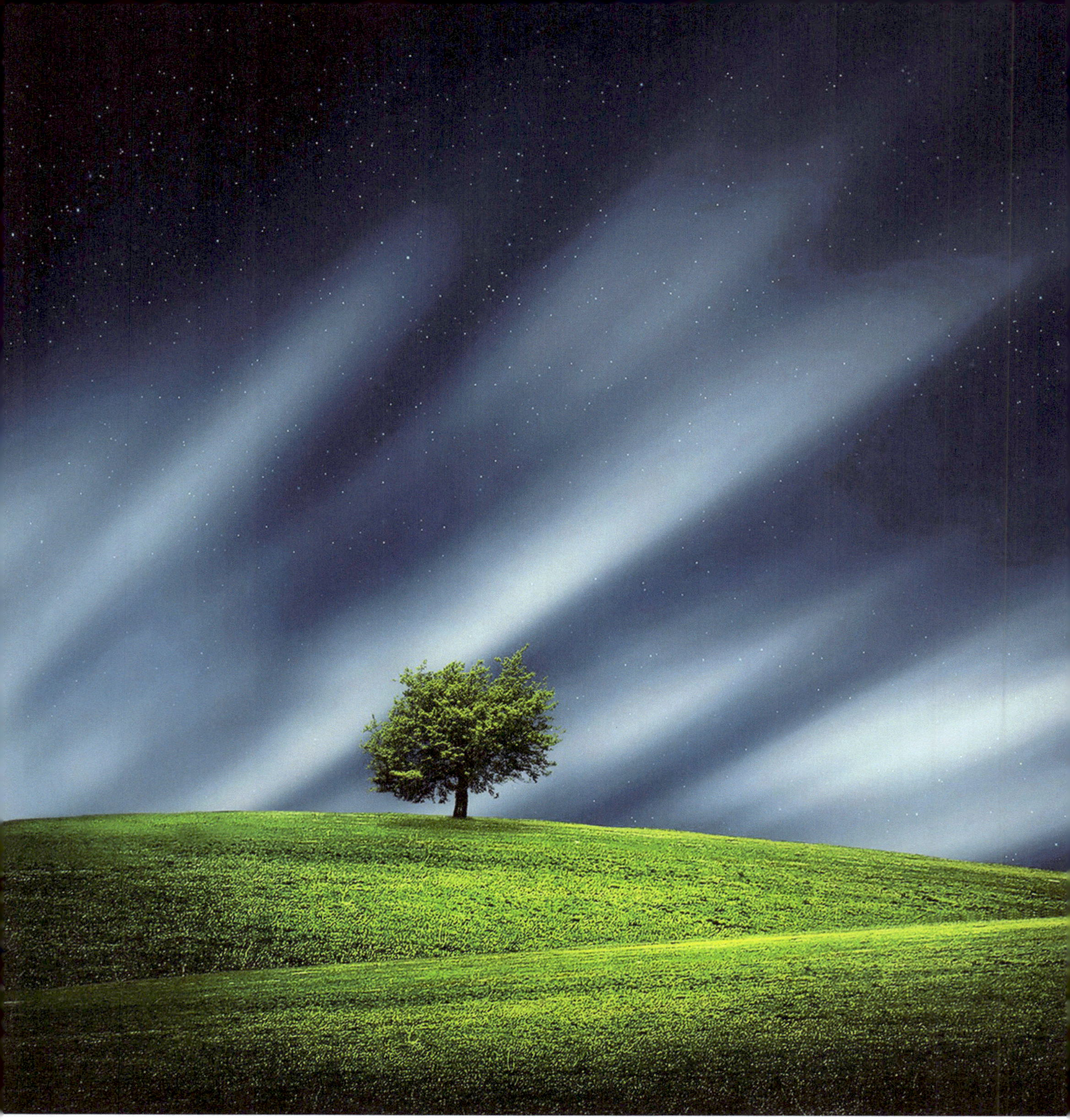

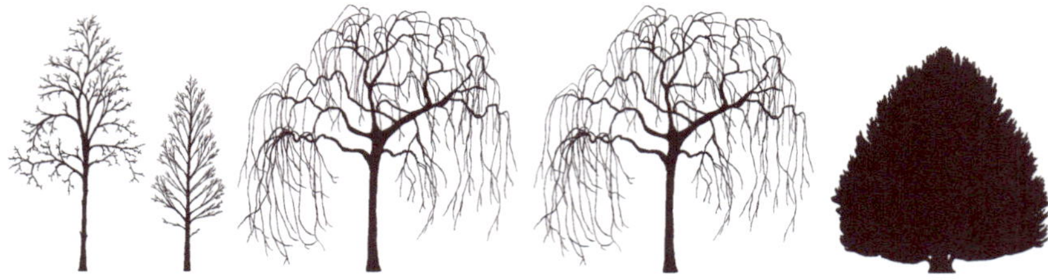

Image by Bessi from Pixabay

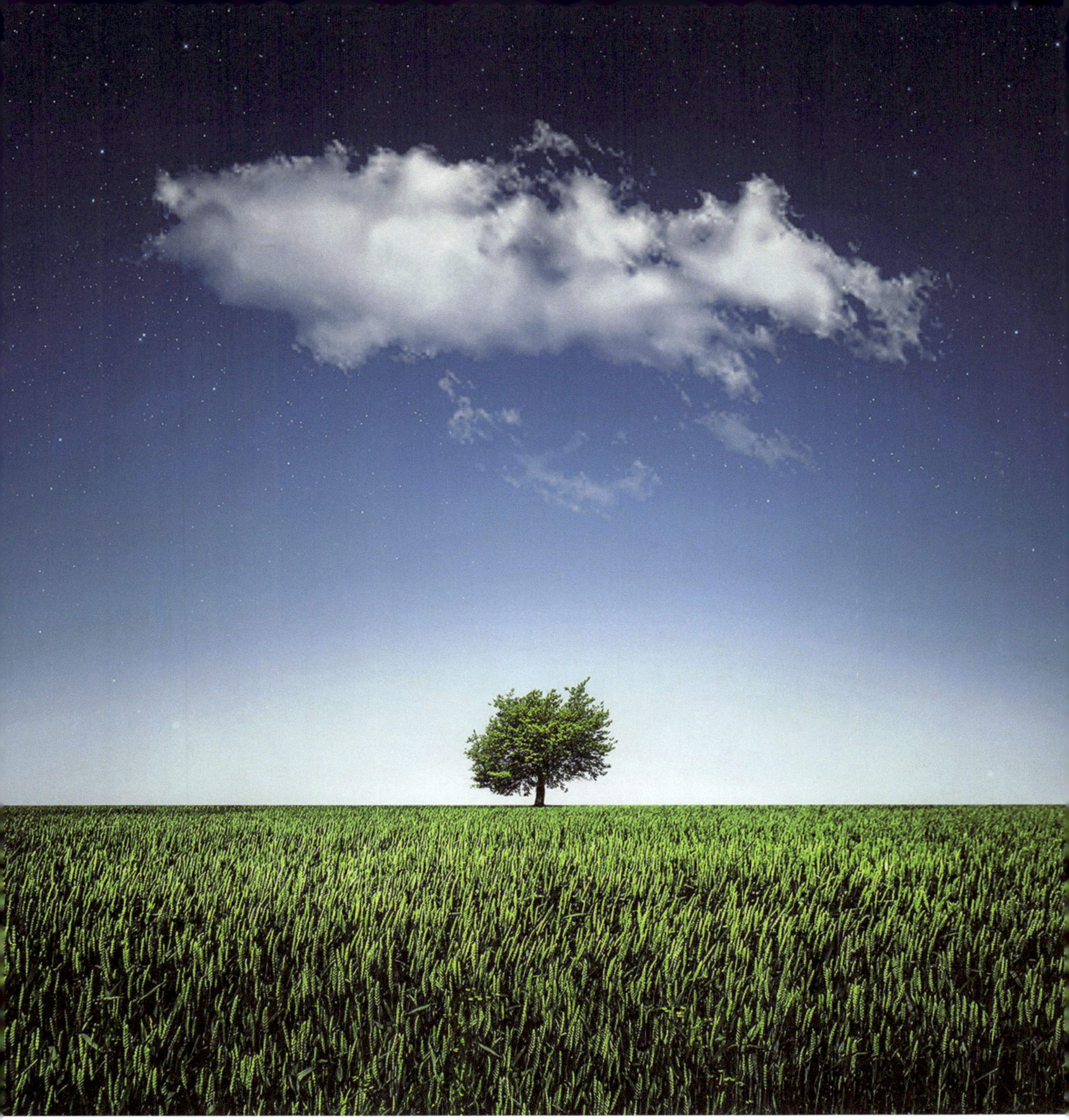

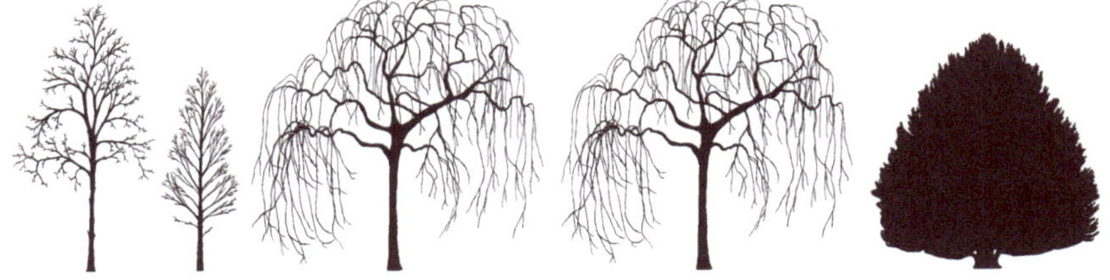

Image by Bessi from Pixabay

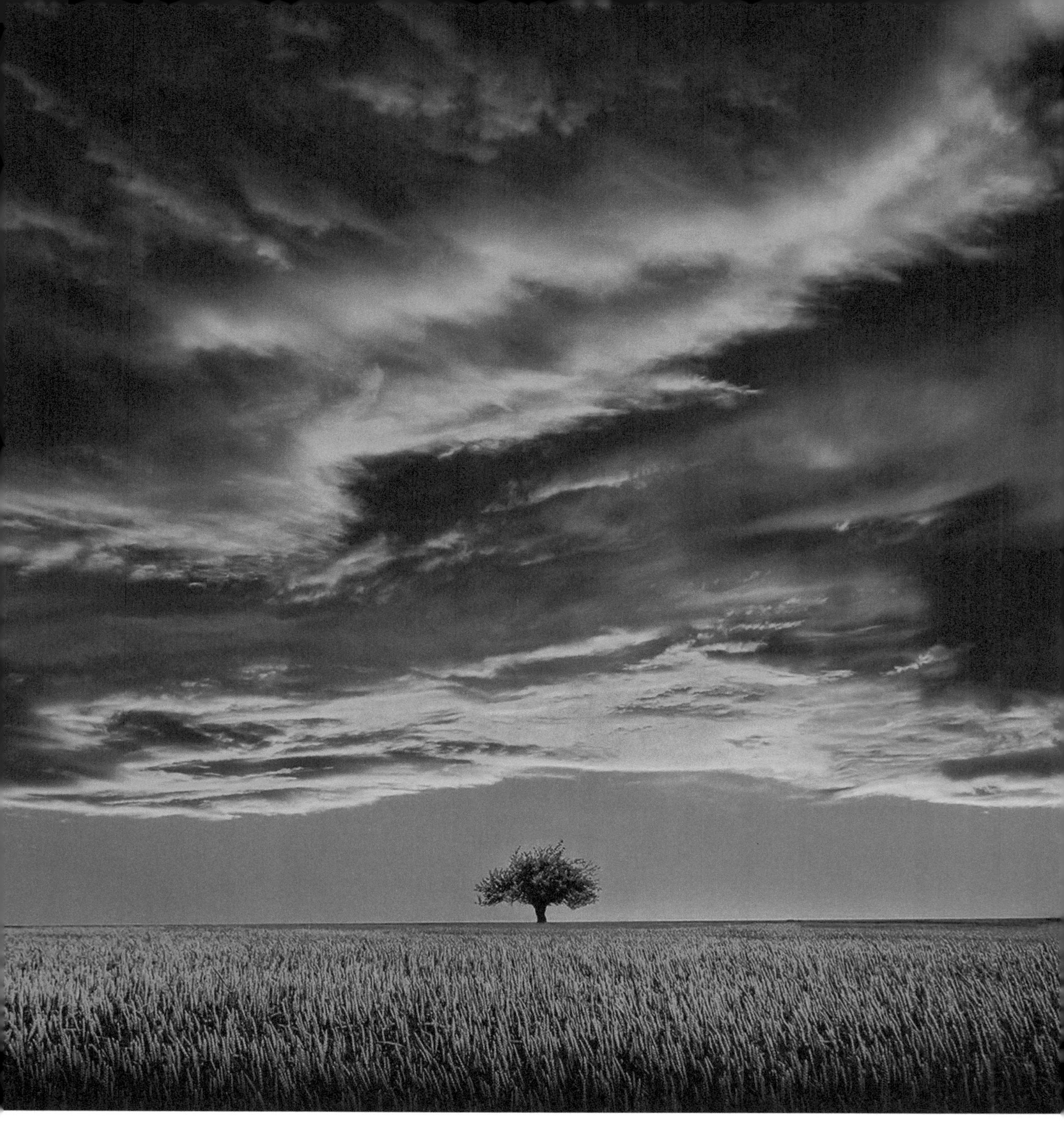

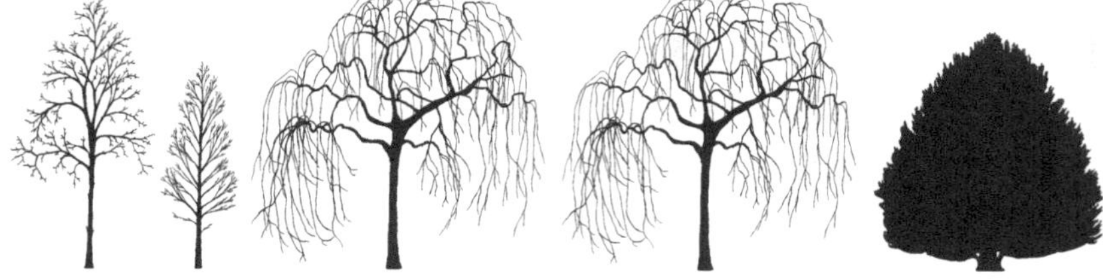

Image by Bessi from Pixabay

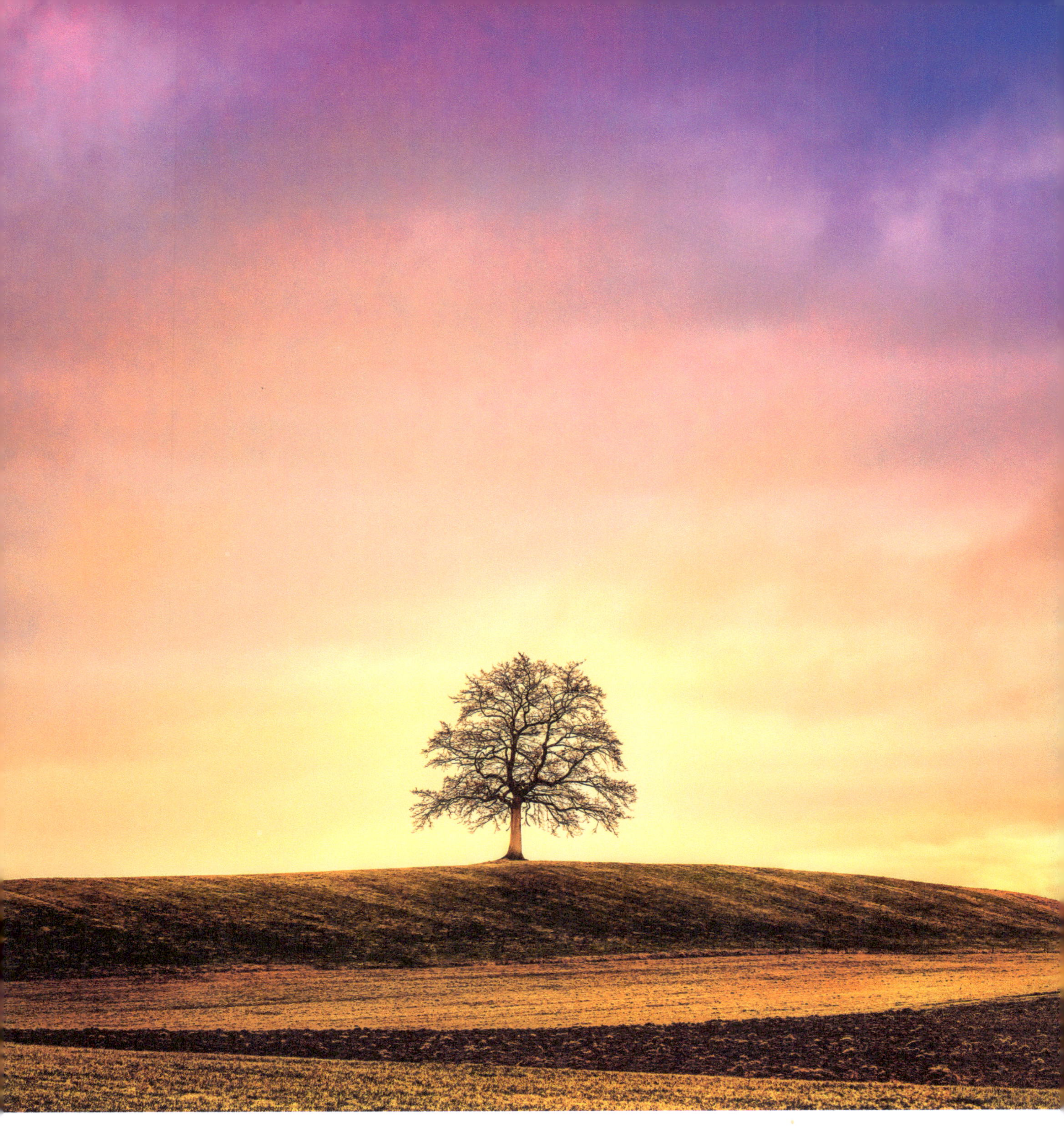

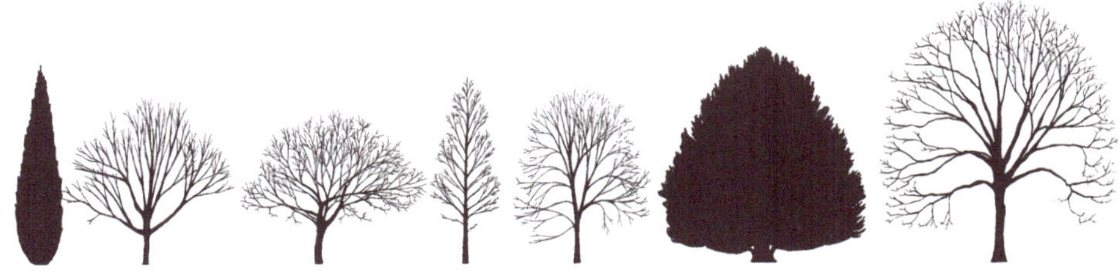

Image by Jplenio from Pixabay

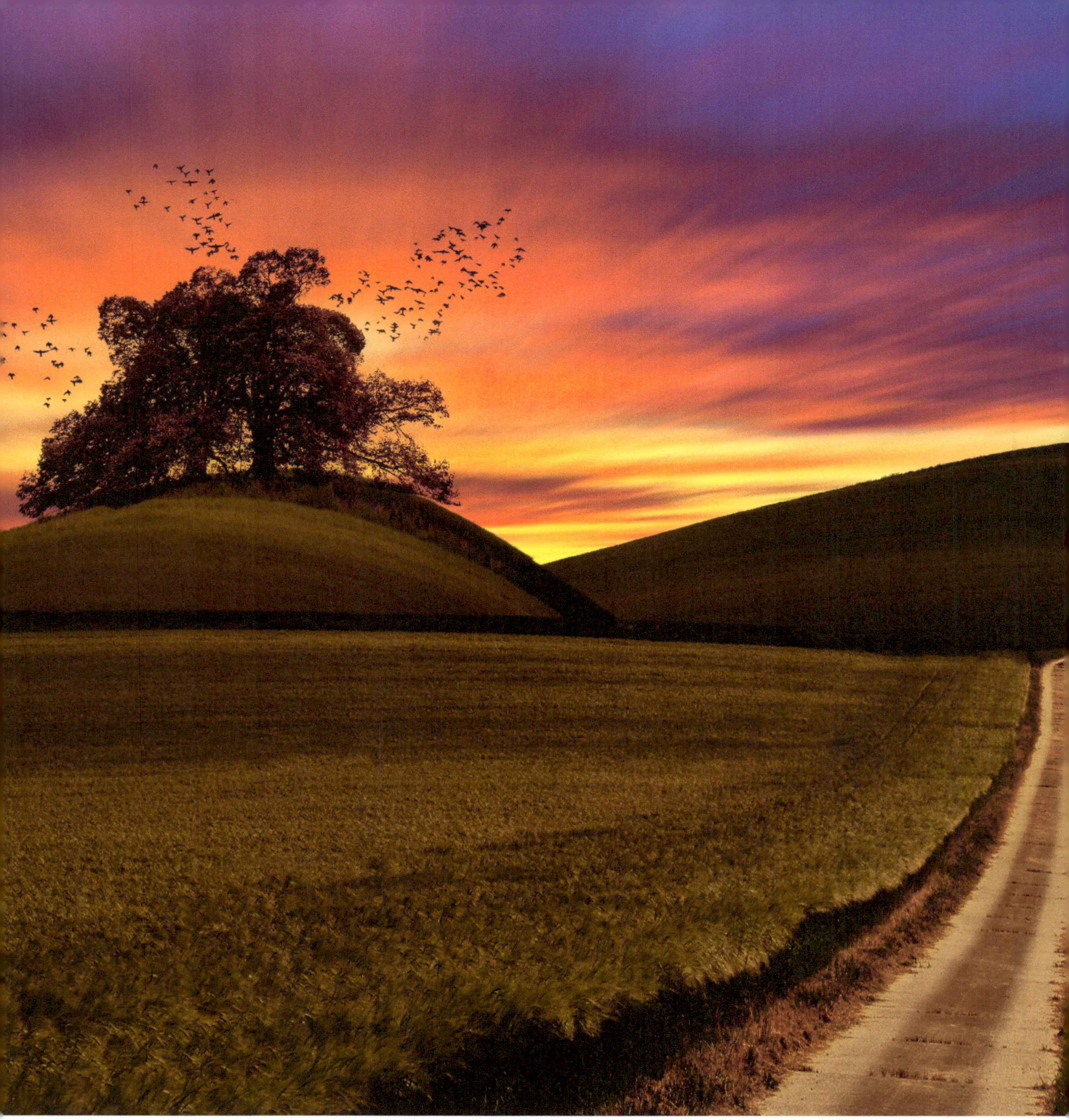

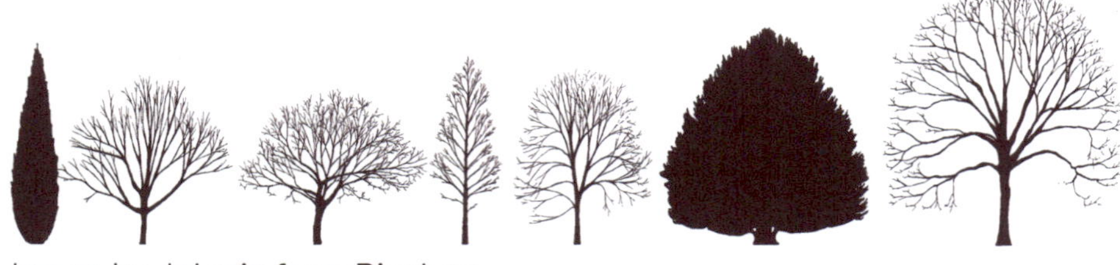

Image by Jplenio from Pixabay

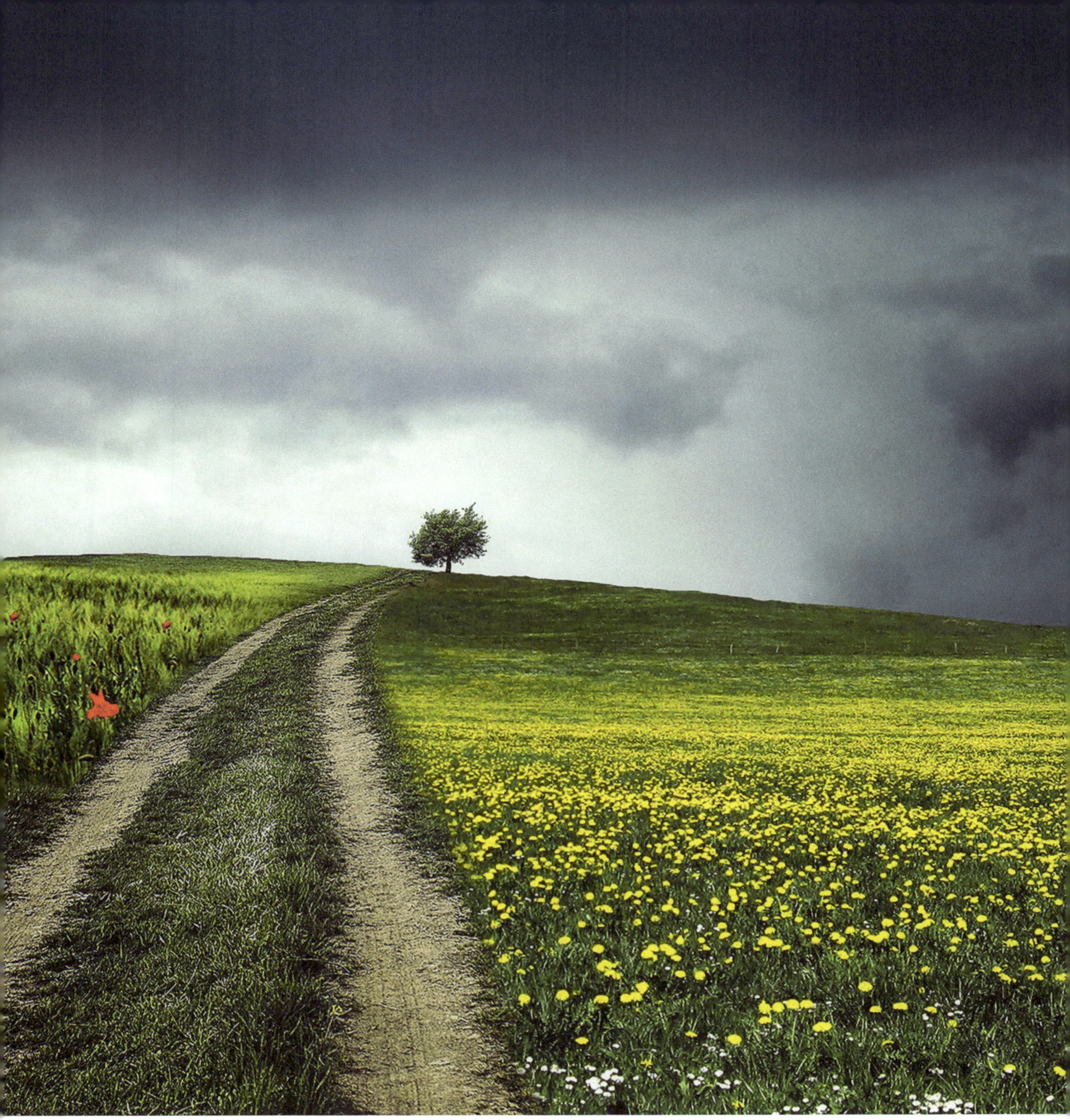

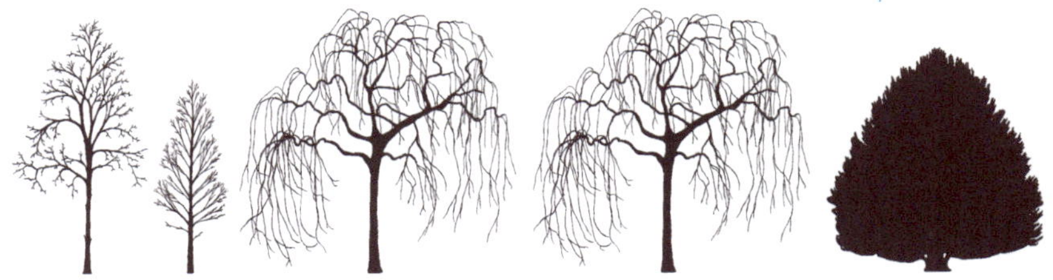

Image by Bessi from Pixabay

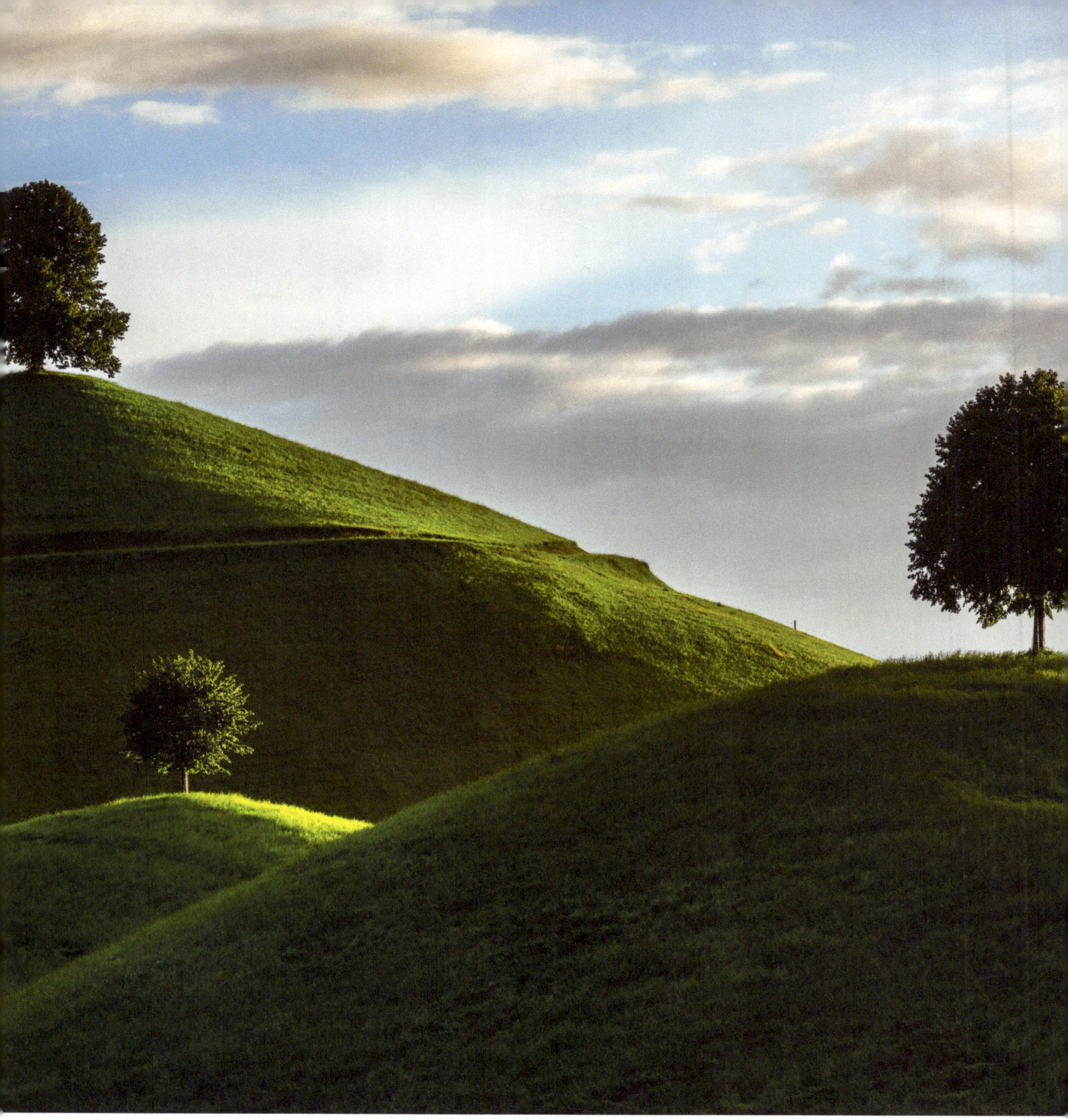

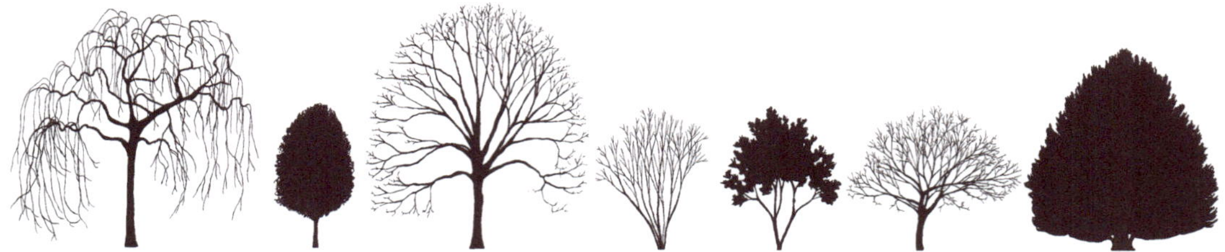

Assemblages of drumlins / Image by Susanne Stöckli from Pixabay

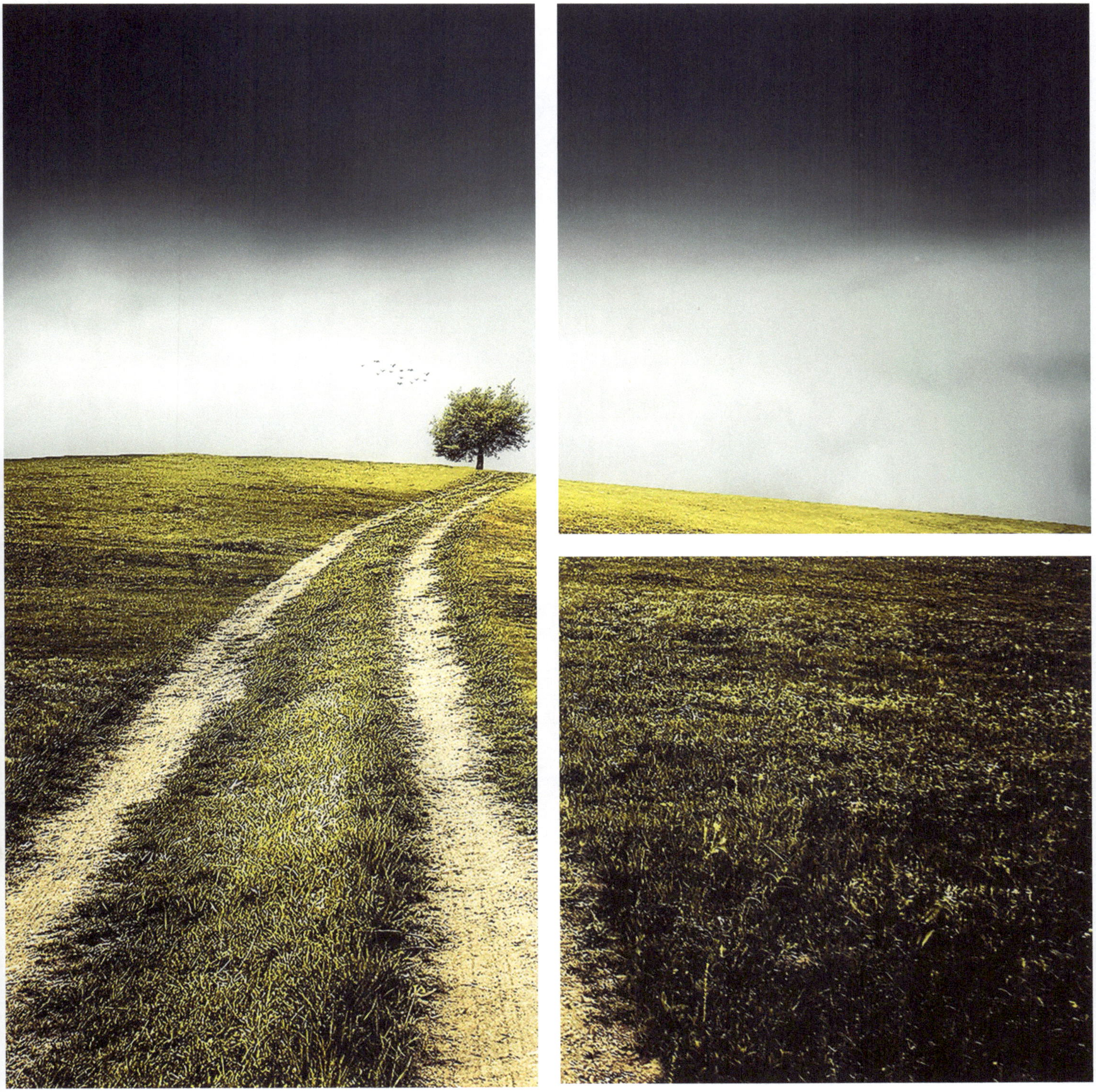

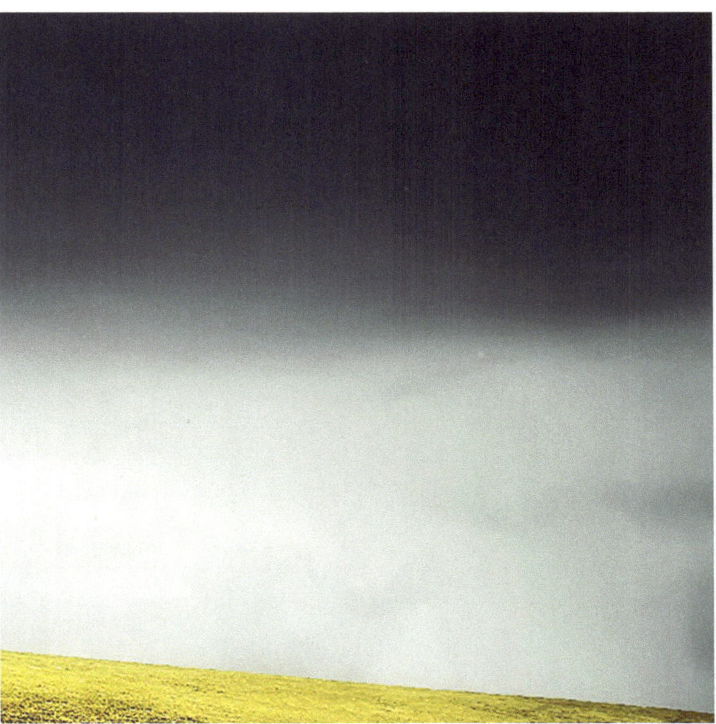

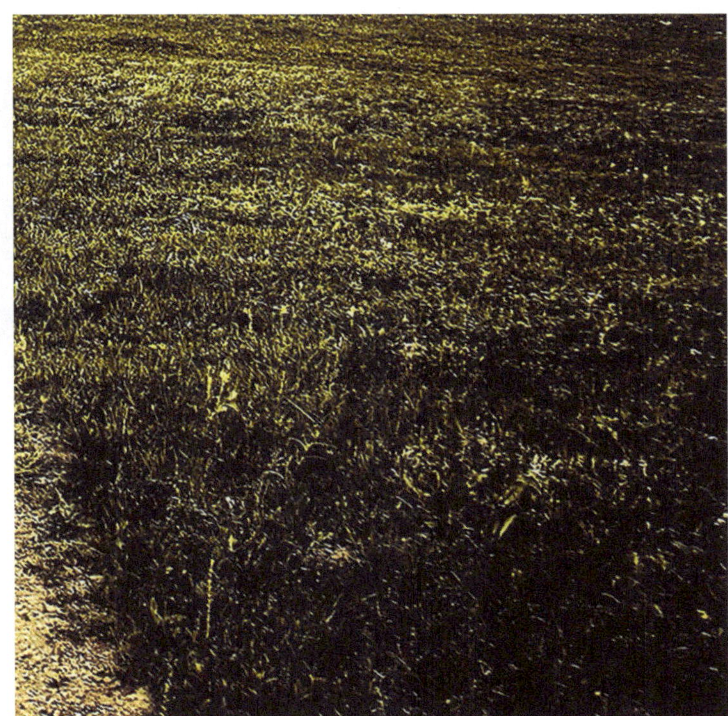

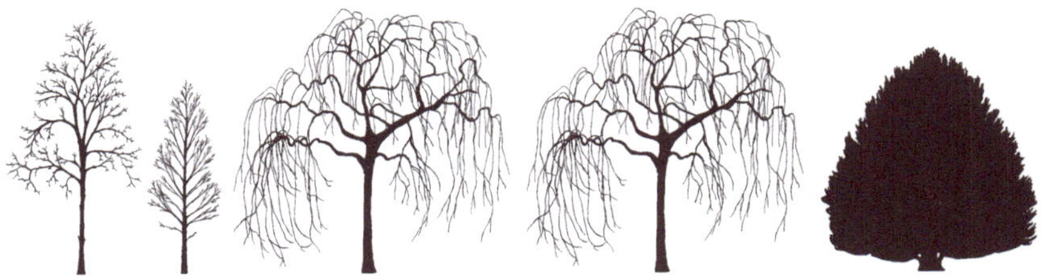

Image by Bessi from Pixabay

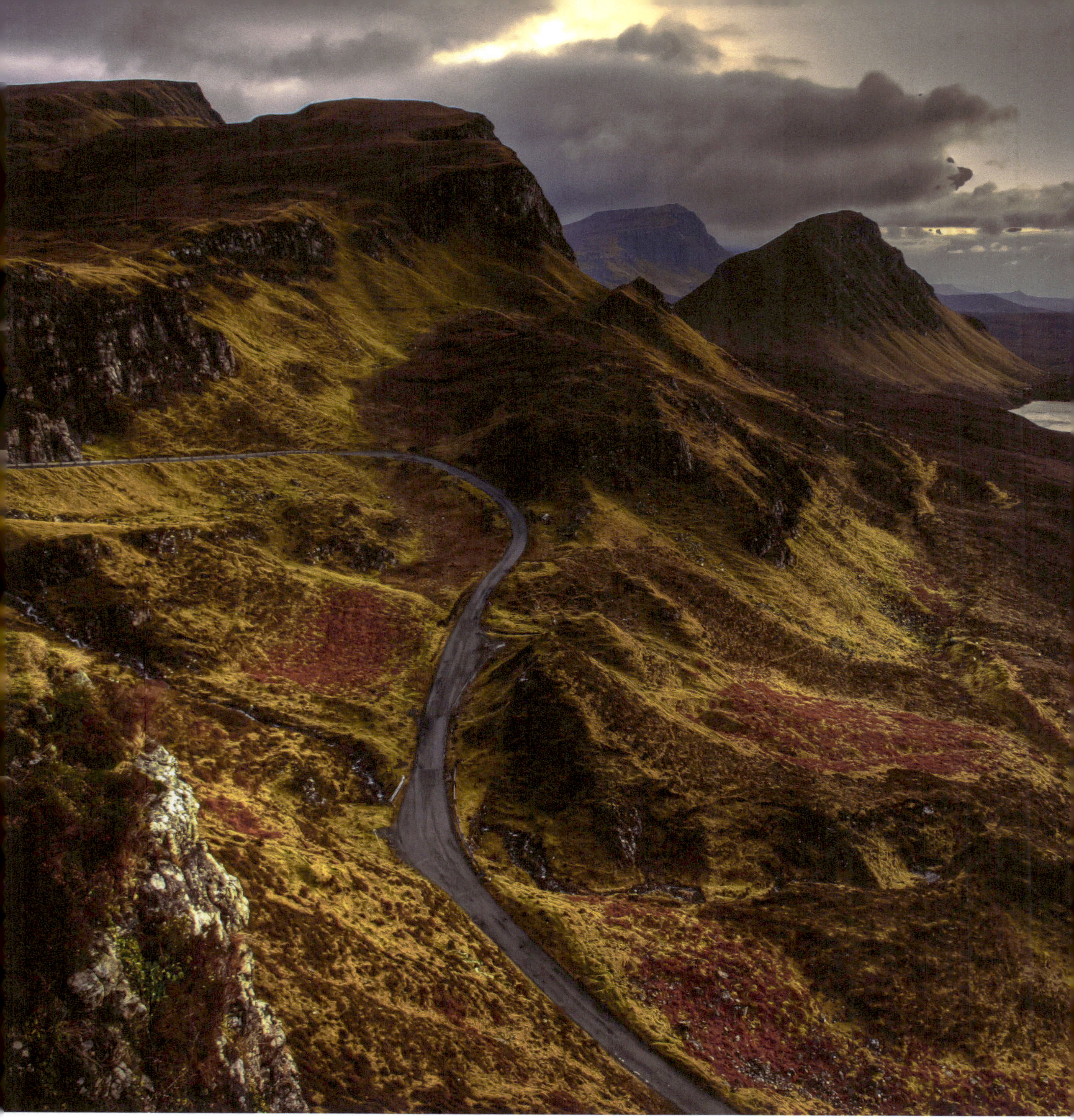

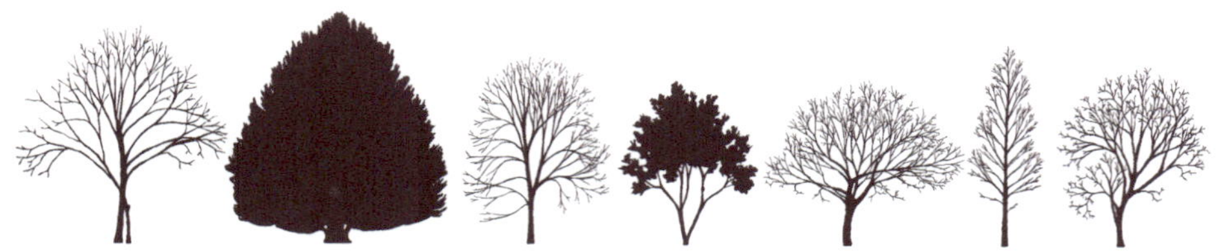

Quiraing (Meall na Suiramach), Isle of Skye, Scotland / Image by Frank Winkler from Pixabay

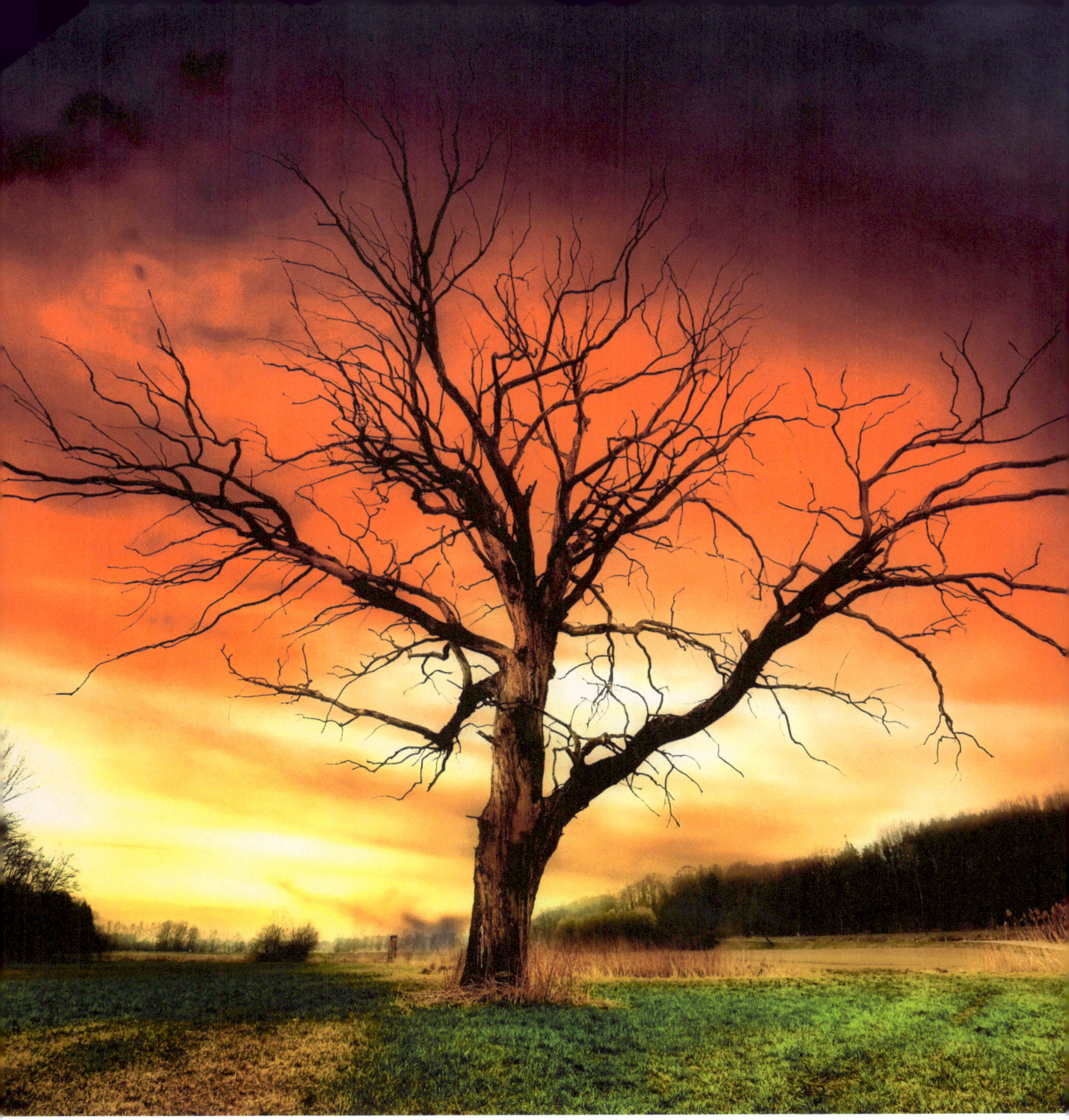

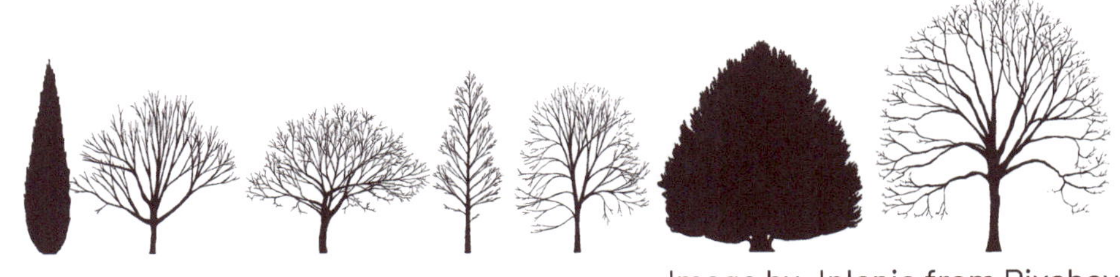

Image by Jplenio from Pixabay

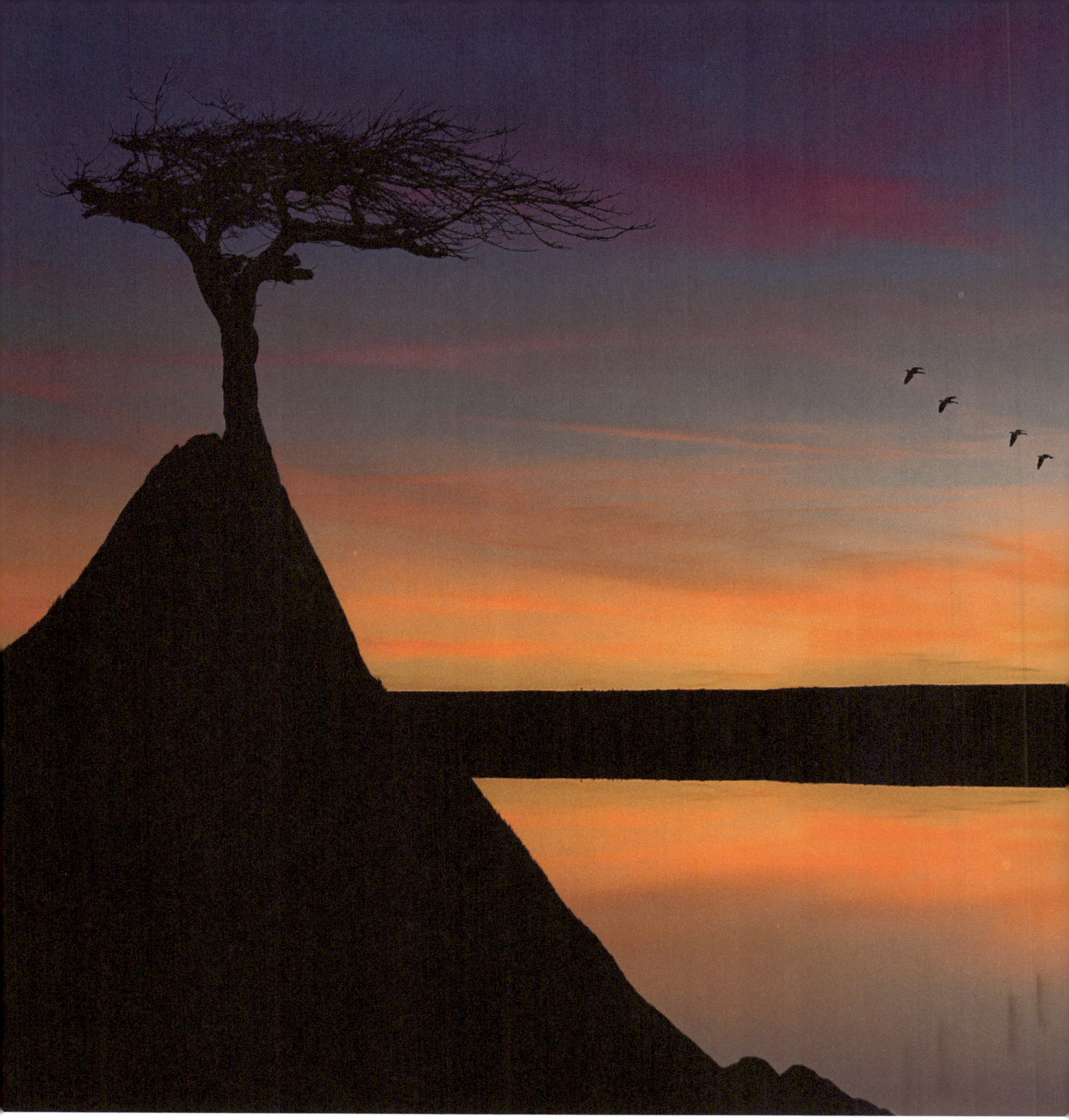

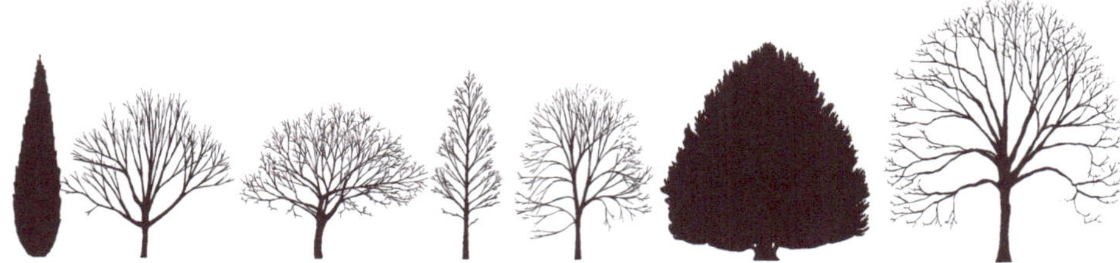

Image by Jplenio from Pixabay

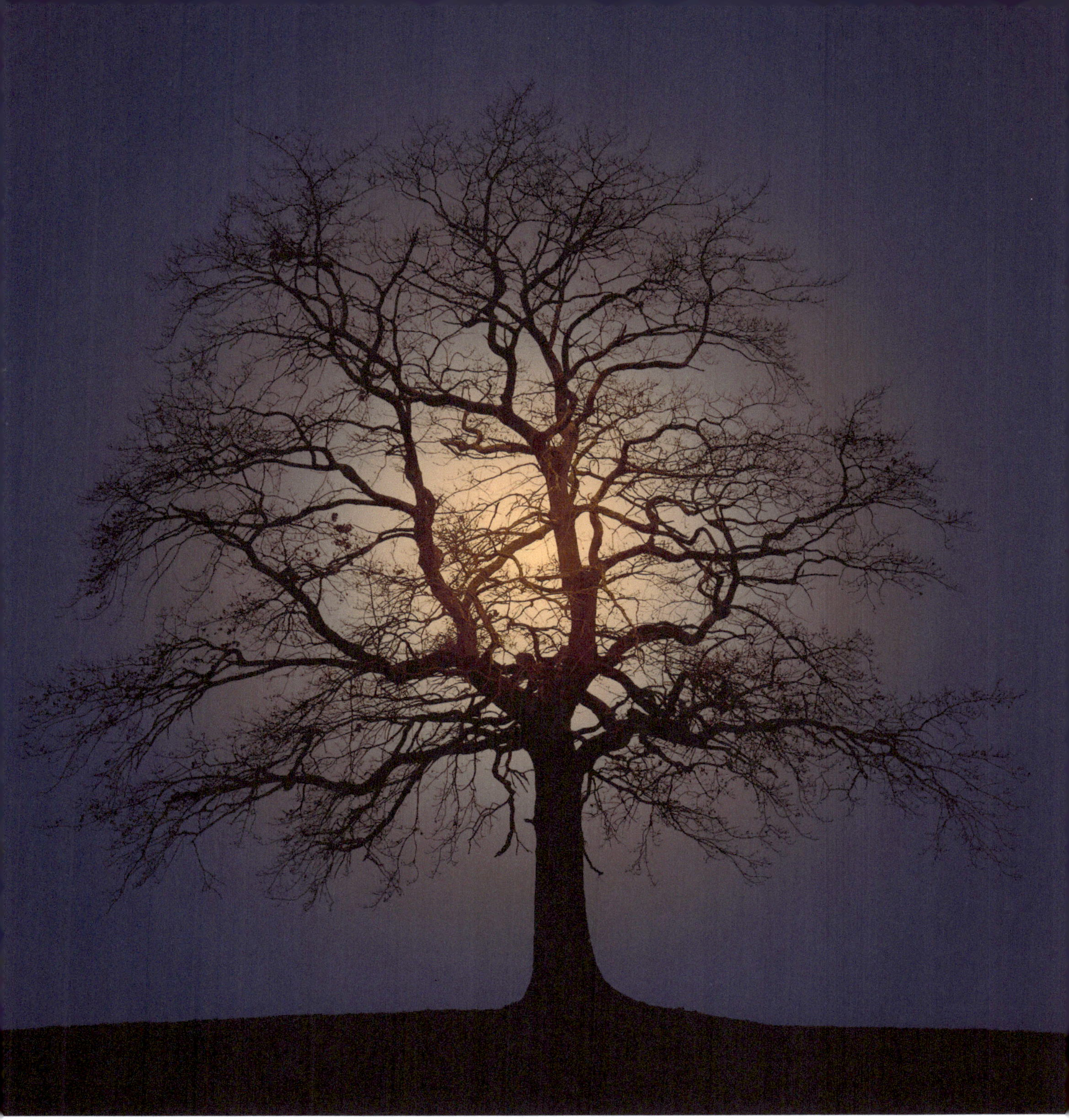

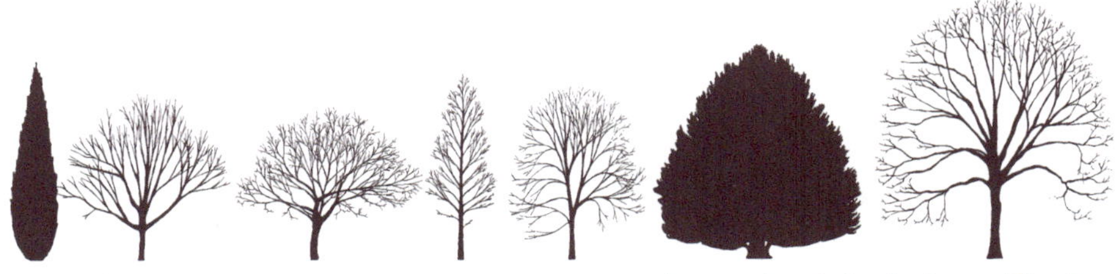

Image by Jplenio from Pixabay

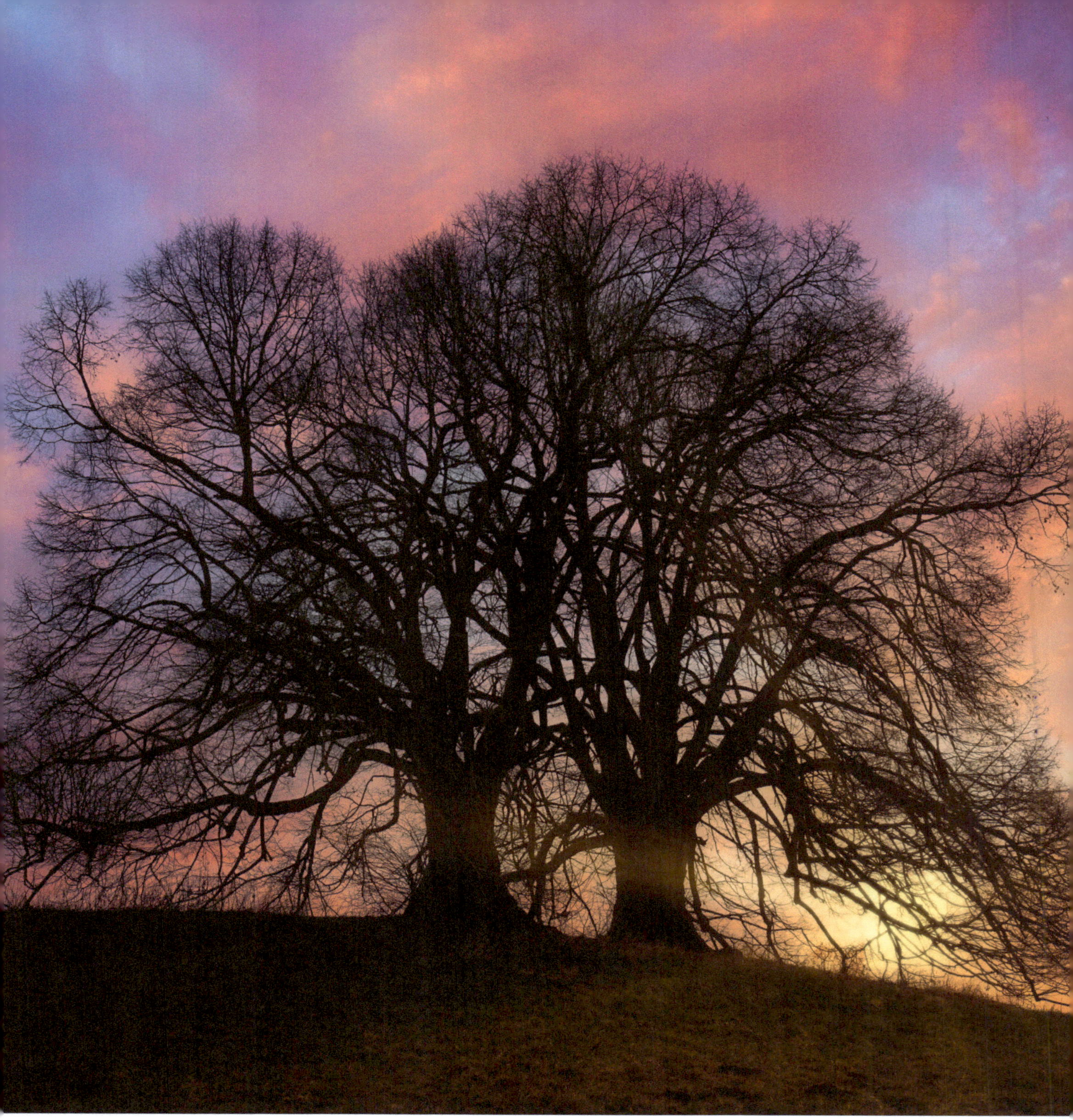

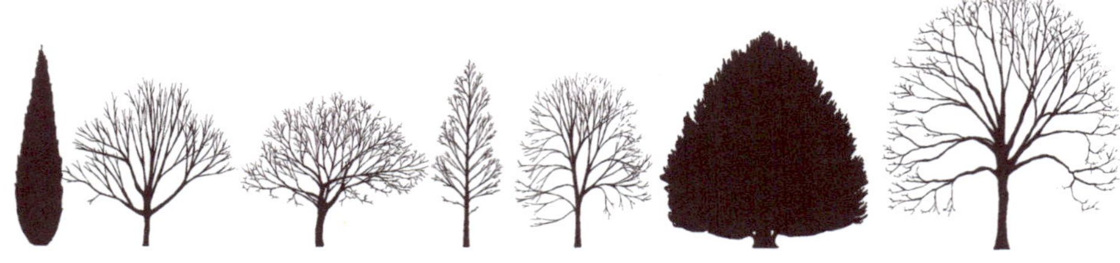

Image by Jplenio from Pixabay

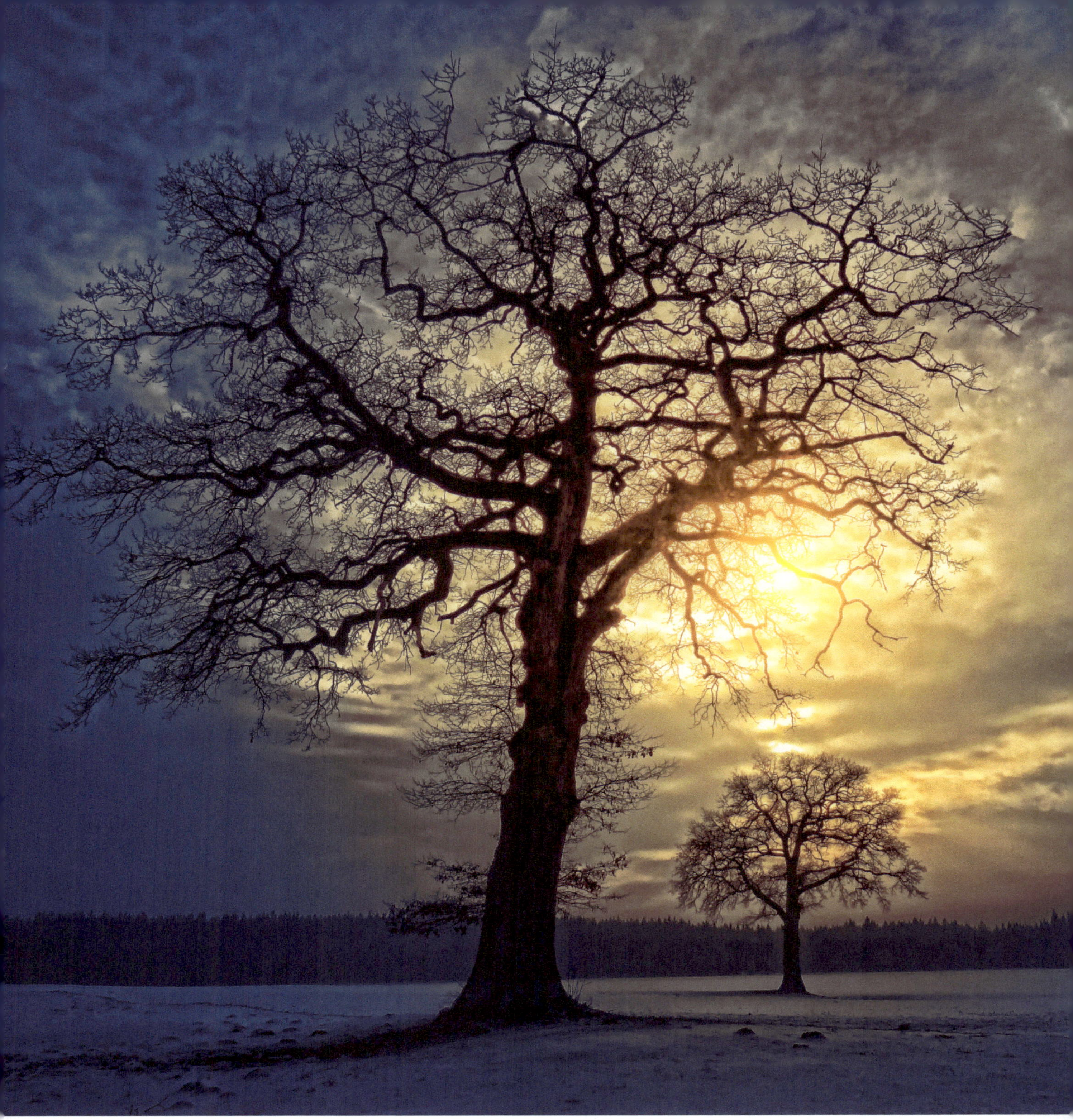

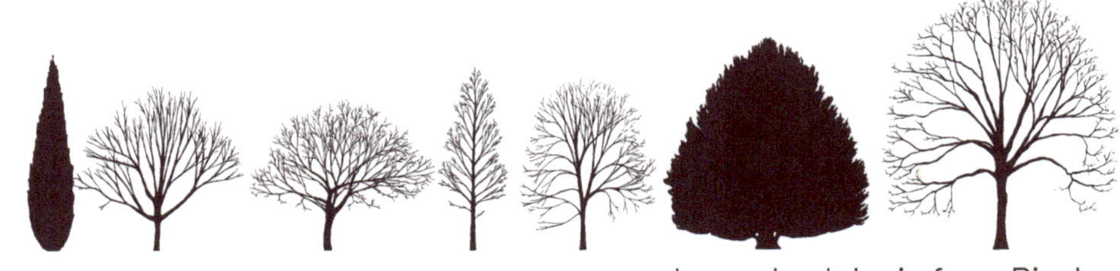

Image by Jplenio from Pixabay

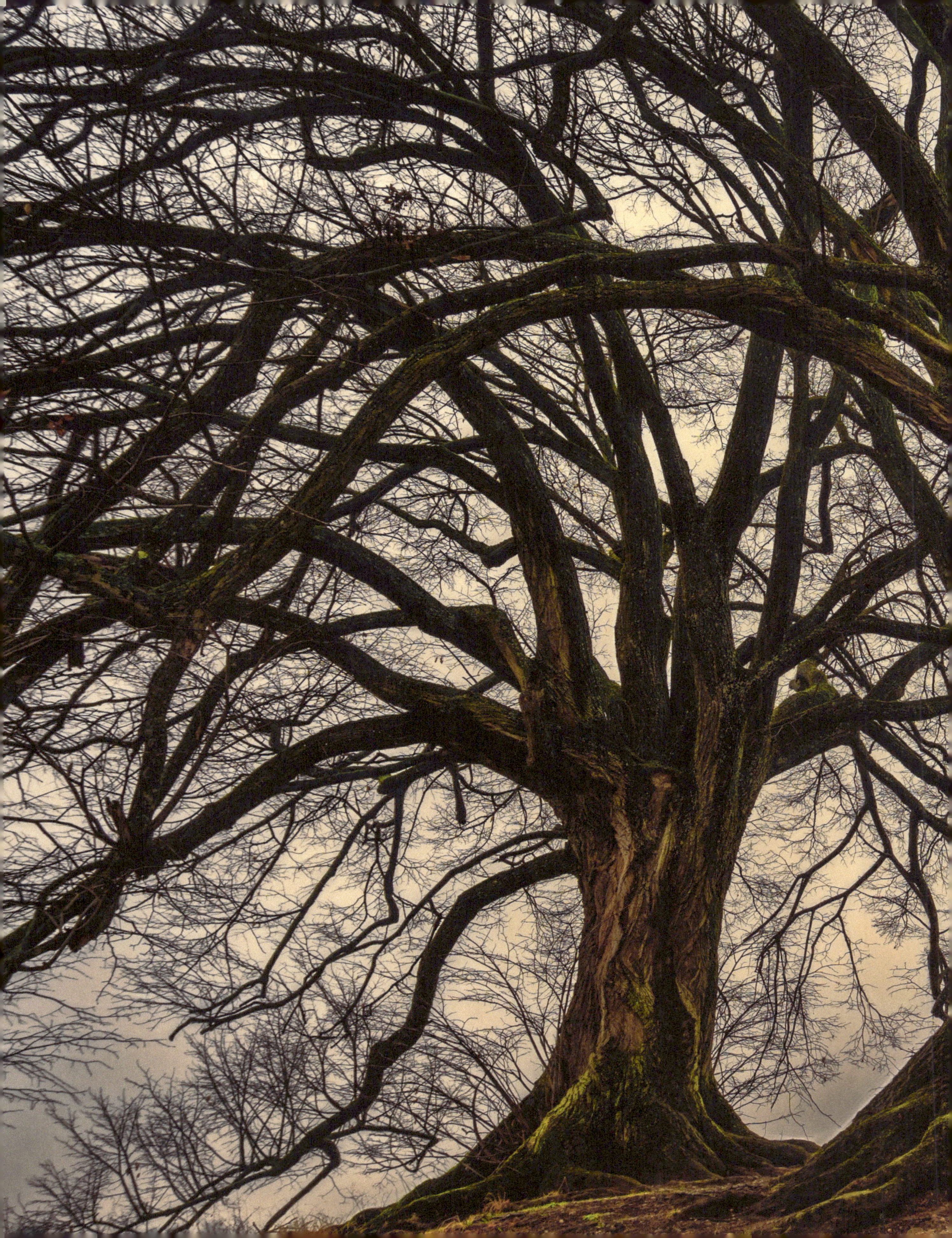

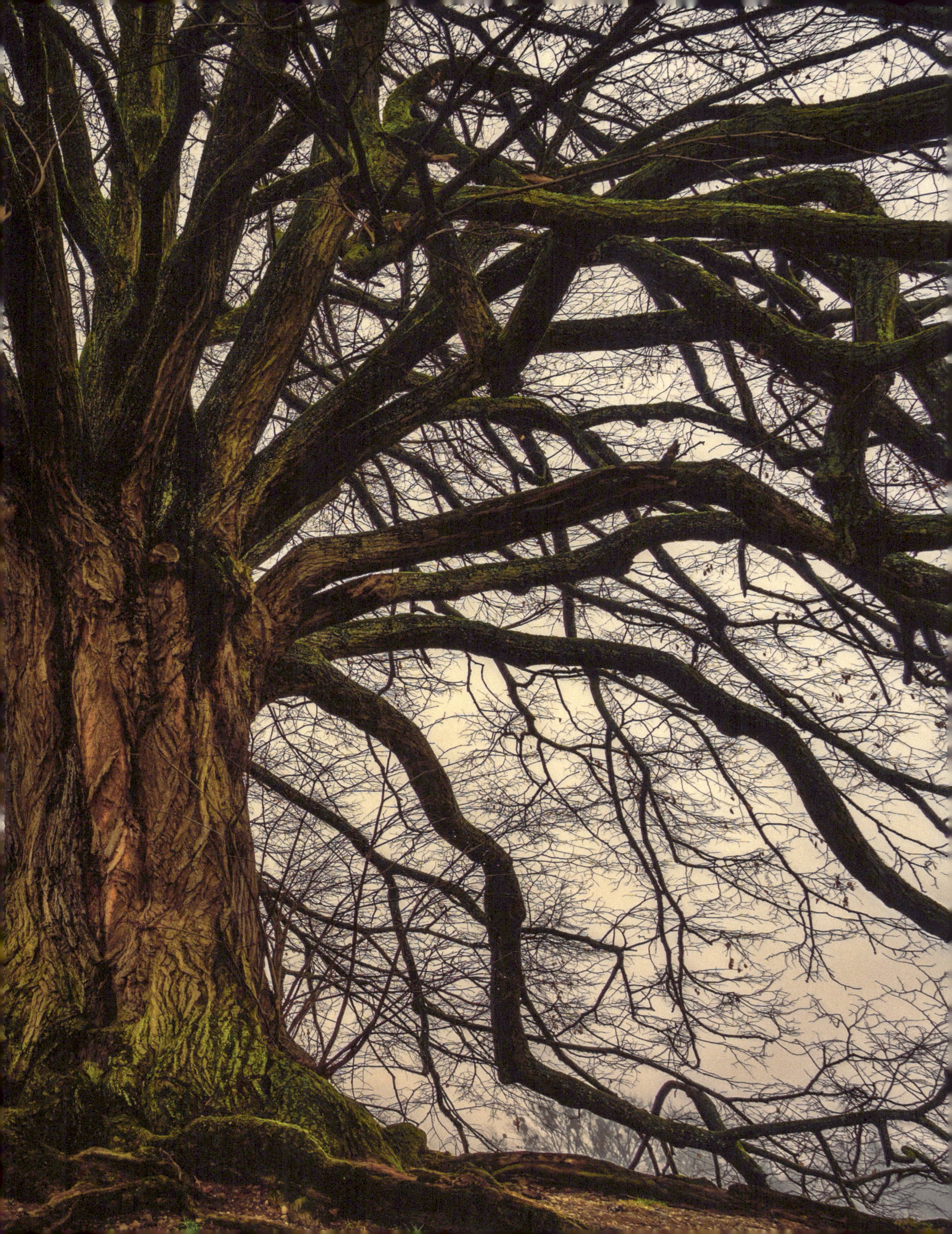

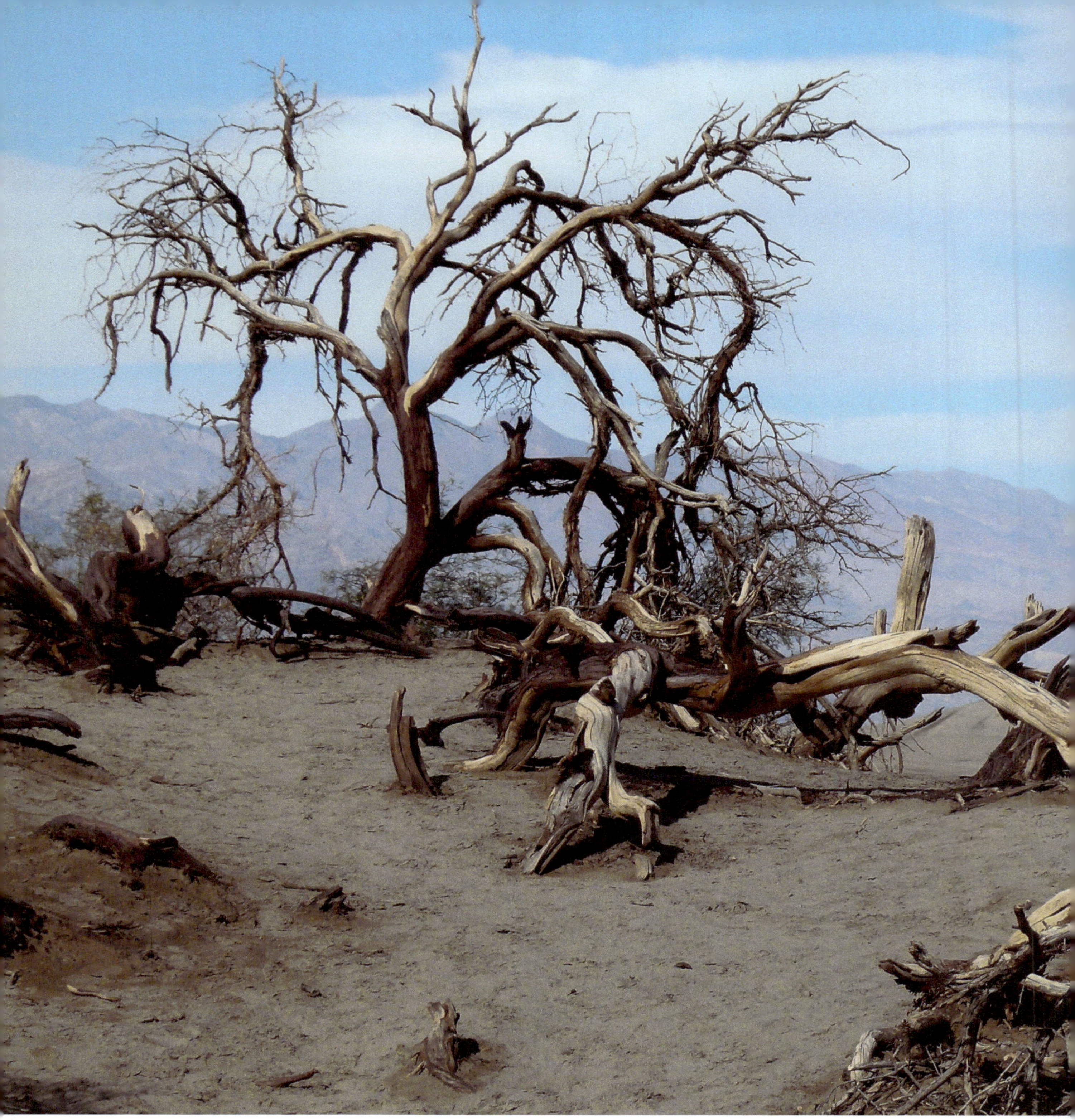

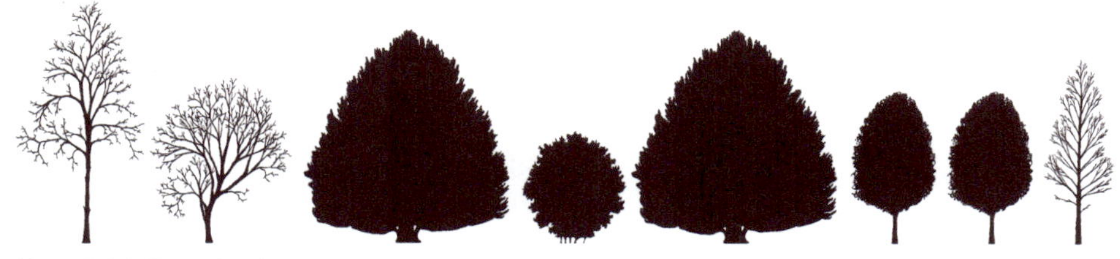

Death Valley, California, USA / Image by Brigitte from Pixabay

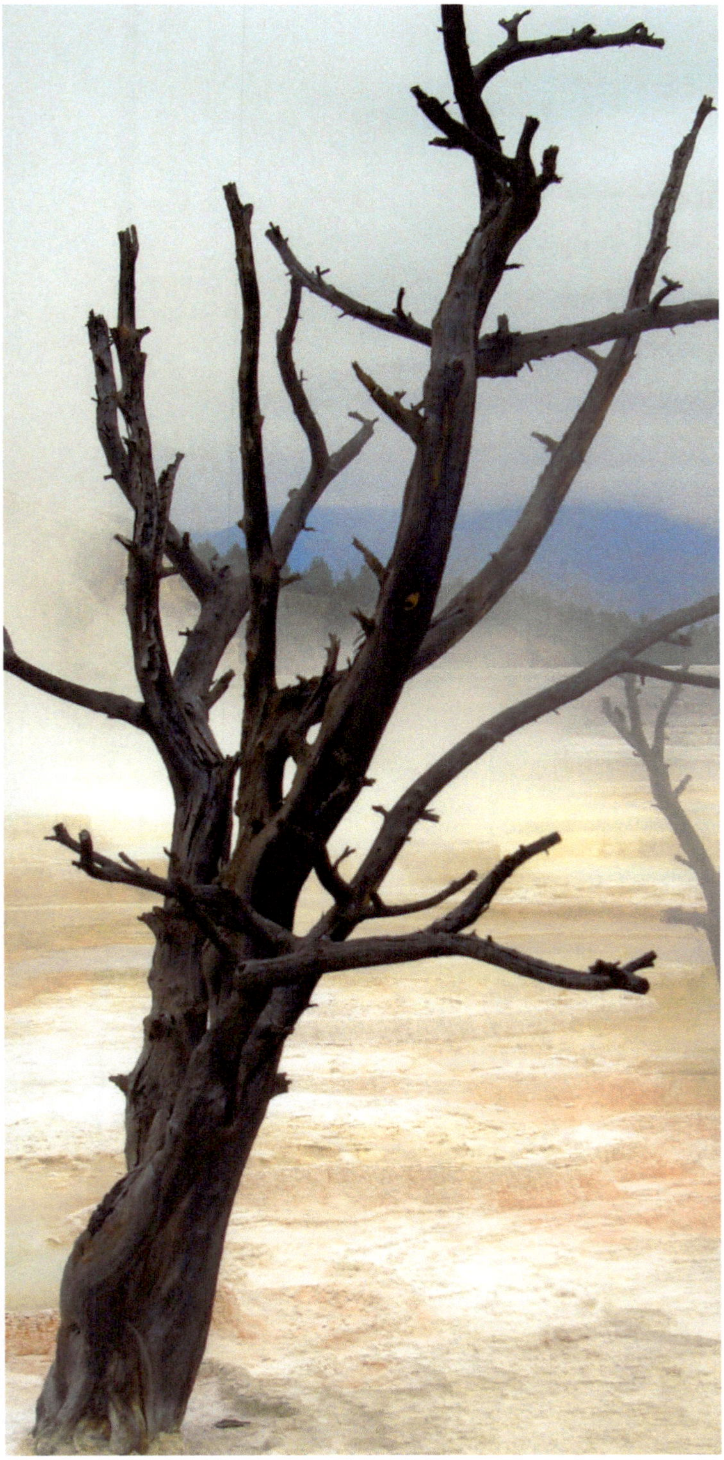

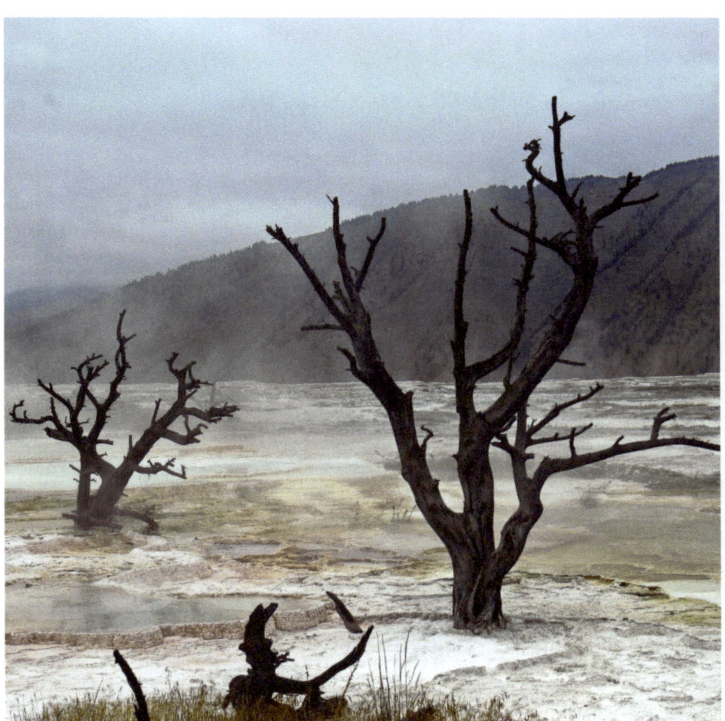

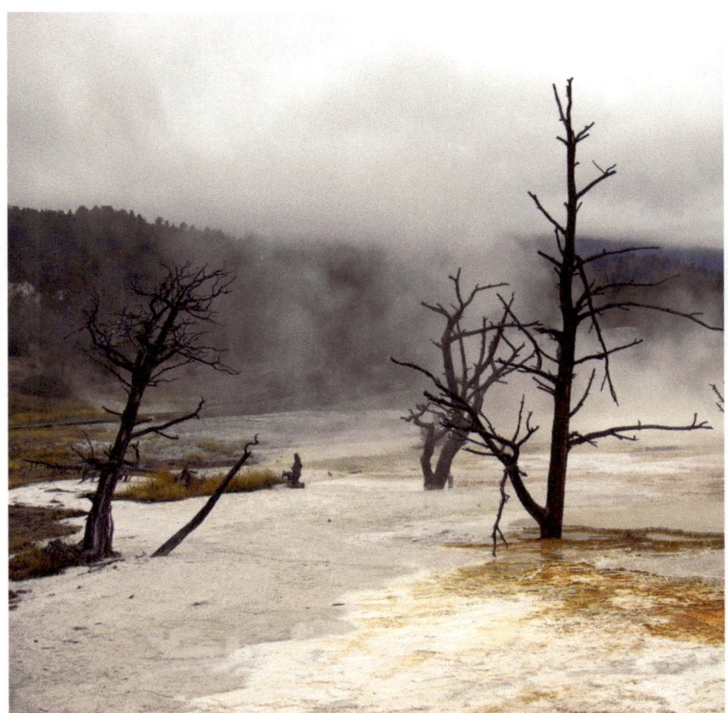

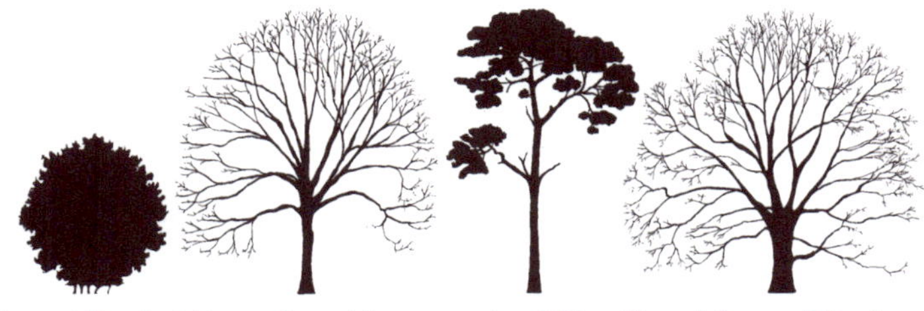

Canary Spring, Yellowstone National Park, Wyoming / Images by Mike Goad from Pixabay

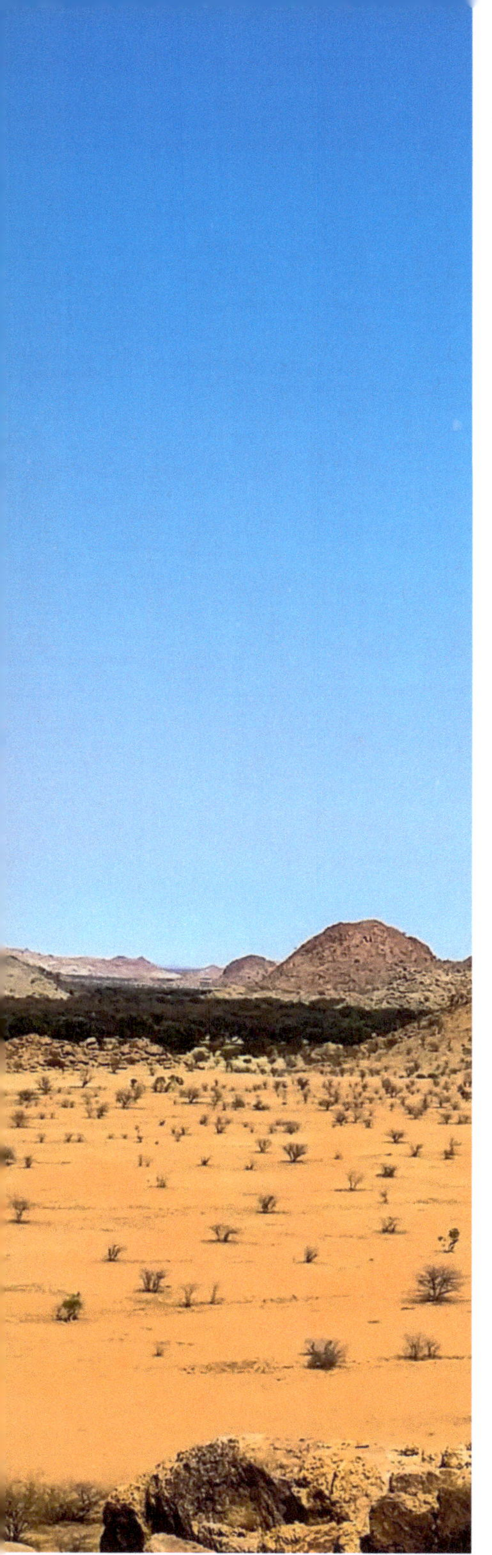
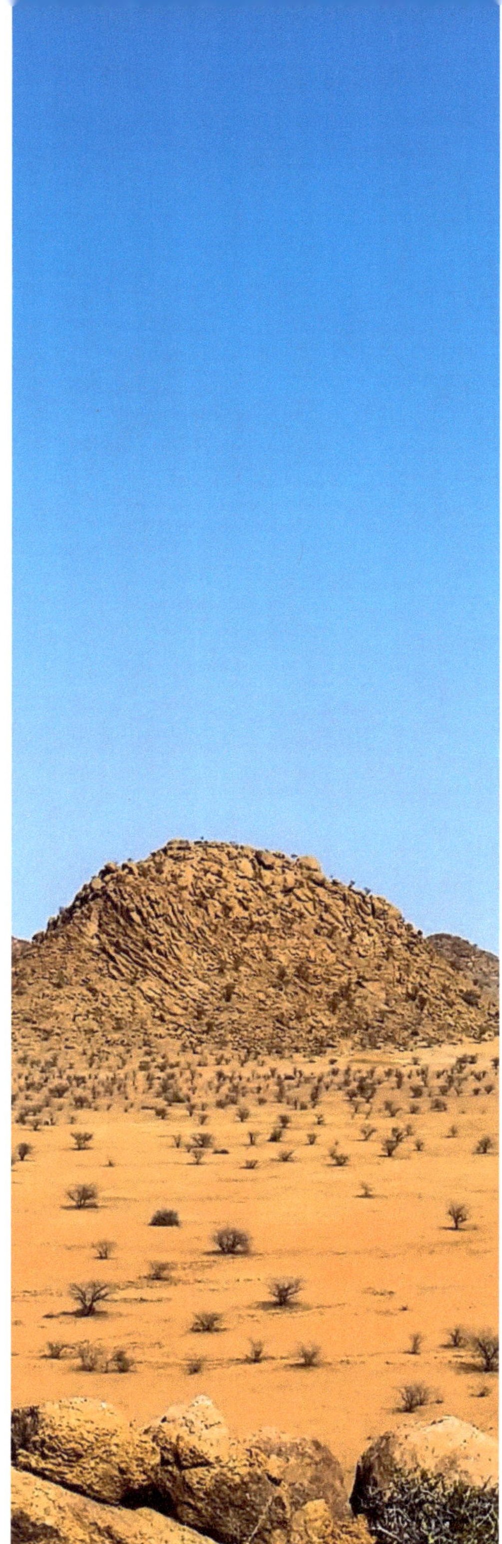
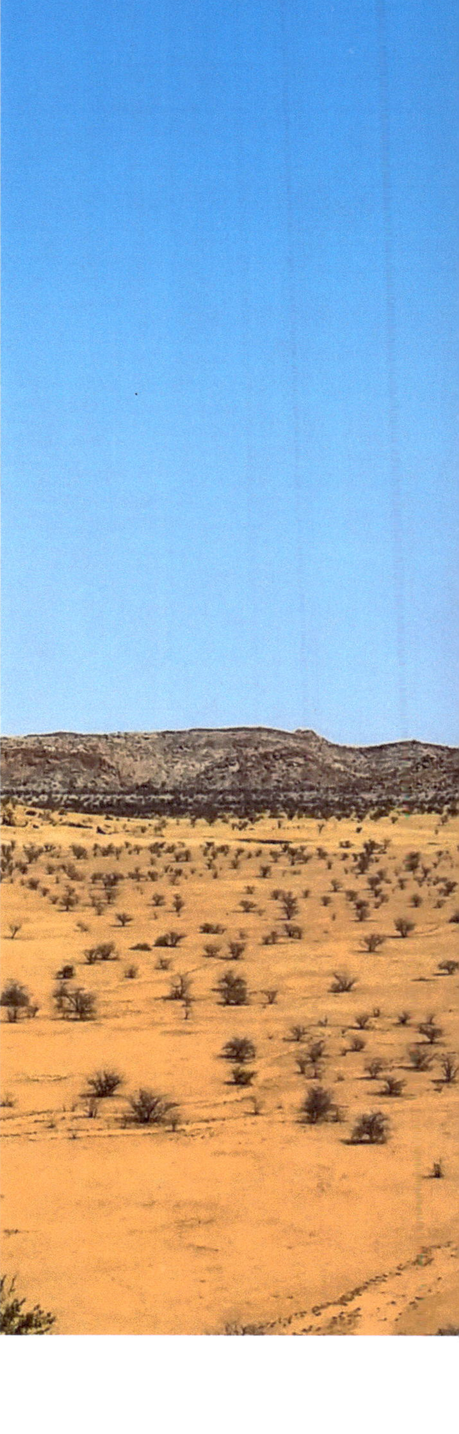
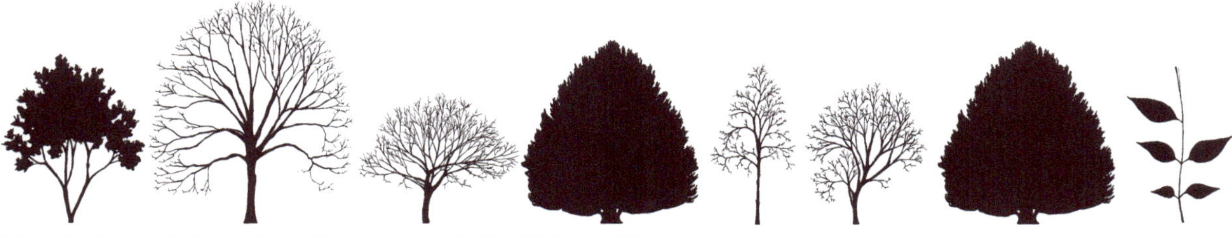

Namib Desert, Namibia / Image by Kolibri5 from Pixabay

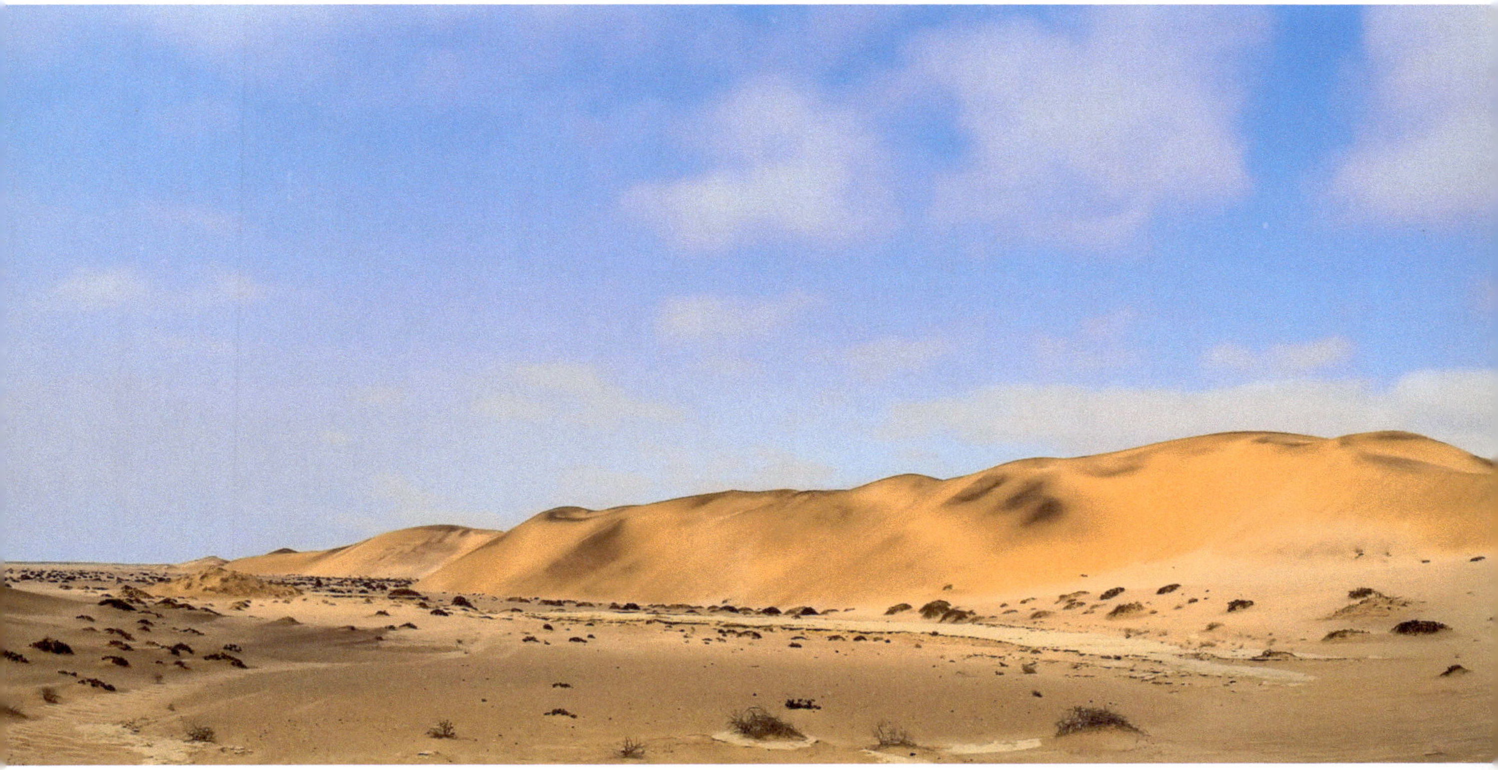

"The best time to plant a tree was twenty years ago.
The second best time is now."
(Chinese proverb)

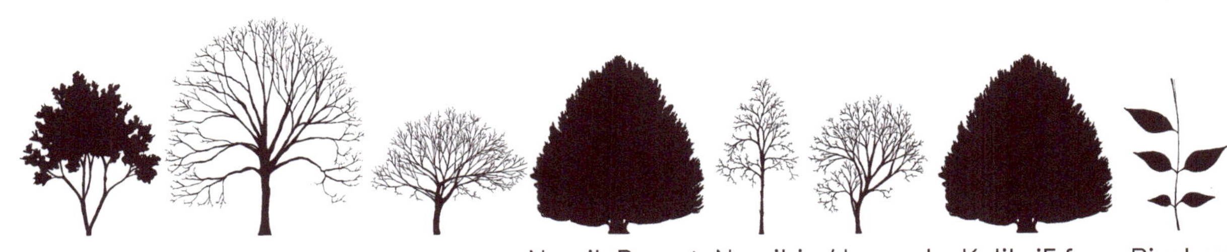

Namib Desert, Namibia / Image by Kolibri5 from Pixabay

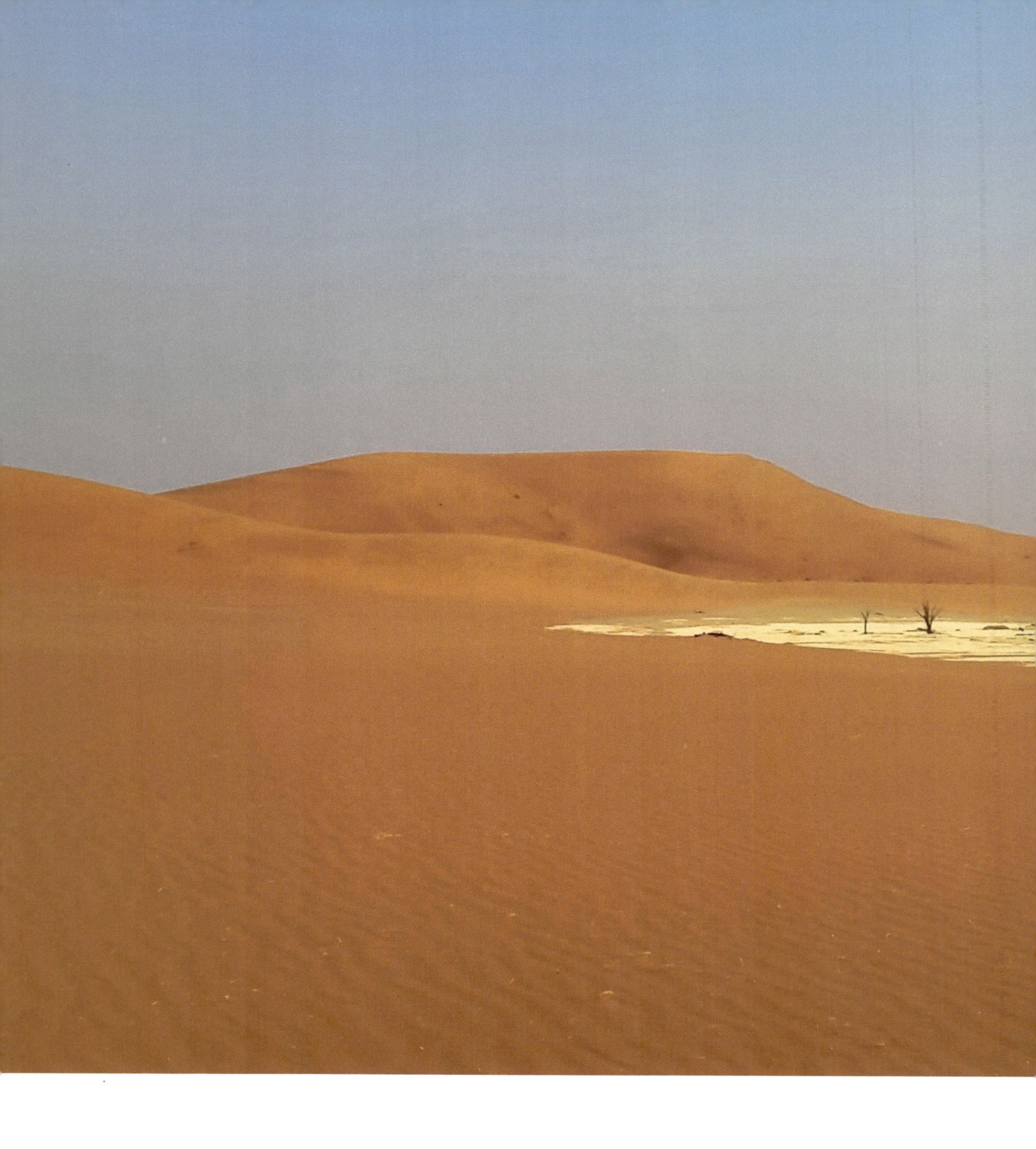

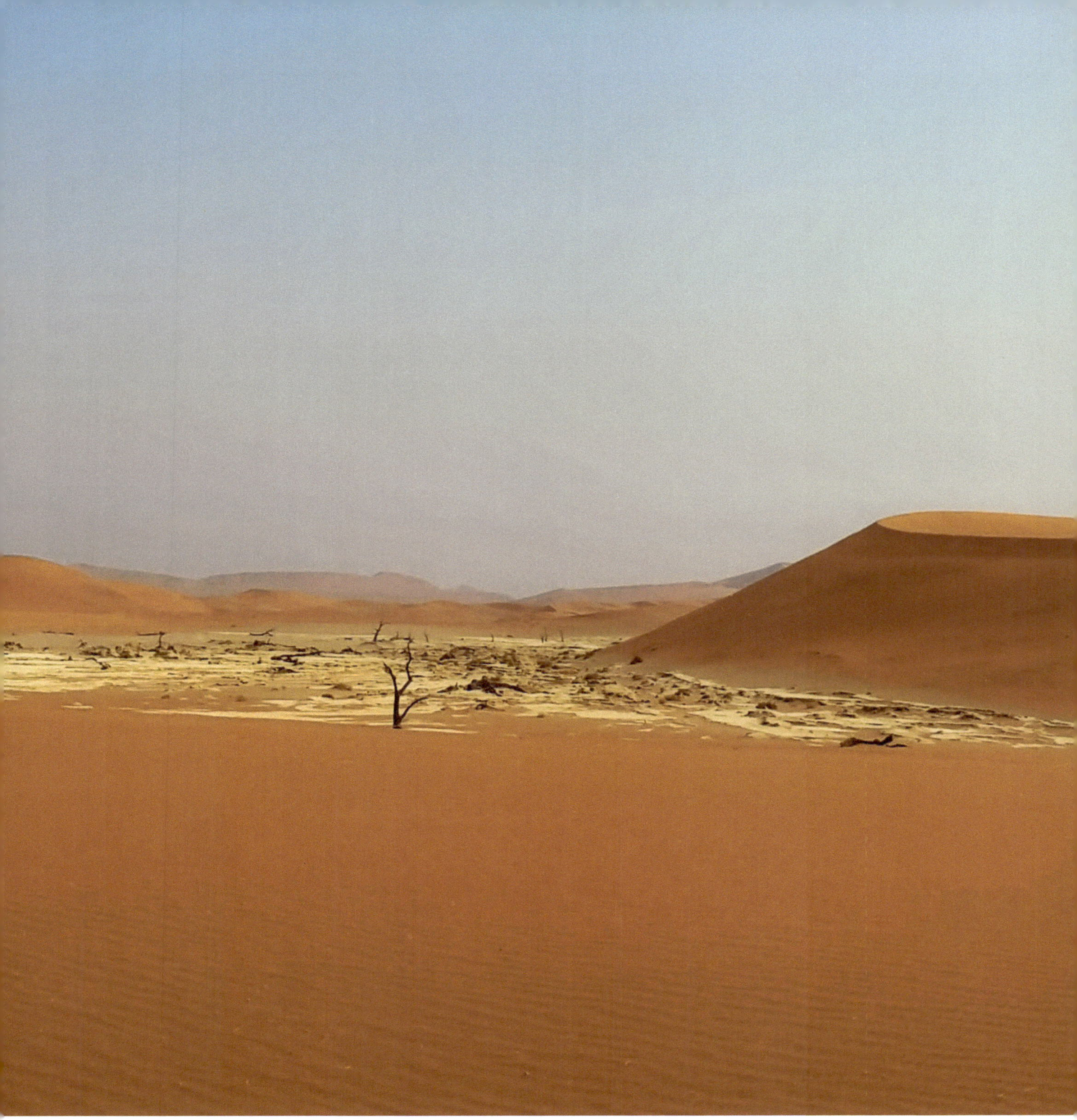

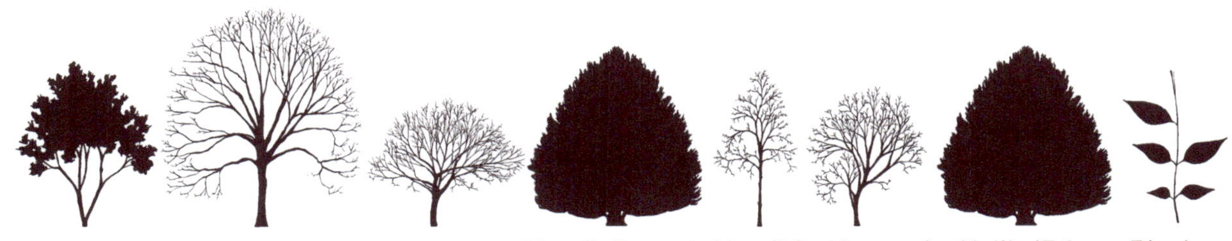

Namib Desert, Namibia / Image by Kolibri5 from Pixabay

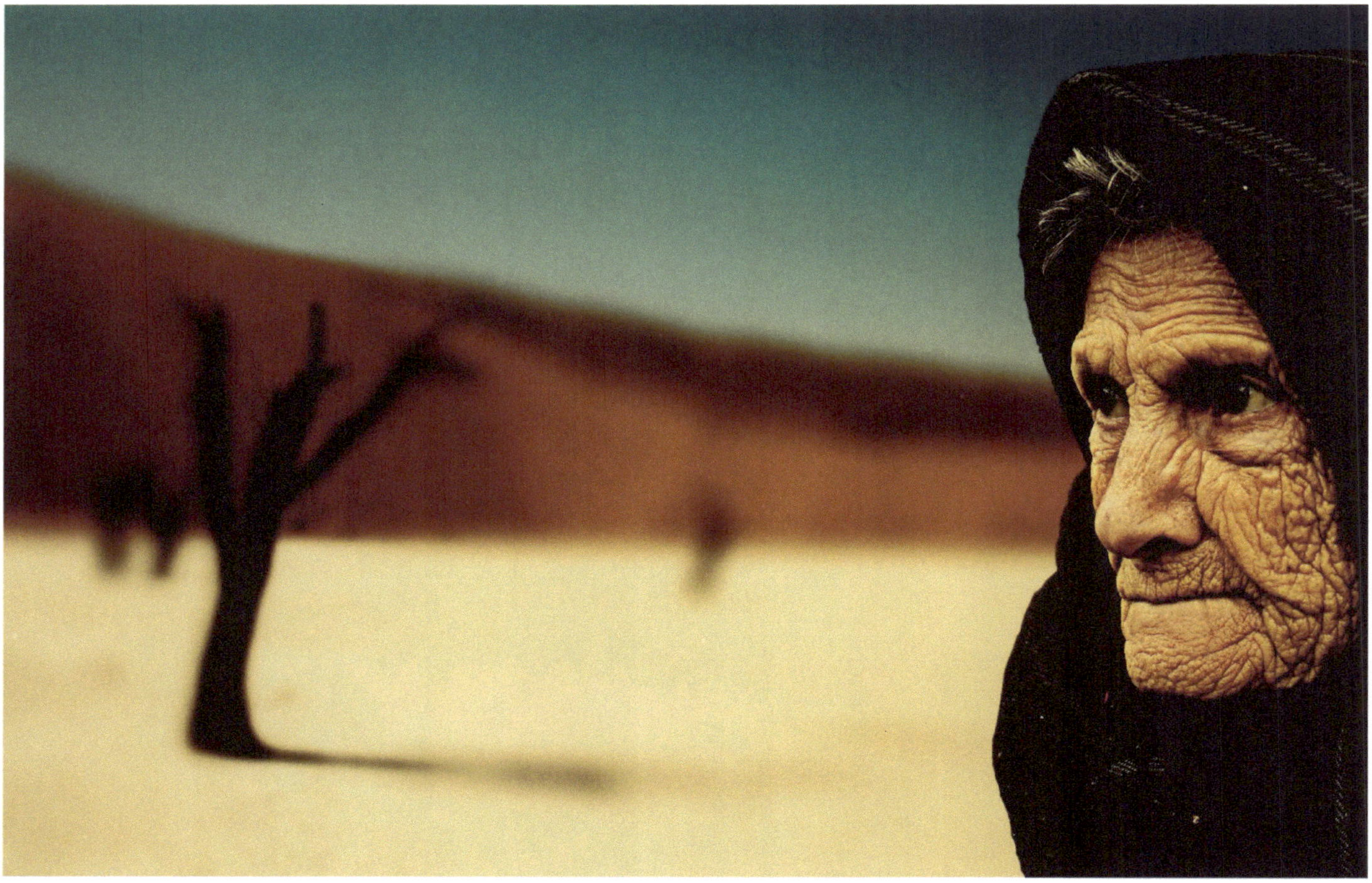

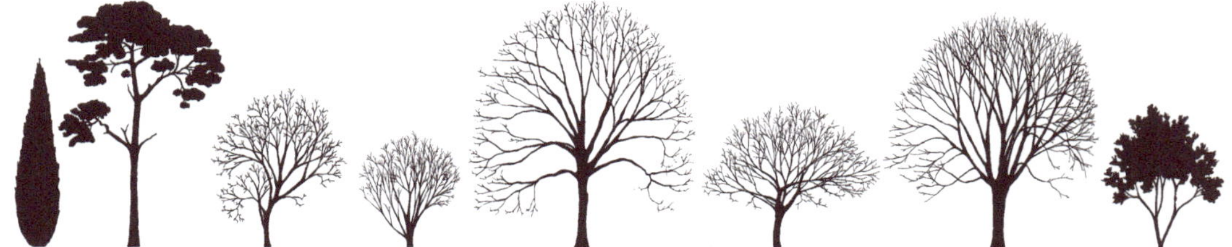

Namib Desert, Namibia / Image by Michal Jarmoluk from Pixabay

It's up to you!